ORIGINAL MAN

THE TAUTZ COMPENDIUM OF LESS ORDINARY GENTLEMEN

By Patrick Grant

gestalten

Contents

LIBERTINE

STYLIST

Extraordinary Gentlemen

by Nick Sullivan

I was struck, thumbing digitally through the advance layout of this fascinatingly inspirational rogue's gallery, how very few of the men have beards. Even Peter Beard doesn't have one. In these interesting times for men's fashion, a beard of any style (except perhaps a goatee) is a positive asset, possibly the only one you might need. In the panoply of possibilities there are grizzly mountain man beards, 70s German porn star beards, Victorian pugilist beards, marooned U-Boat captain's beards. Take your pick. Many a male model has carved out a career in front of the camera or on the runways of Milan or Paris simply by being in possession of carefully cultivated facial hair. Such has the beard become a token of cool that the man behind the right beard du jour, we like to joke, is almost immaterial, merely the carrier.

At the pond-life level of experience, such things mean something. But true style at its finest is none of this transient nonsense. It is doubtful that many of the icons listed in this delightful book would have troubled themselves over such fleeting notions. Anyone who has ever grown up and tried to become a man learns only by experience that the lasting measure of style is not about how he shaves his chin or even how he dresses, but who he is and what he does.

When I was a boy, my first heroes came from Ladybird Books, short and rather facile primary school tales of Scott of the Antarctic, Alfred the Great, Horatio Lord Nelson—the Great British men of the past. There was in those simpler, less revisionist times a relative paucity of significant foreigners. The few there were (Napoleon Bonaparte and Julius Caesar spring to mind), were implied chez Ladybird not to have amounted to much.

Fortunately, I grew up and read a little more broadly than Ladybird. As adults the scales fall from our eyes and we naturally see our heroes in 3D, warts-and-all as it were. As we experience the world more widely and more deeply, it's invariably the unconventional that attracts us.

5

What best unites the men in this book, I think, is that all of them can be said to have been in full possession (most of the time) of their own egos. Tyrannical and vain, passionate and determined, unapologetic (especially when wrong), bloody-minded and, no doubt, at times downright difficult to live with. Now that is a skill set to emulate!

What we're really looking for, I think, in the fantasy football team of inspirational heroes we nurture in our minds is a point of reference to something vital and tangible: a beguiling creative talent, grim-faced determination, a personal victory in the face of insurmountable odds, or even just one fleeting moment of luck that defines a lifespan, with a dash of balls-out eccentricity to make things interesting.

Because it's not just about achievement. Or if it is, it's not so much the thing itself as it is the manner of its delivery. We might not agree with Churchill's politics, but can admire the eloquence with which he communicated them. Though we may not wish to dress quite like Quentin Crisp, we're rather glad that someone does. We might instinctively shy from the arrogance of the cocksure, yet we secretly wish we had the same unshakable self-confidence.

What we don't seek in life is perfection. Because, as the men in this book show, there is nothing quite so boring as doing everything by the book.

A Note From the Editor

Patrick Grant

I have always been drawn to the stories of incredible men. As a youth it was mostly straightforward action types that I most admired; sportsmen, adventurers, military heroes and such. Swashbucklers, dashing types begrudgingly admired by men, swooned over by women. But as I got older the veneer assumed less and less importance. It was thoughts and actions that came to define the men I admired. Their endeavours were what counted, not their appearance. These were men that women admired, and other men adored.

As I set about re-invigorating the old Savile Row tailoring house of E. Tautz after a thirty-year hiatus, I wanted to try to define the kind of man I aspired to clothe. I recalled a line from *Herzog* which grabbed my attention at the time. Striving to define himself and his existence, Saul Bellow's eponymous anti-hero tells himself, 'I am Herzog. I have to be that man.' It struck me that the men I most admired, like Herzog, were simply being, or trying to be, the very best version of themselves. Quentin Crisp's *How to Have a Lifestyle* establishes a manifesto for a more considered way of life, stressing the need to work at one's personality and to strive constantly for betterment. 'What is needed,' he says, 'is greater intensity of living.' It is the men that follow this doctrine, whether consciously or unconsciously, that I was drawn to. Be your own man, be him completely, and devote all of your energy to this pursuit. Too many men in the public realm seem to seek universal popularity. That attitude surely only leads to mediocrity; the original man accepts from the offset he is likely never to be admired by many. But following the less conformist path, he may well end up being adored by a select few.

Behind my desk was a large pin board on which I stuck images of men doing the sorts of things I thought men ought to do. Two Frenchmen sitting on wicker chairs on the polar ice drinking champagne, their stricken ice-bound ship in the background. An English couple picnicking in a field in black tie attire next to some cows. Young men in a cavernous nightclub dancing, sweating, roaring. Men whose faces all spoke of a determination to

wring the last drops of joy out of life. I began collecting quotations and pinning those up too. Malcolm Bradbury—'I like the English. They have the most rigid code of immorality in the world.' Chesterton—'An inconvenience is only an adventure wrongly considered.' Crisp—'Vice is its own reward.' The words of men possessed by a single-mindedness, and a facility to look at the world obliquely.

I have always enjoyed reading biographies and obituaries. The first one I remember reading is David Niven's engrossing *The Moon's A Balloon,* which I found (nicotine stained) on a bookshelf in my father's study-come-smoking den sometime in my mid teens. Niven's life was preposterously charmed, and greater than any fiction. The best biographies and diaries often are. I began writing very brief highlights of the lives of these men I admired, and posting them on the E. Tautz social media pages. Their stories seemed to resonate with men and women alike.

These collected biographies suggested no single type or characteristic that unified the men that I revered. But what they did have in common was uncommon-ness, non-ordinariness, or simply put, originality.

Years later I met a tall bearded German at a party, a taller, better-looking version of myself. We got to talking about my stories of original men and he suggested that a selection of these might make for a worthwhile and interesting compendium. So this is what we have jointly created.

This book is a very small selection of the many notable men whose stories have brought me great enjoyment. The selection is heavily 'Western', around half being from the U.K., a quarter from the United States, and most of the remainder from Western Europe. This is nothing more than a reflection of the fact that I was born and raised in the U.K. and have lived, worked, and travelled most extensively in the United States and Europe, with a little bit of time spent in Japan and China. There is a strong bias towards the British, but then again we seem to breed original characters (or celebrate them more vocally) at a rate which belies our relatively small population.

This list could easily have been comprised very differently, and there are men that I will certainly come to regret not including. Amongst those who did not make the cut are a huge number of incredible characters. Whittling the list down to a manageable number was not easy and there are some omissions about which there has been some disagreement. But in this list, originality and historical precedence trump prowess. There are few young men in this selection. The youngest, born in 1973, is the comedian and artist Noel Fielding. This may be partly because I am no longer young myself, but inclusion in this book requires sustained effort, not just a brief burst of activity. Some men on the list died young, but they did shine very brightly and consistently during their brief lives. It also might be argued that as time goes by it becomes harder to do anything new, but I don't think that this is the case. The world changes, new opportunities present themselves.

The list also contains a few men with a seedier, less savoury side; those well-known for being drunks, drug addicts, womanisers, and in rare cases, abusers. Those flawed personalities are celebrated despite—not because of—these traits. It is not the frittering away of life that we celebrate, but the style with which it has been frittered. Those that are included have achieved greatness despite their habits, and there are very few who did not at some stage seek redemption or salvation. Often their stories are rather sad ones, like that of snooker player Alex Higgins, and one might hope that their tales are precautionary as much as laudatory.

For the purposes of this compendium, our subjects have been grouped, but no attempt has been made to rank them. These groupings are arguably a little arbitrary and many of our men could easily sit within two, three, or all of the following collectives. 'Stylist' here means men who live with great style, not those who are well dressed, though some are. 'Libertine' here means men who lead lives of a fairly reckless nature, largely absolving themselves of the usual moral principles—a mixture between what might at one time have been called a gallant, and a 1960s hellraiser. 'Artists' are simply those whose living is made in the arts of any kind: architects, painters, writers, filmmakers; men who have made their way in life through creativity and intellect. 'Hero' does not necessarily describe those whose actions are bravely heroic, but rather those men who have achieved something outstanding in their line, whose indefatigability, obstinacy, sublime physical prowess, or courage has been their most defining feature.

These tales of lives less ordinary are a celebration of the joy of living. I tell them in the hope that the efforts of these extraordinary men might make us seek to try and live more interesting and original lives ourselves.

CHAPTER I

Artist

The artistic professions, unlike any others, allow for complete freedom of style. More than this, originality of style, in work and self, goes hand in hand with artistic creativity and is a requirement for any artist.

Our selection encompasses that which the ancient Greeks attributed to the goddesses of human creativity, the nine Muses. The Greeks universally accepted the benefit of art on mankind: they believed these Muses would enrich people's lives, stimulate learning, and promote civic harmony. The nine Muses were the inspiration for literature, science, and the arts, the personification of art, and the source of all knowledge and creative power in the fields of music, astronomy, poetry, and dance. For our purposes we have added architecture and industrial design, professions that unite science and art.

In my early twenties, architecture became my greatest passion. Through John Pawson's book *Minimum,* I was drawn into the reductivist world of eminent twentieth-century architects such as Le Corbusier, Ludwig Mies van der Rowe, or Frank Lloyd Wright. Having graduated with a degree in engineering, I went back to night school in Liverpool to study for my A level in Art and was offered a place at the prestigious Liverpool School of Architecture—one I didn't, for mostly cowardly reasons, take up. I felt great affinity with the somber-suited architects, trustworthy men with tidy haircuts and heavy rimmed spectacles, no less unique for an absence of flamboyance. Originality does not necessarily require ostentation, but it was hard not to feel there was something more wildly exotic about their contemporaries in the visual arts. Paint daubed, bewhiskered bohemians. They lived as they chose, free from personal censure, unburdened by the tedium of the office, the nine-to-five lifestyle, and the stultification of commerce. The great London artists of the 1960s and 1970s, Bacon, Auerbach, Freud, caroused in Soho's Colony Room (or Muriel's as it was known to its older clientele) squeezing up the dingy staircases past MPs, spies, and gangsters. It is hard not to love the free-loving ideal espoused by the patrons of this Dean St. institution. Extraordinary characters were nurtured there in an atmosphere free of inhibition, free of judgement. As Bacon himself said of the Colony Room, 'You could always be yourself.'

Musicians, more than any artists, seem to understand and embrace the need for originality. Their persona, both on and off stage, enriches our experience of their music. The music becomes inconceivable without the man, the art inseparable from the artist. My father liked soul. On the long drive south down the A68 to my school in County Durham, we'd pass through tough colliery towns with names like Kiln Pit Hill. He'd chain smoke Dunhills and play James Brown on the tape player. I loved Brown for his wild dancing and his awesome hair as much as for his music. Listening to John Peel on an illicit radio, I came to know The Smiths, The Fall, The Pogues. The music was often raw, but the frontmen, enigmatic and charismatic with unruly hair, bad teeth, and second-hand clothes, were remarkable. Before any of this, in the late 70s, I was into Queen—their frontman one of the most musically gifted and enigmatic men of all. Like many other great musicians of the last half of the twentieth century, his persona (as well as his name) was a theatrical facade.

Art has enormous value in our culture, it is an integral part of what we consider to be pleasurable in life. The men that follow represent a very small sample from the massed ranks of incredible and original artists, whose life stories, like their art, are both life affirming, and life enriching.

ANDY WARHOL

On 3 June 1968, Andy Warhol was shot and seriously wounded in his New York City studio by radical feminist Valerie Solanas. It may seem an odd way to begin a biography of Warhol, but his mid-life brush with death provides the perfect introduction, for as George Bernard Shaw once said: 'Assassination is the extreme form of censorship.' Warhol could not be censored though; the 1960s were the zenith of his work, his breakthrough decade, and his era of expression. The attempt on his life, which he survived, profoundly affected him and represents the height of Warhol's visibility and vivacity, perhaps only returning in the 1980s.

This, however, was not Warhol's first brush with death, even if it is undoubtedly his most dramatic—even his actual passing was unspectacular in comparison. At a young age, Andrew Warhola was diagnosed with the sometimes fatal Chorea disease, leaving him bed-ridden for months and making him a social outcast at school, but also helping him form a close bond with his mother who would fund his interest in drawing and later photography. Warhol's father would die in 1942, when Warhol was 14 years old.

Warhol graduated from high school and studied pictorial design at the Carnegie Institute of Technology. After graduating in 1949, Warhol moved to New York where he would set up his studio, his life, his art, and his persona. New York quickly recognised Warhol's peculiar talent and within a year, Warhol had procured commissions from *Glamour Magazine, Harper's Bazaar,* Tiffany & Co, and *Vogue.* In the 1950s, Warhol also began practising as an exhibition artist, with his first show in the Hugo Gallery, and later exhibiting work at the prestigious Museum of Modern Art in 1956.

In the 1960s, Warhol catapulted the pop art movement that had flourished a few years earlier in England. With an emphasis on the quotidian, a desire to blur boundaries between high and low culture, to commercialise and commodify, pop art under Warhol's guidance was a well-oiled business machine. Warhol himself noted, 'Once you "got" Pop, you could never see a sign the same way again. And once you thought Pop, you could never see America the same way again.' His first foray into pop was his reproduction of Campbell's canned soup. Glamourised by their multitude, this was Warhol's attempt at capturing what he considered to be quintessentially American. One of the most striking pieces from this period is the print of the electric chair, and then there were Warhol's famous pop art portraits as well, which embodied the artist's obsession with celebrity.

The 1960s also saw Warhol begin his work in film at his studio in New York that became known as The Factory. He produced around 60 films and many more screen tests of the various members of his entourage. His film work is mainly considered avant-garde, with some pseudo-documentary elements at times. His most famous film, *Chelsea Girls,* was the first underground film to make its way into commercial theatres. He would also propel The Velvet Underground and Nico into fame, producing their debut album with its iconic banana cover.

Warhol was a socialite, very often seen in New York City nightclubs fraternising with stars. From art and music to film and books, and eventually even television with a show on MTV in the 1980s, Warhol was simply an indomitable global force. The 1970s saw Warhol rounding up his patrons and showing his entrepreneurial spirit. From the Shah of Iran Reza Pahlavi to Mick Jagger, there were few who did not want their portrait made by the great Warhol. Warhol would continue to travel and exhibit globally throughout the 1980s until his sudden death in 1987 after routine gall-bladder surgery.

Ever-protective of his trademark silver wig, Warhol was buried wearing it. A practising Ruthenian Catholic inspired by his religion and apparently a non-practising homosexual who remained a virgin, Warhol was nothing if not originally complex. His sexuality undoubtedly influencing much of his work, many of his films opened in gay porn theatres. From a quiet, bed-ridden, often bullied young boy to the world's first international superstar artist, Warhol's life trajectory has a poetic brilliance to it. HB

'I want to die with my blue jeans on.'
Andy Warhol

Andy Warhol

Peter Beard

PETER BEARD

It seems that wherever Peter Beard finds himself, from top London night clubs to rural Kenya, he cannot help but be surrounded by booze, drugs, and beautiful women. During his life, defined by his career as one of the greatest photographers of modern times, Beard has consistently and unrelentingly moved from experience to experience with the speed and frivolity only possible if one is living on a trust fund. Beard's lineage includes the American tobacco magnate Pierre Lorillard IV who popularized the tuxedo, and his great-grandfather, James Jerome Hill, who made his fortune as the founder of the Great Northern Railway at the end of the nineteenth century and left millions to Beard after he died; this money has facilitated the rock-star lifestyle Beard has fully embraced.

Jerome Hill was a keen patron of the arts and this strand ran throughout the family, inducing Beard's great love for all manifestations of beauty, and probably providing the roots for Beard's exceptional talent behind the camera lens. Beard went to Yale University and initially studied medicine before switching his major to art history. His earliest artistic impulses were directed towards the diaries he started keeping at the age of 11, comprising photographs, drawings, smears of animal blood, his own transcribed telephone messages, and more. These diaries are a window onto the mind of the man: messy, disorganized, a juxtaposition of high society with nature, always busy and forever full. The diaries have inspired the work of many of Beard's friends and admirers from Andy Warhol to Francis Bacon, and his rakish charm has attracted friends in the Kennedy and Rockefeller families as well as supermodel bedfellows. Beard later began specializing in photography, focusing mostly on African wildlife, but also photographing supermodels and rock stars such as David Bowie, Mick Jagger, Iman, and Veruschka. He never stopped writing and compiling his diaries which continue to be the true, day-to-day embodiment of his artistic impulses.

A fascination with Africa led Beard to travel there in his teens, and around a decade later to purchase the 'Hog Ranch' at the foot of the Ngong Hills in Kenya, where he would spend most of his adult life. Beard's existence at the ranch has comprised mainly of photography, drugs—marijuana and cocaine in particular but not exclusively—and endless sex. Rarely seen without a beautiful woman on his arm, Beard has embraced the remoteness offered to him by Kenya, free from the constraints of life in the West.

His work photographing wildlife has served to draw attention to the increasingly desperate state of his beloved continent. Beard's photography simultaneously indicates the beauty and vulnerability of nature, and the role which humans will play in either the preservation or destruction of the natural world. His work is thus some of the most influential of its kind, and allows its subject matter to speak for itself. The story of Beard's art is one of awe and wonder, anguish and despair, and points to the incredible intelligence and depth of imagination of the man.

Beard's time in Africa has been spent dancing with danger. His adventurous spirit has led him to think little of swimming with crocodiles, watching fellow adventurers be devoured, and famously winning a footrace away from a charging rhino with a safari guide, Terry Mathews, who was gored and thrown by the beast. In 2009, Beard's luck ran out while he was photographing elephants on the Tanzanian border in Kenya. Beard managed to aggravate a mother elephant, who charged at him. Beard's strategy was to cling on to the leg of the charging elephant in the hope he could escape her tusks. Though he managed to grip the leg, the elephant loosened Beard's grip and he fell to the floor, where she crushed him with her skull. Beard's pelvis was broken in five different places and he sustained a serious gash to his thigh. Beard arrived at the hospital to warnings that he would bleed to death, and entered the operating room with no pulse. After a few hours, Beard was fitted with an external scaffold which was pinned to his hip bones through the skin, and his bleeding was stopped. Beard was to make a full recovery, and would return as soon as he could walk to the drink-and-drug-fuelled adventures that he seems unable to resist, despite the obvious perils.

Beard is a drug enthusiast who seems unable to function without at least inebriation, and an adventurer who is oblivious to the danger in which he places himself, which make it easy to forget Beard's true importance as an artist. His work has sought to highlight one of the most pressing international issues, and provides a constant reminder of Beard's artistic brilliance. GE

JOSEPH BEUYS

Born in Krefeld near Dusseldorf in Germany, Beuys grew up during the Third Reich. He was a member of the Hitler Youth, partook in a Nuremberg Rally in 1936, and in 1941 he volunteered for the Luftwaffe. Stationed in the Crimea, Beuys's plane was shot down and his own account of his survival has become an integral element of his persona. He claimed to have been rescued and resuscitated by the nomadic Tatar tribes who nursed him to health using fat for warmth and wrapping him in felt to keep him insulated from the cold. Beuys's extensive use of these two materials in his work, animal fat and felt, derives from this story. This narrative has been questioned, proven false by some, and merely accepted by others, yet its veracity is perhaps not of importance. What it says more than anything about Beuys is that he understands the power of historical myth-making in the art world.

After the war, Beuys returned to live with his parents, still imbibed with the ideas of being an artist and sculptor that he had picked up while young. Joining the Dusseldorf Art Academy, Beuys became deeply influenced by the notion of anthroposophy, a philosophical and spiritual doctrine espoused by Rudolf Steiner that centred on the development of a supersensory consciousness not tied to the five senses, but nonetheless based on a scientific method. Beuys became entangled in the world of science, in particular its intersection with art, finding inspiration in polymaths such as Galileo and Leonardo. He was also deeply moved by James Joyce, and he would later fill six exercise books with drawings based on Joyce's *Ulysses*. Indeed, Beuys suggested that Joyce himself had commissioned him to illustrate the work as an extension of the novel itself, which given Joyce's death in 1941 attests to the complex and esoteric creative process Beuys worked by—it is known that Beuys only began working on the drawings in the early 1960s.

By the mid-1950s a potent combination of poverty and artistic insecurity led Beuys into a state of depression which he would emerge from by the time he was appointed professor of 'monumental sculpture' in Dusseldorf in 1961. Here Beuys began to express himself as the eccentric many know him to be, abolishing entry requirements for his course and beginning to associate himself with the Fluxus group. The group was described by its founder as 'a fusion of Spike Jones, gags, games, Vaudeville, Cage, and Duchamp'. If that were not explanatory enough, then the group was a loose collection of artists using various media in an attempt to destroy the gap between art and life. In this regard, the group often considered themselves anti-art, and Beuys's contribution would indeed lead to the ubiquitous question 'What is art?' or perhaps more pertinently 'What is not art?'

Punched in the face and bloodied is how some will know Joseph Beuys. In the middle of a performance piece in 1964, a student attacked Beuys leaving him bloodied, to which he produced a toy model of Christ on the cross and held his arm aloft in what has become one of the most enduring images of the artist. Here was Beuys openly sacrificing himself for his audience. Performance art was only one aspect of his contribution; he also included so-called traditional art in his works and art theory.

As Beuys gained international artistic currency and the fascination with him increased, he performed his first solo show *How to Explain Pictures to a Dead Hare,* which is regarded as his signature piece. Here Beuys could be seen covered in honey and gold leaf with an iron cast on one foot and felt tied to the other, cradling a dead hare. He sat and soothingly murmured explanations of his works to the dead hare.

He continued to use both felt and animal fat throughout his work representing the dichotomy between the man-made and the natural. His work would grow increasingly strange with a turn toward the growing conceptual art scene of which he was an itinerant part. 'Social Sculpture' as he called it was the form he continued to employ even after being dismissed from his academic post. His death in 1986 from heart failure did not stop his final project from being completed. *7000 Oaks,* a work of land art, was finished by others after Beuys's death.

An unashamed believer in the democracy of human expression, Beuys thought that everyone was essentially an artist. He was convinced that art is a fundamental expression of the human being, meaning it should not be curtailed by institution or training and that it must address the political, the social, and most importantly the personal. HB

**'Every man is a plastic artist who must
determine things for himself.'**

Joseph Beuys

PETER BLAKE

Sir Peter Blake is responsible for some of the most iconic images of modern times, and his presence can be strongly felt throughout contemporary popular culture. Blake's emergence on the art scene would coincide with the birth of the 'swinging sixties', and his pioneering contribution to the emergence of pop art cemented him as one of the most original artists of our day. Part of a generation of great artists which included R. B. Kitaj and David Hockney, Blake has become most famous for his work on a number of different album sleeves, including those of the Beatles's *Sgt. Pepper's Lonely Hearts Club Band* in 1967, the Band Aid single 'Do They Know It's Christmas?' from 1984, The Who's *Face Dances* of 1981, and Paul Weller's *Stanley Road* in 1995. Blake was appointed a member of the Royal Academy in 1981, awarded a CBE in 1983, and knighted in recognition of his services to art in 2002.

Born in Kent in 1932, Blake attended art school from the age of 15, and was given a place at Gravesend Technical College and School of Art after failing the entrance examinations for local grammar schools. Though not his first choice, the varied education Blake would receive at Gravesend played a significant role in the shaping of his artistic output later on in his career. In 1950, Blake's painting of his sister entitled *Portrait of Shirley Blake* earned him recognition from the Royal College of Art, and he was awarded a place to further his studies there. Blake would enrol at the RCA in 1953 after a brief hiatus serving in the Royal Air Force, carrying out his compulsory National Service.

Exhibiting at the John Moores Liverpool Exhibition in the Junior Section, Blake received First Prize, and this recognition led to a number of successful shows in the following years, including the first exhibition of the Brotherhood of Ruralists in 1976, of which Blake was a founding member. Alongside this, Blake experimented enthusiastically with what he termed 'found art', comprised of collages and collections of banal everyday objects such as match boxes, cigarette boxes, and photographs. Blake's ability to conjure captivating and popular art from the amalgamation of usually meaningless objects speaks volumes about his talent. His position in the public consciousness, and his place in the hearts of his fans, stems from his extraordinary ability to grab the attention of all who lay eyes on his pieces.

Blake claims that he is motivated by the desire to create new accessible art, similar in its tone to the popular music of the late twentieth century. As such, Blake has mentioned in an interview that he 'wanted to make an art that was the visual equivalent of pop music.

Peter Blake

When I made a portrait of Elvis I was hoping for an audience of 16-year-old girl Elvis fans, although that never really worked.' This is perhaps the reason for his enthusiasm for album covers, a clear example of the parallels between visual and audio art. Nonetheless, his iconic Beatles cover, one of the most recognizable pieces of pop art, has earned Blake little more than fame, as it emerged recently that he would receive no more than the £200 he was paid at the time, even though the album was to become one of the best selling of all time, recording over 14 million copies sold to date. In fact, the story of the Sergeant Pepper cover is a perfect representation of Blake's brilliance. Transported all over the world, on the shelves of millions of households, the album represents more than the Beatles. Through his work on its cover, Blake not only helped to elevate the album to critical acclaim with his embellishment of what was already a masterful musical product, he achieved his artistic raison d'être: to make beautiful and exciting art accessible to millions. When one holds a copy of any album to which Blake has lent his art, one is not only holding a piece of musical history, but holding a piece of Blake's mind, and it is this pervasive influence that grants Blake a place among our most original and influential minds. GE

'I wanted to make an art that was the visual equivalent of pop music.'

Peter Blake

Peter Blake

RICHARD BUCKMINSTER FULLER

Science can be a tough mistress. Of those who have achieved eponymous immortality in the sciences, relatively few have transcended interdisciplinary obscurity, and even fewer have done so with a name as unwieldy as that of prolific inventor, engineer, and futurist Richard Buckminster Fuller.

During quite a unique career at Harvard University, Fuller had the singular distinction of having been sent away twice, the first time for general irresponsibility, namely spending the entirety of his annual allowance on taking the chorus line of a local musical, some thirty girls, to dinner, and the second for 'lack of sustained interest in the processes of the university'. Coming from a distinguished yet relatively poor family, Fuller found himself alienated by the culture of clubs and brotherhoods and increasingly at odds with a university that seemed to care more for the rich than the outstanding.

Having served time in the United States Navy, and having worked various jobs including in the meatpacking industry and in a textile mill, Fuller then developed the Stockade Building System with his father-in-law. But overcome with depression, prone to drinking, and in a state of financial desperation, Fuller claimed that he contemplated suicide. He was then struck by a vision in which he was suspended above the ground in a sphere of light and a voice spoke to him informing him of his importance to the world and of his obligation to enrich it.

Fuller began investigating structures based upon his own theory of Dynamic Maximum Tension, Dymaxion for short, using physical principles from nature to derive structures both lightweight and stable. One of his first efforts was a safer, more aerodynamic Dymaxion Car. His Dymaxion House received great interest but was never commercialized. During the 1940s, Fuller began working on his idea of the geodesic dome, and in 1949 built his first complete structure, wowing viewers by dangling several of his students from the structure. His work was immediately put to use, one of his first customers being the U.S. military. Huge international acclaim followed, and Fuller received the Presidential Medal of Freedom. Many hundreds of thousands of Geodesic Dome structures have since been built around the world.

Fuller was also one of the world's great recorders. Claiming that he could not judge 'what was valid to put in or not', he decided to put everything in, recording his life every fifteen minutes from 1920 to 1987, amassing a pile of paper said to be 80 metres high, now

housed at Stanford University. Language and its use was a subject of great interest to Fuller. In 1927, he gave up the use of speech altogether for a period of two years claiming to have become suspicious of words and wishing to avoid the 'weakness of being a parrot'. Fuller wrote and spoke in a style entirely of his own devising. Examples of his rather elastic use of the English language include terms such as 'livingry' and 'thinkaboutable', and he substituted the words 'up' and 'down' for 'out' and 'in' respectively, as they 'better represent an object's position relative to its gravitational centre'.

He combined this eccentric vocabulary with a tendency to attack multiple topics; geometry, engineering, anthropology, philosophy, and more, the result of which lead to sentences such as 'the hierarchy of hierarchies of synergies' and 'things = events = patterns = somersaults = intertransformability systems' in his texts. Not lacking at all in conviction, Fuller claimed that where Malthus, Darwin, and Marx had been wrong, he had a plan to eliminate housing shortages and secure universal wealth for all. If further evidence of the multiplicity of Fuller's brain were needed, he famously chose to wear three watches: one for his current zone, one for the zone he had recently departed, and one for the zone to which he was going.

Fuller died in 1983. His last day was spent with his wife who was dying of cancer at the time, and who passed away just 36 hours after he did. Perhaps muddled and eclectic at times, his body of work is that of a truly remarkable man whose relentless drive to question, redefine, and improve was an embodiment of the spirit of science and progress, and whose desire to do whatever he could to protect the planet, his 'Spaceship Earth', was way ahead of its time. PG

'things = events = patterns = somersaults = intertransformability systems'

Richard Buckminster Fuller

MILES DAVIS

Born in 1926 when a new form of music known as jazz was just beginning to make waves in big urban cities, Miles Dewey Davis III arrived like a prophet to the bourgeoning genre. At age 13 he picked up a trumpet and within four years was performing with legendary musicians Charlie Parker and Dizzy Gillespie. His rise was meteoric, his talent grandiose.

At 18 Davis left Illinois, the city of his birth, for New York to enrol at the prestigious Julliard school. The institution lacked the dynamism that the jazz scene provided and it was in the heated nightclubs of Harlem that Davis found his true expression. It was there that he would meet his future band mates and there, in supple smoke-scented bars, that Davis would find the inspiration for bebop, the fast-paced virtuosic musical form influenced by 1930s swing. A year into his time at Julliard, Davis left to become a full-time musician joining the Charlie Parker Quintet which ended in unceremonious fashion as Parker fell foul to a drug addiction, foreshadowing Davis's fate.

Davis nonetheless continued to make musical waves with his nonet, a nine-piece group that included a French horn and a tuba. Davis was so smitten by this group that he turned down an opportunity to play with the Duke Ellington Orchestra, and despite the group's commercial failure, they would be retrospectively remembered as the pioneers of cool jazz. The nonet was Davis's first recording contract granted by Capitol Records, a milestone moment in his career.

From the early 1950s, Davis began struggling with a heroin problem that he would not recover from until 1955. The stresses of Davis's various relationships with women and his lack of acclaim in the music industry contributed to the development of his addiction. He continued to play, but mainly in Detroit where drugs were harder to come by. He recorded albums and music for both Prestige Records and Blue Note Records in this period, yet his personal manner became erratic and he was known to be withdrawn. His relationship with the press and music critics in particular was problematic, and they reciprocated this frustration by publicising his near fight with Thelonious Monk and other similar instances of unpredictable behaviour.

After his recovery, Davis continued to flit between bands with varying formations including his own quintet. It was however with his sextet that he would create what is widely considered to be one of the best albums ever made—not only in the genre of jazz. *Kind of Blue,* Davis's magnum opus, is the largest selling jazz album ever recorded, having gone platinum four times. It is a 46-minute concoction of improvised brilliance in which Davis makes his statement as one of the greatest musicians of all time.

In Davis's own words: 'It's not about standing still and becoming safe. If anybody wants to keep creating, they have to be about change.' Jazz fusion was to be Davis's next project, inspiring artists such as Jimi Hendrix, Sly & the Family Stone, and James Brown. This spawned the experimental record *Bitches Brew,* in which Davis used various electronic elements and disposed of jazz rhythms in favour of an even more improvised style. The revolutionary sound of the record led Duke Ellington to describe Davis as the 'Picasso of Jazz'. Davis would become the first jazz artist to be on the cover of *Rolling Stone* magazine.

Davis's albums increasingly polarised fans and critics. The music was unforgiving on the listener, demanding attention and patience as a riposte to those who had claimed that Davis was only interested in being popular. Another bout of drug abuse from the mid to late 1970s left Davis out of the music game until his return in the 1980s. Marsalis's critique of Davis as moving away from 'true jazz' was representative of the perception that Davis had fought against his entire career. For him, there was no true jazz, indeed 'Good music is good, no matter what kind of music it is.'

Miles Davis died in 1991, but his influence is so far reaching that in various genres of modern music, Miles Davis is still undoubtedly present. Modern jazz, hip-hop, rock, and soul are amongst the genres that owe much to Davis's impassioned desire to experiment, explore, and exchange tradition for innovation. A man never content to settle for the singular, Davis would say that 'sometimes it takes you a long time to sound like yourself'. HB

'A legend is an old man with a cane known for what he used to do. I'm still doing it.'
Miles Davis

Throughout his life, Marcel Duchamp continued to define and redefine himself in terms of original intellectual and artistic endeavours. Widely accepted as one of the most influential revolutionary artists of the twentieth century and a certified Chess Master, Duchamp's mind was forever searching new stimulation, and refused to fall into complacent acceptance of the status quo. Such was his influence, in fact, that fellow artist Willem de Kooning described Duchamp as a 'one man movement'.

Duchamp was born in 1887 in Normandy, and grew up surrounded by innovative and creative personalities. Marcel was one of seven children, four of whom grew to be successful figures across the art world, with his brothers Jacques and Raymond becoming painters and sculptors respectively, and his sister Suzanne also carving a career as a painter.

Duchamp studied art at the prestigious Académie Julian in Paris from 1904 to 1905, but chose to spend more time playing billiards than attending his lessons. Throughout his time at the Académie, Duchamp produced satirical and humorous cartoons, which he sold to the public. These drawings are perhaps the first tangible evidence of the keen sense of the subversive, coupled with intelligent humour, which came to define much of Duchamp's later work. The frequent use of puns, both verbal and visual, and symbolism indicate the power of Duchamp's intellect beginning to permeate through his early work.

Duchamp's family connections helped him in 1908 when, through his membership to the illustrious Académie Royale de Peinture et de Sculpture, Jacques secured the exhibition of Marcel's work in the 1908 Salon d'Automne. This was followed by the Salon des Indépendants of the following year, in which Duchamp's work also featured. The art critic Guillaume Apollinaire criticized Duchamp's work in the show, commenting that his nudes were 'very ugly'. Apollinaire would later become a great friend of Duchamp, as would the famously extravagant artist Francis Picabia. The two met at the 1911 Salon d'Automne, and Picabia's exuberant lifestyle rubbed off on Duchamp, who began to follow a social life in international high society, characterized most obviously by Duchamp's flourishing love affair with Cuban cigars.

Perhaps Duchamp's most famous work, or at least his most influential was *Fountain,* which he submitted to the Society of Independent Artists exhibition in 1917. The piece was composed primarily of a mounted urinal. Traditionally, all works submitted to these exhibits were displayed and were not judged on their artistic content, but the show's committee rejected Duchamp's piece from the show, insisting it was not art. The result was an uproar across the artistic community and Duchamp's resignation from the Society of Independent Artists. *Fountain* is indicative of Duchamp's broader attitude toward art; he was determined to redefine what could be perceived as art, and indeed the way perceptions of the function of art permeated society. His progression towards 'readymade' art, that is, pieces composed from everyday objects, illustrates a desire to subvert traditional artistic values, and to challenge viewers of his work to think as he thought himself. *Fountain* was declared the most influential artwork of the twentieth century in 2004 by a board of 500 internationally renowned historians and artists— it encapsulates Duchamp's revolutionary artistic conceptions.

A crucial part of Duchamp's subversion was his approach to humour. In 1919, he composed a parody of the Mona Lisa. Duchamp's version included a moustache and a goatee adorning an obviously cheap knock-off of the famous image. Duchamp signed the work 'L.H.O.O.Q.' The inscription, superficially innocuous, is an insight into Duchamp's mind. When read aloud quickly in French, it sounds like 'Elle a chaud au cul', which loosely translates as 'Her ass is getting hot', meant to insinuate sexual restlessness.

Duchamp spent much of his later life pursuing another of his great talents—chess. Travelling to Buenos Aires in 1918, he began carving his own wooden chess set. After moving between Paris and the United States in the following years, he largely disappeared from the art scene. While participating in the 1925 French Chess Championship, he earned the right to be called Chess Master. Obsessively playing to the exclusion of most other activities, Duchamp declared 'I am still a victim of chess', a view with which his first wife obviously agreed, as she took to gluing his pieces to the board to grab his attention. 'I have come to the personal conclusion that while all artists are not chess players, all chess players are artists,' Duchamp said. Perhaps he was right, but he was certainly both. It is clear that the link between Duchamp's two most successful pursuits was his indomitable intellect—he could not escape the urge to think, create, subvert, and imagine. GE

FEDERICO FELLINI

Born on 20 January 1920 in Rimini, Italy, Federico Fellini has left a great mark on contemporary cinema. His films are imbued with his razor-sharp wit, wild imagination, candid realism, and passion for the joys of life.

Fellini enrolled as a law student at the University of Rome in 1939, primarily to please his parents. Nevertheless, Fellini never attended a class at the university. Instead, Fellini primarily spent his time drawing and writing, teaming up with the painter Rinaldo Geleng, who would become a lifelong friend, to produce sketches of restaurant and café patrons. During this period, Fellini and Geleng were desperately poor, though Fellini managed to secure regular employment writing for the *Marc'Aurelio,* an influential bi-weekly surrealist humour magazine. Just four months after Fellini published his first article for the magazine, he joined its editorial board. Achieving notable success writing a column entitled 'But Are You Listening?', the magazine was Fellini's main occupation during the years 1939–42, and is often perceived as a seminal point in his life. The circles in which Fellini was able to move while at the *Marc'Aurelio* not only opened his eyes to the entertainment industry but also presented him with the opportunity to foster personal relationships which he would build upon throughout his career.

When Mussolini declared war in 1940, Fellini was just 20 but was developing an ever-growing interest in the greats of literature and drama, including Kafka, Steinbeck, and French cinematographers Marcel Carné, René Clair, and Julien Duvivier. In 1941, he published a self-penned booklet of ten chapters depicting the surreal adventures of Pasqualino, Fellini's alter ego. In 1942, Fellini started a new chapter in his writing career when he travelled to Libya, occupied by Fascist Italy, to work on the screenplay of *Knights of the Desert*. Fellini was forced to make an escape on a German military plane when Tripoli fell to the British, but his experiences there were the first that marked him as a reporter in the field, as well as a craftsman behind a desk.

Fellini's success continued to grow with his age, and he received his first Oscar nomination for the screenplay of *Rome, Open City* in 1947, and an Academy Award for the 1957 *Nights of Cabiria*. It was the 1960 *La dolce vita,* however, which he is best known for. The film's orgy scene was inspired by the increasingly prolific instances of paparazzi photographers capturing celebrities' behaviour while they were working on Italian film sets, and the film itself was heavily influenced by the improvised striptease Aïché Nana, a Turkish dancer and actor, in an Italian restaurant. The event, attended by countless Italian and foreign

celebrities, was immortalized by the candid photographs of Tazio Secchiaroli. Fellini's choice to reimagine the event in the film, depicting an orgy at a party in one of the final scenes, is a testament to his effortless ability to blend reality and the imagination. The film broke all box office records, and crowds queued for miles to view the movie, which had been branded as subversive and immoral by critics. *La dolce vita* reflected Fellini's original take on society, blending the cold light of reality with the warm glow of fantasy, and producing an idiosyncratic take on human life which is simultaneously ephemeral and firmly grounded.

Fellini received five Oscars during his career, setting the record for the most Academy Awards for the best film in a foreign language, including a special award for his remarkable service to the film industry. His work encourages deep thought and consideration from its audience, not without its fair share of controversy and criticism, and this surely is the main occupation of an artist—not only to think originally, but to inspire original thought in others. Fellini's films depict life as a circus, a party, and a dream, and have inspired modern greats including Tim Burton, Luis Buñuel, and David Lynch to pursue filmmaking in a similar vein—film whose dreamy substance reflects a sincere and long-running fascination with life itself. GE

**'There is no end. There is no beginning.
There is only the passion of life.'**
Federico Fellini

JEAN-LUC GODARD

A man whose life and work has come to be defined by originality of thought and of production, Jean-Luc Godard's influence on the arts is inestimable. Though they tackle a wide range of topics including Marxism, war, social upheaval, and love, to name an easy few, Godard's films have also made themselves their subject. His canon of work is amongst the first to attempt to consider the entire history of cinema and to reflect on the nature of the art itself. Littered with references to popular culture, historic cinema in particular, one cannot escape the sheer potency of intelligence that emanates from a Godard production. Godard stands not just as a producer of great twentieth century cinema, but as one of its chief architects.

Born in France to a wealthy Swiss family on 3 December 1930, Godard spent most of his early life in Switzerland. He did not go to the cinema as much as one might expect during this part of his life, but was an interested reader of film criticism and specifically attributes his introduction to the industry to a reading of *Outline of a Psychology of Cinema,* an essay by French novelist, art theorist, and Minister for Cultural Affairs, André Malraux. After the war, in 1946, Godard moved to France to study at the Lycée Buffon in Paris but moved back to Switzerland in 1948 after failing his baccalaureate exam. Godard passed the baccalaureate on his second try in 1949 and registered for a course in anthropology at the Sorbonne in Paris. This plan was short-lived as Godard did not attend any classes, perhaps distracted by the connections he was starting to make in this period, most notably in groups of young critics in the Parisian ciné-clubs. The members of such groups would go on to found the New Wave movement in French cinema—Godard was becoming drawn to the art which would define the rest of his life.

Criticism embodied Godard's active introduction to cinema, and he was amongst the three, with Jacques Rivette and Éric Rohmer, who founded the journal *Gazette du Cinéma* in 1950. After five issues of the *Gazette,* Godard began writing for the *Cahiers du Cinéma,* in which he made some of his earliest influential contributions to cinematic criticism. The next ten years saw Godard slowly progress to the production of his own films and, following a number of short films through the 1950s, he produced his first feature film *Breathless* in 1960.

It is perhaps unjust to draw a line between Godard's filmmaking and his criticism, as the films he made are works of criticism in themselves; each one a commentary on the nature of film. Throughout the 1960s, Godard made groundbreaking work that reimagined the

way in which cinema could be produced. The incorporation of jump-cuts and the use of a wheelchair to film tracking shots in *Breathless* and a constant tracking shot lasting eight minutes in *Week End,* demonstrate the attention Godard pays to progressive and original cinematic production, and are a testament to the versatility of his methods. Though Godard would move away from cinematic films later in his life, and towards more abstractly realised narratives and conceptually-based subject matter, this period of his work was revolutionary.

Towards the end of the 1960s and throughout the 1970s, Godard's productions became more radical. Increasingly reflective of extreme political views, especially his growing interest in Maoist ideology, much of Godard's work throughout this period remains unfinished, and many of the films that were completed were refused screening. In 1978, whilst commissioned by the government of Mozambique, Godard accused Kodak films of inherent racism as they did not fully reflect the depth of colour and colour variations in the skin of his African subjects; for Godard, a film and its medium are the embodiment of his understanding of the world. Godard's work continues, and has returned to its more traditional roots, but this period of radicalism is indicative of the extent to which Godard's personality infects his work.

Godard once said, 'All you need for a movie is a gun and a girl.' Perhaps this is true, but Godard has taken the simple ingredients of cinema and conjured a finished product that is unmistakably avant-garde. The originality of his thoughts and his dedication to their realisation has placed Godard amongst the finest artists ever to live—filmmaking is more than a profession for Godard, it is his existence. His films will forever continue to influence the industry. GE

'Art attracts us only by what it reveals of our most secret self.'
Jean-Luc Godard

Jean-Luc Godard

WALTER GROPIUS

As the founder of the Bauhaus movement, Walter Gropius was a modernizing, innovative, and inspirational force in the architectural world. He changed the face of society by rethinking how it presents itself.

Born in Germany in 1883, Gropius lived at a time when the Western world was experiencing significant and sudden shifts in its composition and outlook, and while living through two World Wars, numerous governments, nations, and cultures, Gropius played a crucial role in these changes.

Gropius studied architecture from a relatively early age. Between the years 1903 and 1907, he studied primarily in Munich and Berlin, before gaining employment with Peter Behrens in 1908. Behrens's studio was responsible for the AEG Turbine Hall, an imposing structure of glass, concrete, and steel, which marked a turning-point in modern architecture and clearly sowed the seeds of much of what was to come from Gropius's work. One of the most prominent examples of industrial architecture, the AEG building spoke volumes of its context. Practical and functional, the building exuded the growing role of industry in the modern world, dispensing with decoration and embellishment in favour of clean, simple design which spoke of intelligence, clarity, and efficiency.

By 1910, Gropius had established his own architecture practice in Berlin, designing the Fagus Works in Alfeld. The Fagus plant is another crucially important example of early modern architecture. Commissioned by owner Carl Benscheidt, the new works were designed as an overt break from the past, a revolutionary statement in German industry and its architecture. The building featured, for the first time, facades completely conceived in glass, unsupported corners, and thin, unobtrusive pillars. The result was a building whose design was at once recognizably industrial but strikingly open and modern, with straight, cubic lines and an effortless mix of basic outlines and contemporary materials. This is perhaps the first true example of Gropius's remarkable talent; the ability to blend revolutionary modernizing elements with simple structures and standard shapes.

The foundation of the Weimar 'State Bauhaus', a school that taught this modernizing architecture in 1919, gave Gropius his first opportunity to extend his influence beyond buildings towards the direct instruction of other great minds. With Gropius himself at the helm, the school employed Johannes Itten, Gerhard Marcks, and Lyonel Feininger as

Walter Gropius

its first three teachers, and immediately pursued an ethos of radical innovation. Though the Bauhaus school did not have an architecture department during these early years, its intention was to create 'total' works of art in which all composite disciplines, including architecture, would be brought together. The core curriculum was composed of preliminary courses and workshops, designed to inspire its students to create works which were simultaneously beautiful, simple, and easily produced. Having both artists and craftsmen as professors was what made the Bauhaus school so revolutionary, as it forced the combination of conceptual innovation and practical creativity. The Sommerfeld House in Berlin is the first tangible product of the school, designed by Walter Gropius and Adolf Meyer in 1921–22. It was furnished with the original creations of the students.

Gropius continued to expand the Bauhaus movement in the following years, especially after he was forced to move away from Germany during the Nazi government, as they claimed that Bauhaus, with its modernizing and collectivizing artistry was a 'centre of communist intellectualism'. He moved to England in 1933 and to the United States in 1937, taking a top professorship at Harvard. Becoming a U.S. citizen in 1944, the States played host to much of Gropius's innovations in his later career, and he is widely considered to be one of the most influential architects in the nation's history. Upon moving to the United States, Gropius designed his new family home, later named 'Gropius House'. Though modest in size, the house was a perfect example of the revolutionary impact of the Bauhaus movement. It integrated the traditional design of Gropius's new hometown, Lincoln, Massachusetts, namely wood, brick, and stone, with materials and craftsmanship rarely seen in domestic architecture. The house, whose glass block, acoustical plaster, and chrome banisters spoke of Gropius's indomitable desire to innovate, was built with maximum efficiency and simplicity of design. The house received enormous acclaim and was made a National Landmark in 2000.

Gropius's place in the common memory is secured by the physical works he and his school produced, but they are an allusion to a much greater substance. After all, the work of an artist can be no more than the physical embodiment of their intellect. Gropius is one of the great modern innovators and purveyors of original thought. He chose to rethink the way man could express himself through the buildings in which he worked and lived, founding a movement which has influenced almost all Western architecture and design. GE

ALFRED HITCHCOCK

Known as the Master of Suspense, Hitchcock is a giant of cinema. One of its most profound and provocative practitioners, Hitchcock is nothing short of an utter genius. Born in Leytonstone, London in 1899, Hitchcock was brought up a Roman Catholic. A 5-year-old Alfred Hitchcock could be seen in the local police office with a note from his father asking to lock him up for five minutes as punishment for bad behaviour. This parental tactic would instil a lifelong fear of policemen in Hitchcock and unjust accusations would become a strong theme throughout his life as a film auteur.

Rejected from the military due to his size (sometimes described as obesity), Hitchcock worked in advertising for a cable company called Henley's where he would contribute to the in-house magazine, the *Henley Telegraph*. Even these early pieces of creative fiction show some of Hitchcock's trademarks, thematically violent and often with plot twists at the end. His move into cinema began as he worked for a film company that would later become Paramount Pictures, designing title cards for silent films.

Hitchcock's early cinematic efforts were a spate of unfortunate commercial failures. His first attempts throughout the early 1920s saw him working in Germany, and Hitchcock was greatly inspired by German Expressionist film-making which he would take back to London with him as he became one of the first members of the London Film Society formed in 1925. A year later, Hitchcock released his first commercial success, the thriller titled *The Lodger: A Story of the London Fog*. Telling the story of a serial killer in London, the film would introduce some of Hitchcock's characteristic film traits. The same year as the film was being finished, Hitchcock married his assistant director, Alma Reville, who would retain central importance in all of Hitchcock's films due to her meticulous eye for detail. Years later, it would be Reville who would notice Marion Crane's dead body slightly twitching in a scene from Hitchcock's most famous film *Psycho*.

In 1929, Hitchcock began directing his tenth film, *Blackmail*, which would be converted from a silent film to a talkie in a landmark moment in British film history. Both the silent and the sound versions of the film were released concurrently as many theatres were not yet equipped for sound technology. The film also included a cameo by Hitchcock himself, the first of many in his illustrious filmography.

The rest of Hitchcock's early films in the 1930s, from *The Man Who Knew Too Much* to *The Lady Vanishes*, saw the director build both his reputation and stylistic palette. These were

commercial and critical successes in Britain and were beginning to garner praise from the United States as well. Hollywood was calling for Hitchcock, and David O. Selznick, who had just produced the massive hit *Gone with the Wind,* pulled off another master-stroke in signing Hitchcock to a seven-year deal in March 1939. The relationship between the two would be fraught by their mutual desire for creative control.

Despite the tension, Hitchcock would make his American debut in 1940 with *Rebecca,* starring Laurence Olivier and Joan Fontaine. The film won an Academy Award (picked up by Selznick) for Best Film. The 1940s once again saw Hitchcock dabbling in genres with *Mr and Mrs Smith,* a comedy with old-fashioned romance, and only two years later Hitchcock was directing *Shadow of a Doubt,* a psychological thriller. The latter is something of a landmark Hitchcock moment, considered by many his best film, and often referred to in interviews as Hitchcock's personal favourite. Commenting on the theme of the film Hitchcock said that 'love and good order is no defence against evil.' A motto that could apply to many of his films.

In Hollywood, Hitchcock would go on to work with various other artists, enlivening scripts by Steinbeck and dream sequences designed by Dalí, and constantly renegotiating the relationship between a film and its audience. This is particularly prevalent in his 1954 classic *Rear Window.* Admired by academics, auteurs, and amateurs, Hitchcock will remain a vast trove of entertainment, fear, analysis, and appreciation. His death in 1980 came four years after his last film release, at which point Hitchcock had already secured his position as a titan of cinema and perhaps the greatest director of all time. HB

'Television has brought back murder
into the home—where it belongs.'
Alfred Hitchcock

DAVID HOCKNEY

'The mind is the limit', David Hockney said. 'As long as the mind can envision the fact that you can do something, you can do it.' This is an insight on the life and outlook of the man. Putting one's imagination first and allowing it to control the direction of one's life is a mantra which Hockney has embraced fully over his career, prompting the personal style and a staggering life's work which has placed him amongst the most influential creative minds of all time.

Born in Bradford, England, on 9 July 1937, Hockney was educated at Bradford College of Art and the Royal College of Art in London. It was whilst at the latter institution that Hockney met the great R. B. Kitaj, and was featured in the exhibition 'Young Contemporaries' with Peter Blake, which signalled the arrival of British pop art. Hockney always maintained that he felt at home and enjoyed his years spent at the Royal College, but his time there did not pass without incident. The College initially insisted that Hockney would not be allowed to officially graduate, as he had refused to write an essay for his final grade—insisting instead that he be marked solely on his painting. Hockney produced his now famous piece *The Diploma* in protest and would not be moved on the matter. Ultimately, it was the RCA who was forced to concede and, in recognition of his startling artistic abilities and flourishing reputation, rewrote their regulations and allowed Hockney to graduate.

Hockney's work only grew stronger after his time in London, and precipitated a number of long spells living in the United States where he blended painting with travelling, copious beloved cigarettes, and an avid exploration of the American gay scene. Hockney once said 'Sex doesn't dominate my life at all, really. I think painting does', but that's not to suggest that sex didn't play a large role in the life of the man who has become known as the playboy of the art world. From his subtle early nods to sexuality, as seen in *We Two Boys Together Clinging,* to the overt expressions of his own homosexuality whilst in America, such as *Peter Getting Out of Nick's Pool,* the love and sex which filled his private life have never been far from Hockney's work.

The work Hockney produced whilst in the States is some of his most cherished and distinctive, and includes *Beverly Hills Housewife,* a 12-foot depiction of philanthropist Betty Freeman standing by her pool in a long hot-pink dress, which sold for $7.9 million at Christie's in New York in 2008 and set a new record for the sale of a Hockney painting. This move to the use of acrylic produced a series of similar paintings of swimming

pools inspired by his time in California, and these provide the most pertinent examples of Hockney's highly realistic, vibrant style. Hockney has only ever faced minimal, if any, criticism of his work, and this is perhaps because it seems to clearly represent the happiness and confidence of the man; the bright colours and easily digestible subjects of his art are a window onto Hockney's exuberant persona.

Hockney's impact has been felt across a much broader span of the creative world. He has played the role of unsolicited muse to a list of British designers too long to list. Vivienne Westwood, a close personal friend, sought also to stamp Hockney's name on the fashion world in 2012 by naming a jacket after the man. His personal style does not go unnoticed either. Indeed, in earlier years it seemed to form an extension of his painting style. Today, Hockney frequently appears in collations of best-dressed men, including those of the *Guardian* and *GQ* magazine.

Hockney's creative flair and impeccable style, partnered with his determination to never pass on the opportunity to broaden his horizons, puts him in perfect opposition with his famous statement that 'we grow small trying to be great'. Hockney has never tried to be great, but he exudes greatness with infectious and inspirational reminders of the originality of his character. Hockney is certainly not small—he is the embodiment of a spirit so seldom found, but so often desired. His life and work are the unique result of a man combining happiness, untold talent, and candid reflection on life, love, and the real meaning of things. As such, Hockney has not only provided an example of greatness, but he has enjoyed the process. GE

**'Drawing is rather like playing chess: your mind races
ahead of the moves that you eventually make.'**
David Hockney

AUGUSTUS JOHN

According to folklore, Augustus John's genius was the result of a swimming accident. Whilst diving into the sea on holiday in 1897, John seriously injured his head, and emerged from the water with his personality starkly changed. Whether or not this is true we may never know for certain, but we can be sure of two things: John's artistic brilliance and the hedonistic bohemian lifestyle from which it originated. After the accident, John grew a large beard, developed a deep love for travelling and an interest in the gypsy lifestyle, and engaged in sex with a vast number of women (so many that it became fashionable to claim that he had fathered one of your children), and was almost always drunk. His new adventurous lifestyle imbued his art, and this style of painting led to him becoming one of the most successful British artists of all time, winning the Slade Prize in 1898.

Born in Tenby in Pembrokeshire, John was the third of four children in his family, which includes his sister Gwen, an influential artist in her own right. John was educated in Wales, where he attended the Tenby School of Art for a short time, and later left Wales for London, studying at the Slade School of Art at University College London. Whilst at the Slade, John enjoyed impressive success, especially under the tutelage of his drawing teacher Henry Tonks, and was recognized even before his graduation as the most talented in his generation.

After his marriage to Ida Nettleship in 1901, encouraged by the prospect of having to support a family, John took up a teaching position at the University of Liverpool, though the Liverpool Art School (allegedly attached to the University) proved to be little more than a collection of sheds and outbuildings. This post did not last long, as John preferred to travel, often in a gypsy caravan with his family, drinking heavily and having numerous love affairs. By 1910, John had fallen in love with Martigues, a small town in Provence, France, which he had first seen from a train on the way to Italy. He purchased a house in Martigues, and lived there for some time before he felt the town had lost its charm, upon which he sold his property and moved to pastures new.

During the First World War, John had been conscripted into the Canadian army as a war artist, allowing him to keep his bohemian facial hair. He was the only officer in the Allied forces, aside from King George V, to have a beard. John's foray into the war was short-lived, however, and he was sent home in disgrace after only two weeks for his role in a drunken brawl in France.

By the end of the war, and certainly by the 1920s, John was Britain's leading portrait painter, and his subjects included a litany of famous faces such as Thomas Hardy, T. E. Lawrence, and George Bernard Shaw. Such was his renown that an international uproar was prompted when John was snubbed by Lord Leverhulme who had not appreciated his portrait, cut the head from the painting, and sent it back to John in the mail. In Paris, a 24-hour art strike which involved artists, models, and framers was called due to the insult that had been made to John's genius. In Italy a huge soap effigy of Leverhulme was ceremoniously burnt, and in London students marched carrying an enormous decapitated torso.

Many critics have suggested that John's talent went to waste in the later years of his life, and it is certainly true that his work did not match that of his younger years. Nonetheless, it is unjust to refer to waste when discussing such an influential character. On the contrary, such a personality as John's could not stay occupied by the same vocation forever. John's later life saw the pursuit of an increasingly hedonistic lifestyle, with no less drinking and promiscuity, as well as political activism which led him to join the Committee of 100's anti-nuclear weapons demonstration in Trafalgar Square, London on 17 September 1971.

When John died, on 31 October 1961, he left behind an incredible legacy. Not just his portraits, which are a permanent window onto his talent, but the legacy of his personality and lifestyle. John was more than the best painter of his generation—to judge his influence on his portraits alone would be to miss the idiosyncratic appeal of one of the greatest characters in the world of twentieth-century art. GE

'I belong to no definite school and I am not sure that any would be complimented if I did!'

Augustus John

LE CORBUSIER

Le Corbusier was a visionary yet controversial architectural figure, and amongst the twentieth century's most original thinkers. His views continue to divide those whose job it is to oversee the creation of our buildings and cities.

Charles-Edouard Jeanneret-Gris was born in 1887 to an affluent watch-making family at La Chaux-de-Fonds in Switzerland. At age 13 he entered a local school of arts and crafts and at 18 he and 15 contemporaries built a house for their teacher. Fascinated by architecture, he left to study abroad; in Italy, Austria, France (where Auguste Perret introduced him to concrete constructions), Germany (at Behrens's studio), Greece, and the Middle East. The communal architectural planning of the latter became a lifelong inspiration. He finally settled in Paris where he worked in a factory but continued to practise architecture (as well as painting and journalism) on the side.

His career in architecture began in earnest in 1922 when he, along with his cousin Pierre Jeanneret, established his first architectural practice using the name of his maternal grandfather, Le Corbusier. In that year they exhibited the Citrohan House, a new housing idea built on the principle that houses should be capable of being mass produced, and manufactured using existing industrial production, and should thus offer sustainably affordable housing. Houses, he contended, should be considered machines for living in.

Le Corbusier strived for simplicity, and a perfection of scale in his buildings. Following the Golden Ratio principle, he created a unit of size based on the height of a man with his arms aloft which he called the Modulor. Le Corbusier claimed that any structure based upon multiples of the Modulor would achieve perfect proportions.

In 1928 the pair began to work on the Villa Savoye. This was a time of great technical progress, which Le Corbusier embraced; steel-reinforced concrete allowed buildings to be hung from pillars, allowing for complete freedom internally. Roofs could be usable spaces, and huge glass windows would illuminate interiors. Commissioned by the Savoye family, the design for the structure followed Le Corbusier's 'Five Points', the basic tenets of his new architectural philosophy. The building garnered international importance and would go on to have a profound effect upon international modernism. The Savoye family was taken to a concentration camp in the Second World War, and the building was eventually passed into the ownership of the French state. Surviving several attempts at demolition, the Villa Savoye was eventually designated a national historical monument.

Le Corbusier

Le Corbusier applied his considerable intellect to the matter of urban planning. He railed against the cancerous spread of the suburb, arguing that man's love of nature and space was leading to its annihilation. Instead of sprawling sideways, he argued, towns should be built upwards creating large open spaces, allowing for maximum light and air, and minimum noise. 'The materials of city planning are: sky, space, trees, steel, and cement, in that order and hierarchy,' he wrote. In 1925 he proposed an urban masterplan for central Paris, La Ville Radieuse. Both radical and totalitarian, it was Le Corbusier's blueprint for the creation of a more harmonious society. He contended that housing be assigned on the basis of need, and not wealth. Never afraid of contentious language he decried the 'frightening chaos and saddening monotony' of the current urban environment; his advocacy of 'cleaning and purging' had faintly sinister overtones. 'Architecture or revolution' was amongst his most famous utterances; failure in the former would, he believed, inevitably lead to the latter.

Le Corbusier built some of the most iconic buildings of the twentieth century. Unite d'Habitation at Marseille was a 'vertical garden city', with everything from jogging to shopping available to residents in one integrated high rise. The City of Chandigarh, built from scratch in the foothills of the Himalayas, is as complete a realisation of the ideas within the Ville Radieuse as was ever built, and despite years of neglect it remains a modernist masterpiece. In 1950, Le Corbusier designed what was arguably the most iconic building of his long career, the Catholic church at Ronchamp. Almost impossible to define in style, it is more of a sculpture than a building, completely redefining religious architecture. The Convent of La Tourette, his last European project, was perhaps his most unique; 'a silent dwelling for one hundred bodies and one hundred hearts'.

He died in 1965. His funeral, which took place at the Palais du Louvre, was an affair of international importance. Of Le Corbusier, President Lyndon B. Johnson said, 'His influence was universal and his works are invested with a permanent quality possessed by those of very few artists in our history.' Le Corbusier believed in the power of architecture to create a harmonious society. His ideas were a tough sell to a conservative regime but his conviction was absolute. His biographer Nicholas Fox Weber sums him up thus: 'Compassionate, arrogant, generous, selfish, Calvinist, hedonistic, proud, enraged, ecstatic, sad, Le Corbusier the man was as provocative, and unique, as the buildings with which he changed the visible world.' PG

LUDWIG MIES VAN DER ROHE

One of the true pioneers of twentieth-century art, Ludwig Mies van der Rohe helped to establish a new tone in modern architecture. With contemporaries including Le Corbusier, Alvar Aalto, and Frank Lloyd Wright, Mies, as he was commonly known, aimed to establish a new architectural school which would befit modern times just as the Classic and the Gothic had done before. The ethos 'less is more' does much to outline the thinking behind Mies's work. He sought to create buildings, composed of clean lines and simple detailing, which instead of encroaching upon open space, would blend into it.

Mies was born in Aachen, Germany in 1886, and worked in a number of small companies during the early years of his life. These included his father's stonemasonry business and numerous different local design firms, before he moved to Berlin and joined the interior designer Bruno Paul. He would later join the studio of Peter Behren, in 1908, where he would work alongside great modern architects including the father of Bauhaus, Walter Gropius.

Despite never receiving any formal education, Mies's natural ability was noticed almost immediately, and he began taking independent commissions extremely early in his career. In fact, Mies was largely self-educated and extensively studied the works of great modern and classical philosophers and intellectuals, in order to arrive at a true sense of how best to tackle the changing world of technology and innovation in which he found himself. After the First World War, the old standard of architecture became increasingly prone to criticism, and was held to be the embodiment of an old, aristocratic social system which had long been outdated. Mies spearheaded a movement which chose instead to utilize modern design, innovative materials, and progressive ideology to move forward in the architectural tone of the twentieth century. This move was one away from the decoration and embellishment so favoured by designers such as John Ruskin and William Morris in Victorian Britain, and towards a total abandonment of ornamental design and unnecessary details.

Mies made a bold emergence onto the architectural scene, submitting a design proposal to the competition for the Friedrichstraße skyscraper. The pointed, all-glass design was a significant break from the perceived norm of Berlin architecture and marked the intellectual intentions which would define Mies's future career. One particular work, now considered to be one of his great masterpieces, proved particularly influential: The 1929 Barcelona Pavilion is renowned for its effortless blend of simple architectural forms and eye-catching materials—employing marble, red onyx, and travertine to complete the impressive, modern building. The same minimalism was extrapolated throughout the finished product, and every ounce of the project reflected Mies's intentions. From the walls to the specifically designed furniture, the entire Pavilion is indicative of the pioneering attitude which flowed through Ludwig Mies van der Rohe.

A second iconic building, the Villa Tugendhat, was completed in 1930 in the wealthy area of Černá Pole in Brno, in the Czech Republic. Built from reinforced concrete blocks, and casting a striking impression in white across the land it surveys, the building is heralded as one of the great examples of European modernism. Mies endeavoured to work by the motto 'God is in the detail', and this building is a particularly pertinent example of his success. Although marvellously simple from the outside, the building was constructed using a revolutionary iron framework, which enabled few connecting walls inside, thus creating a sense of space, light, and freedom for the inhabitants. One entire wall of the building is sheet glass, which opens by simply sliding into the floor below. Though the result is a simple and beautiful case of functionality, the power and complexity of the building's intellectual provenance is startling. A testament to Mies's innovative potential, the building represents all that is great about the modernism of the man; it was not only his mind, nor was it his vision of simplicity, it was his ability to combine the two in order to produce tangible results. As with Mies himself, a superficial layer of simplicity and calm disguised the precise workings of an astonishingly intelligent core.

Mies's legacy to modern architecture is profound. Having spent his career striving to produce buildings that preserved the beauty of light and open space, restricted only by minimal structural impositions, his fervour has inspired the present creative world. His work speaks of modernism in forms not existent during his lifetime, and is present in the work of great modern designers, from fashion to technology. Ludwig Mies van der Rohe counts among the great pioneers, and unlike so many others, the flame of his influence is not guttering in the modern winds of change. GE

GEORGE ORWELL

George Orwell died at age 46 of tuberculosis originally contracted whilst fighting for the Republicans in the Spanish Civil War. This tuberculosis was considerably exacerbated by his decision to live a most spartan existence in a damp and barely heated cottage on the Isle of Jura during one of the coldest winters of the last century. It was typical of a man for whom immersing himself completely in the harshest of conditions very much characterised the way he went about seeking the truth about the world in which he lived.

Orwell was born Eric Arthur Blair on 25 June 1903 in Motihari, Bihar, in British India where his father worked for the Indian civil service. He was brought back to live in England aged one. His intelligence was notable from very early on and when he was 14 he was awarded a Kings Scholarship to Eton where he stayed for four years. Always at the centre of argument and debate with his teachers, he sought to challenge established knowledge. This desire to defy the status quo ran throughout his life and work.

Orwell is of course best known for his two novels, *Animal Farm* and *1984,* both of which frequently appear in lists of the greatest works of the last century. And these books not only brought Orwell international fame but also at long last the financial stability he so desired throughout his life. In 2008, the *Times* named him second in a list of Greatest British Writers since 1945, behind Philip Larkin.

However it was his journalistic early writing, his documentation of the people and conditions of England, that was most remarkable. He was a great note-taker and keeper of diaries. Many writers have great descriptive abilities, but Orwell went even further. Rather than merely observing, he chose to immerse himself wholly. For *Down & Out in London and Paris* he slept rough with the prostitutes and other down-and-outs in Trafalgar Square, shaved in the fountain, and spent money on shared cups of tea so that he could warm himself in pre-dawn cafés. For *The Road to Wigan Pier* he slept in shared lodgings above a tripe shop.

He was perhaps the greatest chronicler of the English condition of the last century, listing national characteristics as 'suspicion of foreigners, sentimentality about animals, hypocrisy, exaggerated class distinctions, and an obsession with sport'. Under Orwell's pen England ceased to be a place and became a state of mind.

Artist

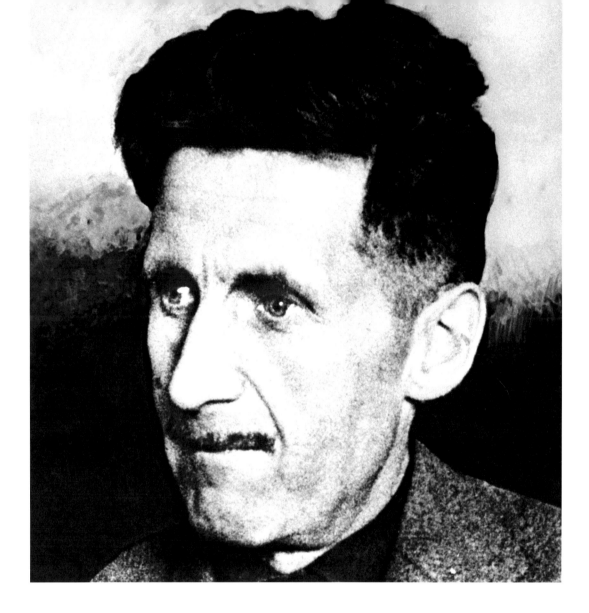

Orwell was above all else a socialist, and his rejection of socialist or pseudo socialist regimes was not a rejection of their goals but rather a rejection of their means, and of the dishonesty with which those in charge set about achieving personal gain over universal good. Honesty and decency were always primordial with Orwell; honesty in research, honesty in writing, and decency in political doctrine.

Orwell is often seen as something of an anti-hero, revered in messianic tones by those who enjoy the cult of the man who walked amongst the needy and the outcasts to achieve brief stardom before an untimely death. But Orwell was not a man who set out with a grand plan to heal the world, he was simply leading the type of life he was comfortable with. PG

VERNER PANTON

Panton was born on 3 February 1926 in Copenhagen, Denmark. His life would see him establish his place as one of the most influential Danish designers of all time, and his work would inspire countless contemporary innovators. During his career, Panton created futuristic and innovative designs for furniture, and employed the entire spectrum of modern materials, such as injection-moulded plastic.

Panton gained considerable experience as an artist in his early life, while living in the Danish city Odense. From there, he progressed to architectural school at the Royal Danish Academy of Art, from which he graduated in 1951. Upon leaving, Panton commenced his career in earnest, taking work from the studio of a fellow architect and furniture designer, Arne Jacobsen. The relationship did not last long, however, as Panton proved to be incredibly difficult to work with, and started his own firm, believing that partnership restricted his individual creative potential. Choosing to travel for some time in a VW camper van converted into a makeshift office, Panton made his way around Europe, meeting colleagues, manufacturers, and traders, and gained an invaluable experience of the industry on which he would leave his mark.

Throughout the mid-to-late 50s, Panton gained a wide reputation for original design. One such design was the Collapsible House which he released in 1955. The design, unprecedented in its concept, was indicative of Panton's ability to think laterally, and to create designs that fell far from the conventional. Other designs followed, including the Cardboard House and Plastic House. The collapsible, plastic, and cardboard houses allude to Panton's incredible ability to challenge the very foundations of design. Panton demonstrated that he was not afraid, nor was he unable, to dispense of the chains imposed on most designers by their artistic heritage. The designs Panton began to produce in this period, and the ones to which they would lead later, demonstrate that Panton's approach was not to adapt preconceived models to better suit the modern world, but rather to begin the creative process with a blank page, and to truly challenge his intellectual and creative potential.

By the 1960s, Panton's reputation largely centred around his designs for chairs. The plans moved increasingly far from accepted norms, including chairs which featured no legs and no arms. In fact, Panton was the first to produce a completely injection-moulded chair, composed of one single part in bright plastic. Though this design is indicative of an overwhelmingly 1960s ethos, especially in its original colours, the 'S chair' persists today, and is the most famous and the most reproduced of Panton's designs. The 'Fantasy Landscape Room' which appeared at the 'Visiona 2' exhibition, hosted by the chemical giant Bayer aboard boats moored at the Copenhagen Furniture Fair, is widely considered as the go-to example of 1960s design.

Though it is certainly true that Panton is a 1960s icon, his influences are broader than this label would suggest. Rooted in the practical functionality of the 1950s, and inspired by the growing change towards modernism which took place throughout this period, Panton's work forms a major piece of a much longer trajectory. He is responsible for harnessing the creative sentiment of a generation or more and using it to transform perceptions of the home and everyday functionality.

Through the 1970s, Panton continued producing examples of the tireless application of processes of original thought to traditional problems, creating more furniture, including lamps, walls, and ceilings which stood out in terms of beauty, functionality, and originality. As his career went on, Panton became increasingly able to seamlessly blend the composite parts of interior design to create a beautiful, simplistic finished product. His designs of the offices of *Spiegel* publishers in Hamburg, which was completed in 1969, and the restaurant 'Varna' in Aarhus in 1970, appear as the most famous examples of this. The seamless integration of walls, ceilings, floors, furniture, and fittings producing a complete unit exudes modernism and simplicity.

Panton's work speaks of a tireless enthusiasm for innovation, and the products are joyous in their presentation. It is clear that not only did Panton have a remarkable talent, he enjoyed the process as much as the world enjoyed the product. From bold colours to unconventional shapes, Panton's work is a decisive move away from the drab and uninspiring work which had come before. Perhaps this is best explained by the conceptualization of Panton not as another step on the ladder towards modernism, but a completely different entity. A true cultivator of original thought, Panton was, and remains, one of the seminal forces in modern creativity. GE

WILLIAM EGGLESTON

This non-conformist southern aristocrat became a pioneer of colour art photography. Much copied in the world of fashion, William Eggleston's influence and originality are unrivalled.

Born in Memphis, Tennessee in 1939, Eggleston's family owned cotton plantations. He played the piano and loved tinkering with electronic gadgetry, collecting cameras and guns which he would take apart, fascinated with the engineering behind them. Eggleston spent six years attending various universities, none of which resulted in a degree of any kind. But it was during these years that his deep love of photography began to take root. Eggleston claimed not to be a fan of photojournalism, but he describes coming across the book *The Decisive Moment* by Henri Cartier Bresson, and being struck by the 'great art, composition like the work of great painters, like Degas'. All of his early work was in black and white but in 1965 he began experimenting with colour film.

Whilst teaching at Harvard, Eggleston was visiting a photo lab. At the top of the price list he saw 'dye transfer printing'. The technique was employed to great effect in cigarette ads and the like, but it had never been used by an art photographer. Eggleston was entranced by the saturation of the colours: 'Every photograph I subsequently printed with the process seemed fantastic.'

In 1976 Eggleston made his artistic breakthrough with a solo show at New York's MoMA. Filled with his trademark photographs of nothing in particular—a dog drinking from a puddle, a lady standing by the side of a road, a child's tricycle, a shower, an oven—it riled many critics. Described by MoMA's curator of photography, John Szarkowski as perfect, one reviewer resonded, 'perfectly banal, perfectly boring'. But it broke new ground, at that moment colour photography became an art form. His style is so frequently copied today that it is difficult to understand the exhibition's ability to shock, but it was profound.

Like a somewhat careworn southern dandy, Eggleston looks a little out of step with modern life and enjoys a highly unconventional private life. He kept two large houses in Memphis, one for his wife and children, the other for his mistress. He once told photographer Juergen Teller, a great admirer of his: 'We have a couple of things in common. Drinking, smoking, and women. Photography just gets us out the house.' At one point he embarked on an affair with Viva, the most striking of the Warhol Factory girls, and it was Warhol who introduced him to video. His friends in Memphis were a gang of

hard-drinking geeks and Quaalude-popping misfits whose lifestyle he perfectly captured on the legendary video work *Stranded in Canton*. His house is riddled with holes from his $6,000 antique shotguns. Primal Scream wanted to use a photo from Eggleston's *Troubled Waters* series as an album cover so they drove to his home to seek permission. There they found him dressed in jodhpurs, leather boots, and holding a rifle with a bayonet attached. Hearing they were Scottish, he sat at his piano and started to recite Robert Burns. On request, they played him a song from their album at which he fell to his knees shouting, 'Bo Diddley, Bo Diddley, y'all love Bo Diddley!' Then his wife took them for ribs. Memphis producer Bill Dickinson describes him thus: 'He wore Savile Row suits and drove a Bentley and played classical piano but was more rock 'n' roll than any of us.'

He still lives and works in Memphis and over the years he has shot thousands of photos of the city, always favouring the commonplace and the banal. Fast food, cars, metal, neon, plastic, the contents of a freezer, and shoes under a bed. He provides a glimpse into the world of the American South. Eggleston's is a rigorously disciplined approach, never taking more than one picture of any one thing. His style is simple but his compositions often appear incomplete, seemingly mis-framed—he has the ability to make the everyday world seem like a very alien place. He photographs what he describes simply as 'life, today', mere hints of a darker world he doesn't want to elaborate on. Always elusive, often abrasive, Eggleston rarely grants interviews. He also dislikes talking about his works, feeling it diminishes them: 'They're right there, whatever they are.'

What Eggleston achieved was startling. He works between gritty photojournalism and high gloss commercial photography, and from that small niche has created a whole art form. In the words of Martin Parr, he photographs 'the gap between everything else'. PG

'He wore Savile Row suits and drove a Bentley and played classical piano but was more rock 'n' roll than any of us.'

Memphis musician and producer Bill Dickinson

I. M. PEI

Chinese-American architect Ieoh Ming Pei's career is defined by modesty and manners. He wears sober suits that are tailored in Hong Kong, as well as crisp white shirts with immaculate French cuffs. He drinks English tea with milk and wears round spectacles in the style of Le Corbusier that magnify his heavy-lidded eyes. Pei is unfailingly polite and respectable, preferring that even his closest associates call him I. M. rather than Ieoh Ming. His colleague Arthur Rosenblatt summed him up perfectly: 'He's like the greatest maître d' at the greatest restaurant in the world.'

It therefore comes as a surprise that what drew someone as upright as Pei from his native China to America was not the reputation of the architecture course at the University of Pennsylvania—to which he had won admission in the 1930s—but rather the elastic slap-stick of Buster Keaton and Charlie Chaplin, and the screwball college films of Bing Crosby. Pei was born in Guangzhou in 1917, and his childhood was trying. His father was a prominent banker and distant, while his mother died when he was 13. It meant that by the time Pei set sail for San Francisco in 1935, he was ready for the glamour and zaniness promised by the movies. 'College life in America seemed very exciting to me,' he later remarked. 'It was all a dream, of course, but a very alluring dream for a young man from Canton.'

It was the Hollywood atmosphere that lured Pei to America, and sensitivity to atmosphere would go on to define much of his subsequent architectural work. Pei studied for a time under the Bauhaus modernist Walter Gropius and his buildings were heavily influenced by the International Style that Gropius and his ilk developed. But Pei's work is not as megalomaniacal, prescriptive, or proselytising as much modernist fare. His 1967 laboratories for the National Center for Atmospheric Research in Colorado are as geometrical and machine-aged as they come, but are also clad in natural rose-coloured stone to help them blend in with the nearby Rocky Mountains. His 1961 Luce Memorial Chapel is a concrete teepee that slips serenely into the surrounding Taiwanese land-scape. 'I became interested in a modern architecture that made connections to place, history, and nature,' Pei once said. 'Modern architecture needed to be part of an evolutionary, not a revolutionary, process.' Indeed the modernism that Pei has spent his career developing is a direct extension of his own mild manners. Pei has never been one to browbeat, more one to gently cajole over tea.

Yet Pei's work has nonetheless been noteworthy for its capacity to offend. His 1979 John F. Kennedy Library & Museum in Boston was well received by critics, but its protracted

I.M. Pei

creation was a lesson in attrition, where a succession of cost cutting, downscaling, location changes, and bitter local opposition soured the project. It was oddly appropriate when the structure ended up being built on top of a major sewage pipe. Pei worked on the ventilation system to compensate.

The difficulties of the Kennedy project paled in comparison to those surrounding Pei's most celebrated project however, the glass and steel Pyramide du Louvre that he completed in Paris in 1988. A new entrance for the city's Louvre museum, Pei's pyramids were modern and contrasted sharply with the otherwise classical architecture of the museum. So unpopular was the design at the time of its commission that Pei was spat at on the streets and Parisians took to wearing badges reading 'Pourquoi la Pyramide?' Ill ease reached farcical heights when false rumours circulated that Pei had constructed the structure out of 666 panes of glass, the number of The Beast. A specific plot point in Dan Brown's 2003 potboiler *The Da Vinci Code* is that Pei embedded these demonic overtones at the 'explicit demand' of France's socialist President Mitterrand.

Even when faced with accusations of satanic, socialist pandering, Pei has always taken setbacks in stride. When spat at in Paris, he reacted with predictable reserve. 'He was very poised,' remembered his daughter Liane. 'His attitude was, "Well, grin and bear it."' It is a natural grace that has led him to win every major honour in architecture, while retaining a studied modesty about his own achievements. Nominally retired since 1990, Pei has nonetheless continued to design major projects such as Doha's monolithic stone Museum of Islamic Art and the meditative Suzhou Museum for ancient Chinese art. It is a prolificacy that reveals the work ethic that has always characterised Pei—a trait that came to the fore particularly memorably in the late 1970s.

In 1978 Pei was commissioned to design a hotel for Fragrant Hills, a former imperial garden and hunting preserve at the foot of the Western Mountains in northwestern Beijing. It was Pei's first Chinese commission and he was keen to impress, abandoning his more familiar modernist aesthetic for a traditional style that reflected Chinese heritage through subtle window and wall tile patterning. Pei had more than 3,000 workers under his command to complete the hotel, but close to the building's opening became aware that there was still much work to be done. Pei felt obliged to intervene to make sure that the project would be ready on time. He and his wife scrubbed floors. Their children made the beds. os

I. M. Pei

YVES SAINT LAURENT

Few fashion designers attain, or aspire to attain the status of national treasures, but Yves Saint Laurent, widely regarded as the seminal French designer of the twentieth century, defied all expectations. If one had predicted at his birth that a sickly, nervous boy would not only match but outstrip his mentor Christian Dior, it might have seemed an outrageous statement, yet Saint Laurent went on to redefine women's fashion in spectacular ways, initially scandalizing and then seducing the notoriously cliquey French haute couture scene. If any man could be said to be responsible for modern dress, it was Saint Laurent.

Born Yves Mathieu-Saint-Laurent on 1 August 1936 to French-Algerian parents, he was a lonely child, more comfortable designing paper dolls and dresses than playing with other boys, who routinely bullied him for his effeminacy. His obvious talents in this area saw him head to Paris at the age of 18, where he won a prestigious prize at the Chambre Syndicale de la Couture for designing a cocktail dress; the runner-up was Karl Lagerfeld. This brought him to Dior's attention, and the older man hired him immediately, proclaiming 'Saint Laurent is the only one worthy to carry on after me.' His legacy came sooner than he might have imagined; Dior died of a heart attack in 1957, and Saint Laurent, at the age of 21, found himself the head designer of Dior.

A lesser man might have panicked and crumbled, but Saint Laurent's physical frailty was matched by both mental toughness and an abiding talent. His first solo collection in 1958 removed much of the stuffiness from Dior's clothes and led to *Le Figaro* pronouncing him France's saviour. However, his subsequent collections, predicting the leather and hobble skirted fashions of the 1960s, were less successful, and Saint Laurent found himself conscripted into the army in 1961, apparently at the behest of Dior's owner, Marcel Boussac, who loathed his designs.

Predictably, his brief sojourn in the army was a disaster, and Saint Laurent had a nervous breakdown in less than a month, whereupon he was incarcerated in a military hospital and given electroshock treatment. However, this ordeal would prove to be his salvation, as he was rescued by a young art dealer called Pierre Bergé, who managed to remove the fragile young man from his hellish surroundings, and, after successfully suing Dior, Saint Laurent established himself as a designer in his own right, with Bergé as his lover, business partner, and intermediary with the outside world.

Freed from the need to conform to a major label's expectations, Saint Laurent spent the 60s experimenting with trendsetting outfits such as his legendary 1966 women's tuxedo suit, 'Le Smoking', and popularizing the beatnik outfits he had experimented with during his time at Dior. His fame and success rose throughout the decade, peaking with the opening of his first Rive Gauche store, selling affordable and stylish *prêt-à-porter* clothing in 1966; his first customer was an early muse, Catherine Deneuve. He hung around in bohemian circles that included the likes of Picasso and Andy Warhol, was an early patron of Studio 54, and spent time in a villa in Marrakech, which offered him both a haven and a source of inspiration.

Unfortunately, success and pressure went hand in hand, and as he ruefully commented in 1968, 'They crowned me king ... look what happened to the other kings of France.' Taking refuge in cocaine and alcohol, his health suffered dramatically, with public appearances at his shows often seeing him having to be supported by Bergé (who he separated from romantically in 1976) and others. He also faced criticism for some of his more outré designs, such as a 1971 spring collection that was felt to glamourize French occupation chic. At his worst, Saint Laurent suffered crippling depression, and increasingly compared himself to his idol Proust, flirting with suicide as a means of escape. He once said, 'I was suffering so much that I considered attaching the heaviest bronze from my collection round my neck and throwing myself into the Seine.'

While the 1980s started well, with Saint Laurent the first fashion designer to be granted a show at the Metropolitan Museum of Art in 1983, it was rumoured that the once-unassailable artist had lost his touch, culminating in a disastrous 1987 show in which models paraded up and down the catwalk in $100,000 casual jackets; at a time of economic unrest, he could scarcely have been further from the zeitgeist. Stung by criticism, he all but retreated from the public eye, putting his *prêt-à-porter* line in his assistants' hands. Thereafter, he became something of a recluse, although a canny one, selling his company in 1994 for a £40 million profit. His final show in 2002 saw him return to the limelight once more for a spectacular farewell, for which tickets sold for thousands of pounds. He spent his final years living quietly until his death caused by brain cancer on 1 June 2008 at the age of 71, survived by the ever-loyal Bergé.

As the release in 2014 of two separate films about his life shows, Saint Laurent remains a towering figure in French popular culture, and the fashion house that bears his name (now owned by the multinational Kering) has a turnover of over a billion dollars a year. This is impressive, all the more so for a visionary man who once claimed that his major regret was not to have invented blue jeans: 'They have expression, modesty, sex appeal, simplicity—all I hope for in my clothes.' Given his peerless accomplishments elsewhere, he can be forgiven this one omission. AL

Yves Saint Laurent

TAKESHI KITANO

'Beat' Takeshi, as he calls himself, is one of Japan's more unusual cultural figures. The lazy might style him as an Oriental answer to Martin Scorsese, given his emphasis on gangsters and crime in his films, but this ignores a remarkably eclectic career that has encompassed everything from stand-up comedy and film direction to painting and video game design. Yet, calling him a Renaissance man seems inappropriate; 'restless man' is closer to the mark, given Kitano's near-endless stream of projects and output. This desire for expression in all its forms has led to accusations ranging from tastelessness to prurience, but he has maintained his signature blank-eyed stare in all situations, leaving his audience to wonder how far he is in on the joke—if it is a joke at all. As he once said: 'Humour is like violence. They both come to you unexpectedly, and the more unpredictable they both are, the better it gets.'

Takeshi Kitano was born on 18 January 1947 in Tokyo. His first public appearances came in the 1970s when he formed a comic double act with his friend Kiyoshi Kaneko as a *manzai* duo, where Kaneko acted as the straight man and Kitano dished out insults to virtually every member of society at high speed. While their act attracted high amounts of opprobrium for the near-the-knuckle and often shocking jokes that they specialized in—often resulting in censorship and eventually a five-year ban from the network because Kitano exposed himself on air—it established Kitano as both reckless and calculating. It also allowed him to develop a successful comic career on television, most notably as the presenter of the slapstick show *Takeshi's Castle,* a light-hearted gameshow in which he played a count who set a variety of challenges for the contestants. Yet even this mainstream show saw him refine a persona as a taskmaster and all-knowing controller, mirrored by his creation of a near-impossible video game, *Takeshi's Challenge,* in 1986, apparently as a result of his disdain for the medium. It sold over 800,000 copies.

He acted throughout the 1980s, most notably in the David Bowie film *Merry Christmas, Mr Lawrence,* but he moved away from the comic roles with which he had become synonymous with his 1989 directorial debut *Violent Cop.* Living up to its title, it combined deadpan black humour with extreme violence, and established Kitano as a critical favourite in Europe. His domestic audiences, who had expected a broad comedy with a popular TV actor, were less receptive. His 1990 follow-up, *Boiling Point,* was his first film to focus on the yakuza, a subject that he would later delve into in his international breakthrough, 1993's *Sonatine.* Its mixture of surrealism and brutality mystified Japanese audiences, who responded angrily to the film. Perhaps in part because of the rejection that he faced at home, Kitano was involved in a horrendous motor accident in 1994, which paralysed half his body and damaged his face; he later described the event as an 'unconscious suicide attempt'.

Recovering from his accident, his career took a different turn. He divided himself into two characters, the film director Takeshi Kitano and the stand-up comedian and TV star 'Beat' Takeshi. As a director, he eschewed the absurdist black comedy that had typified his earlier work in both film and television, and embraced a more meditative direction, taking up painting 'for the sheer joy of it', and making what became his most acclaimed film, *Hana-bi,* which still had little domestic interest but was highly praised in Europe for its serene approach. The autobiographical elements were particularly noted; its protagonist Nishi is, like Kitano, a painter in the pointillist style, and its focus on the hollowness of violence seemed to reflect his feelings about his accident. As he said, 'I intentionally shoot violence to make the audience feel real pain ... I have never and will never shoot violence as if it's some sort of video game.'

'Beat' Takeshi, meanwhile, regained much of the domestic popularity that he had lost with his films through his regular TV appearances on everything from topical chat shows to stand-up comedy programmes. His more recent films have also nodded in a more mainstream direction, notably his 2003 samurai picture *Zatoichi* and a return to the yakuza genre with *Outrage* in 2010, a film that he claimed to have made purely to entertain, with a plot based around the ways in which various characters would be killed. It was successful, and spawned a sequel—the first of his films to do so.

Away from cinema, he has cheerfully attracted controversy in both his private and professional life, while continuing to build a reputation as forthright and uncompromising. When he was photographed leaving a 'love hotel' with a young actress, he and some friends promptly visited the newspaper that published the pictures and attacked the editor responsible with umbrellas, an act that combined surrealism and violence with a flair worthy of any of his films. Treated as a respected auteur by European and American film critics, and as a perennially popular—if sometimes confusing—entertainment figure at home, the suspicion lingers that Kitano will always have the last laugh, even if that laugh is a fairly bleak one. As he said, 'I do all these activities like painting and writing, comedy and films, probably not because I'm good at everything but because I'm not good at any of these things.' AL

'Humour is like violence. They both come to you unexpectedly,
and the more unpredictable they both are, the better it gets.'

Takeshi Kitano

Takeshi Kitano

CHAPTER 2

Hero

In ancient Greek society, a hero was a mortal who had done something so extraordinary that upon his death he left behind him an undying memory and was thereafter worshipped as a god. These early heroes were not always good, but their feats were always beyond the scope of normal human endeavours, and they inspired people to dream of new possibilities for human existence.

You don't have to perform an act of extra-ordinary bravery to be somebody's hero. A hero in politics or sport is every bit as valid as a hero in war. It is also worth noting that heroism does not always carry a moral dimension to it. Some might prefer their heroes to be righteous, but immorality or an unpalatable political or philosophical doctrine doesn't preclude heroic status—unpleasant people do heroic things all the time.

Most of the men who make our list are the *Boy's Own*[1] sort of heroes: military men, explorers, sportsmen, men of physical action. As a younger man I was mad on sport. I struggle to recall any early heroes who were not sportsmen. Most played rugby football. The Scotland team at the time was populated almost entirely with heroic figures. Iain Milne 'The Bear', John Jeffrey of Kelso 'The Great White Shark', Rutherford of Selkirk, Laidlaw of Jedburgh, Renwick of Hawick; hard, honest (mostly moustachioed) men playing in an amateur age for the love of their sport and country. They drove ordinary cars to ordinary homes and ordinary jobs but their actions on the field elevated them to divine status. I would stand outside my garden and wave at the team bus as they passed on their way from the Braid Hills to Murrayfield. Many would wave back. I watched them annihilate England in 1986. It made me proud.

Professionalism has changed sport, driving a wedge between public and players. Today's overpaid sports stars have anointed themselves gods. Footballers perhaps worst of all. Bejewelled and pampered where they were once self-effacing and stoic, with nicknames like 'Iron' and 'Chopper' that spoke of their hardness and spirit. Other sports too were more thrilling and dangerous when sport was closer to its humble roots. Current stars are far too highly paid and too focused to be interesting. It was the ill discipline, the spontaneity, the sense that anything might happen that was so compelling in sport before the professional era. The sheer mortality of the combatants. The sporting heroes of the last century played with a passion that many of today's best paid sportsmen seem to be missing. There was a tangible sense that these magnificent men were still, like us, human, mortal, and that perhaps what was possible for them might be possible for us.

Our selection of heroes also includes military men, explorers, and men who have endured tremendous physical hardship, and in some cases extreme mental torment. The military continues to produce a long parade of heroic figures. However, the men we have chosen to feature stand above the ranks for their extraordinary originality of character, not for their great bravery. There were certainly more successful military figures, and undoubtedly luckier, but few carried out their soldiering with greater élan. Explorers too could fill a tome on heroism. Adamantine adventurers in battered felt hats, canvas cagoules, and damp tweeds. Their obstinacy and determination makes them sublimely heroic.

Henry Thoreau said 'cowards suffer, heroes enjoy'. Happily there are still those who enjoy the suffering, as we can all benefit from a hero. They encourage us to live better and fuller lives. Our heroes help us define our ideals and aspirations. More often than not, they possess the very qualities we most wish for ourselves.

---

[1] The *Boy's Own Paper* was a British weekly paper published from 1879 to 1967 featuring adventure stories, nature, sports, and puzzles for young and teenage boys. Similar titles appeared in the United States and Canada.

MUHAMMAD ALI

Ali was not only the most gifted boxer of his generation, but also became a symbol for the battle against racist oppression and discrimination. His controversial political and religious views at times threatened to make him a public persona non grata, but ultimately people came to adore him and consider him as 'The Greatest'.

Muhammad Ali was born Cassius Marcellus Clay Jr on 17 January 1942 in Louisville, Kentucky. He took up boxing at the age of twelve, winning his first fight that same year. He went on to win six Kentucky Golden Gloves titles, an Amateur Athletic Union National Title, and in 1959 won the National Golden Gloves Tournament of Champions. Ali's amateur record was 100 wins with five losses. In 1960 Ali, a then lanky eighteen-year-old, was selected for the US team for the Rome Olympics and came home with the gold medal in the light-heavyweight division. Ali made his professional debut on 29 October 1960 and over the first three years of his career notched up a record of no losses and 19 wins, 15 by knockout. Ali was gaining as much of a reputation for deriding opponents as he was for boxing. His taunting of opponents was relentless and despite being delivered with a huge toothy grin, it did not endear him to either sports writers or the public, and earned him the nickname the 'Louisville Lip'.

Ali first attended a Nation of Islam meeting in 1961, and in 1962 he met Malcolm X who became a spiritual mentor. It was at this time that Cassius Clay changed his name to Muhammad Ali. Many in the boxing world refused to call him by his new name, and Ali's beliefs drew a wedge between him and much of the population.

By 1963 Ali had emerged as the number one contender to fight then heavyweight champion Sonny Liston. A fight was set for February 1964. Ali called Liston 'the big ugly bear' claiming that he 'even smells like a bear.' 'After I beat him I'm going to donate him to the zoo,' he added. It was in the run up to this fight that he told the world that he intended to 'float like a butterfly and sting like a bee,' saying to Liston 'Your hands can't hit what your eyes can't see'. The outcome was one of boxing's greatest upsets. From the opening bell, Ali danced around Liston, making him look clumsy and lead-footed. Ali landed a combination in the third round, which buckled Liston and cut his eye. The fight lasted three more rounds before Liston refused to come out for the seventh, handing Ali the victory. A rematch in 1965 saw Ali knock down Liston in the opening round by what was later dubbed the 'Phantom Punch'.

Muhammad Ali

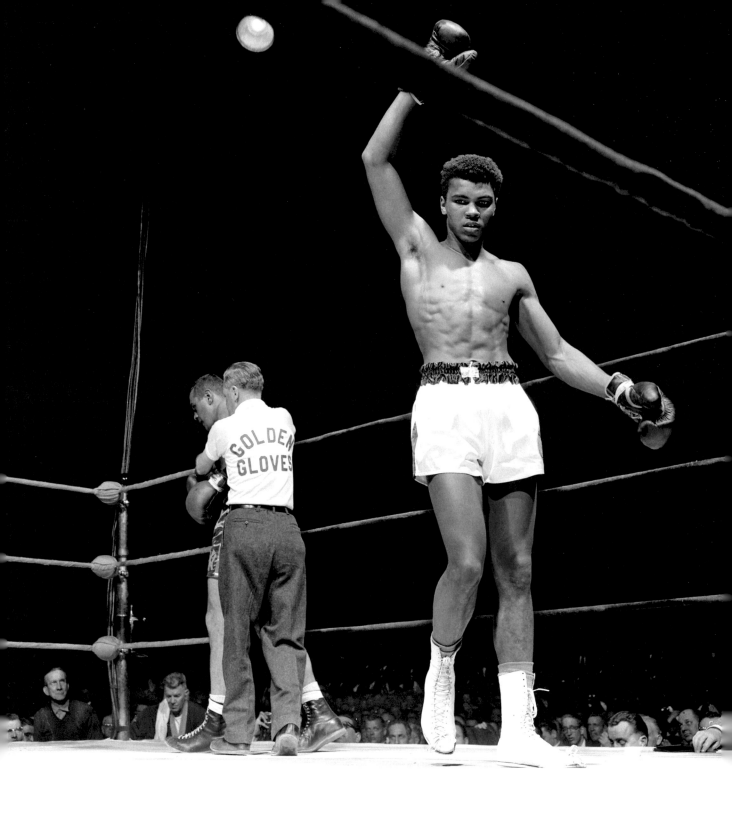

Muhammad Ali

Also in 1965, during the Vietnam War, Ali was made eligible for the draft. Ali claimed to be a conscientious objector on religious grounds, also stating famously, 'I ain't got no quarrel with them Viet Cong.' At his scheduled induction on 28 April 1967 in Houston, Ali refused to step forward when his name was called and was immediately arrested. He was stripped of his boxing licences and his title, and began a period of three years in boxing exile, a time which should have been the prime of his professional career. At the time, Ali was vilified for his refusal to serve but as the years passed public opinion swung against the war. Seen by many as dangerously anti-establishment it was exactly this that made him a hero to so many. In a time when the civil rights movement was gaining ground, Ali became a poster boy for the overthrow of oppression, touring the United States speaking to huge college audiences.

In 1970, he got his boxing licences back and after a couple of lacklustre fights was again lined up to fight for a world title, this time against Joe Frazier in what was touted as the 'Fight of the Century'. In an epic battle, Frazier triumphed handing Ali his first professional defeat. A rematch against Frazier, this time a win, set Ali up for a title fight against then champion George Foreman. The 10 million dollars required for the fight, which went down in history as 'The Rumble in the Jungle', were provided by President Mobutu of Zaire, who was keen to attract the publicity the event would bring. Ali soaked up eight rounds of Foreman's brutal hitting, employing what became known as the rope-a-dope strategy, letting Foreman blow himself out to take the fight and the title by TKO. Ali won three more bouts before fighting what became known as 'The Thrilla in Manilla', a relentlessly dizzying duel with Joe Frazier, which saw Ali triumph. Ali claimed that the fight was the closest thing to dying that he knew.

His career record shows 56 wins and just 5 losses. Three of these were in his last four fights. His penultimate fight, against Larry Holmes should never have been allowed on health grounds, and was a humiliation for Ali, an appalling spectacle. It was an undignified end to a boxing career. In 1964, Ali was diagnosed with Parkinson's Disease but it was not until much later that his health began to decline seriously. In 1996, a clearly struggling Ali lit the flame at the opening of the Atlanta Olympics in front of a crowd reduced to tears. Few would have predicted he would reach the age of seventy, which he did in 2012, when an almost immobile and mute Ali was helped to make a special appearance, touching the flag at the opening of the 2012 games in London. It was simply heart-breaking to watch this man whose balletic grace in the ring had once enraptured generations all over the world. PG

ADRIAN CARTON DE WIART

There are few men one would describe as being amongst the most remarkable in British military history. Fewer still, (recalling Monty python's Black Knight), have done so after being shot in the face, lung, skull, ear, hand, ankle, hip, and leg. And almost none have amassed as many letters after their name as Lieutenant-General Sir Adrian Carton de Wiart VC, KBE, CB, CMG, DSO.

Adrian Carton de Wiart's autobiography is one of the most extraordinary military memoirs. Born into an aristocratic Belgian family, Carton de Wiart was intended for a career in law, like his father before him, but abandoned his studies at Balliol College Oxford in 1899 to join the British Army to fight in the Boer War, falsifying both name and age to be able to enlist.

Wounded in both the stomach and groin, Carton de Wiart was sent home, and despite his father's fury, was allowed (after a brief stint at Oxford) to re-enlist, first in the Imperial Light Horse and then permanently as a second lieutenant in the 4th Dragoon Guards.

Carton de Wiart was exceptionally well connected in European circles. One cousin was the Prime Minister of Belgium and another the Political Secretary to the King of Belgium. He was also thought by contemporaries to be the illegitimate son of the King himself, a rumour which did nothing to diminish his standing. He was a committed polo player and hunted with the Duke of Beaufort's Hunt, where he rubbed shoulders with the future field marshal, Sir Henry Maitland Wilson, and the future air marshal, Sir Edward Leonard Ellington. In 1908 he married Countess Friederike Maria Karoline Henriette Rosa Sabina Franziska Fugger von Babenhausen, further enhancing his royal connections.

Carton de Wiart's outstanding military career saw him in the thick of the action in an important number of campaigns. Whilst serving with the Somaliland Camel Corps in 1915, he was shot twice in the face losing an eye and part of his ear, earning him a Distinguished Service Order. He next fought on the Western Front where he survived many of the most famous battles of the First World War, being wounded an astonishing seven times, losing his left hand in 1915, being shot through skull and ankle at the Somme, through the hip at Passchendaele, through the leg at Cambrai, and finally through the ear at Arras. Carton de Wiart was mentioned in dispatches six times, and in 1916 he was awarded the Victoria Cross, the British armed forces' highest honour for gallantry. With typical modesty Carton de Wiart omitted to mention this honour in his autobiography. Despite all of his wounds, he was later quoted as saying, 'Frankly, I had enjoyed the war.'

In the interwar period, after a stint in the British Poland Mission, Carton de Wiart retired from the army in 1923 and spent 15 years living a peaceful life in the east of Poland. This idyll lasted until the onset of the Second World War, when he was reinstated in his former role as head of the British Polish Military Mission. Narrowly escaping capture as the country fell, he returned to England and served in Norway and Yugoslavia before a plane he was in crash-landed in the sea off the Italian-held coast of Libya, and he was taken to Italy as a PoW. During two years in captivity, Carton de Wiart made many attempts at escape including two by tunnelling, and on one occasion evaded capture for eight days disguised as an Italian peasant.

He played one final part in the war, serving as Churchill's personal representative to Chiang Kai-shek. A photograph taken at the Cairo Conference shows an armless Carton de Wiart surrounded by Chiang Kai-shek, President Roosevelt, Admiral Lord Louis Mountbatten, and Churchill, amongst others.

Carton de Wiart is one of the most extraordinary figures ever to serve the British Army. Highly decorated yet exceptionally modest, it was widely believed that he was the model for the great hero Brigadier Ben Ritchie-Hook in Evelyn Waugh's *Sword of Honour* trilogy. The foreword to Carton de Wiart's autobiography was written by Winston Churchill. Aristocratic and foul-mouthed, he shot, fished, hunted the fox, drank champagne, claret, and port, and was notably successful with the ladies. The *Oxford Dictionary of National Biography* sums him up thus: 'With his black eyepatch and empty sleeve, Carton de Wiart looked like an elegant pirate, and became a figure of legend.' PG

WILT CHAMBERLAIN

Wilt Chamberlain is famous for a number of achievements, but a few stand out from the rest; his prolific point-scoring in the National Basketball Association (NBA), his luxurious and decadent lifestyle fuelled by his enormous salaries, and his claim to have slept with 20,000 different women over the course of his career. During his time in the NBA, Chamberlain was awarded seven scoring, nine field goal percentage, and eleven rebounding titles, and once also led the league for total assists. Atop these, he holds the NBA all-time records in the scoring, rebounding, and durability categories, and is the only player to have scored 100 points in a single NBA game or averaged more than 50 points in a season. Winning two NBA championships, earning four Most Valuable Player awards, the Rookie of the Year award, one NBA Finals MVP award, and being selected for 13 All-Star Games, Chamberlain had one of the most successful NBA careers of all time. He has been commemorated in the Naismith Memorial Basketball Hall of Fame, and was chosen as one of the 50 Greatest Players in NBA History in 1996.

As the first truly high-earning player, Chamberlain's career set the tone for modern NBA stars. His rookie salary of $30,000 in 1959 was $5,000 higher than any before, and he quickly became the first basketball player to earn more than $100,000 per year. During his time playing for the Lakers, Chamberlain earned an unprecedented $1.5 million. His wealth was so great that when Chamberlain played for Philadelphia, he chose to rent an apartment in central New York and commute for training sessions and games. This decision was probably at least inspired by his lifestyle, which became notorious during the 1965–66 NBA season, during which he indulged in lavish parties until the early hours of the morning, never rising before noon.

When playing for the Lakers, Chamberlain used his money to build a home in Bel Air which he called 'Ursa Major', a reference to his nickname 'the Big Dipper' which he earned because he always had to bend in order to fit his seven-foot-one frame through doors. He would frequently hold parties at the house, reminiscent of a small Playboy mansion. Chamberlain's estate was valued at $25 million in 2000, and included an 'X rated' room which was adorned with mirrored walls and a waterbed covered in fur. This room, one would imagine, played host to many of the famous 20,000 liaisons which occupied Chamberlain's life, when he wasn't setting NBA records, of course. Chamberlain's lawyer Seymour Goldberg commented: 'Some people collect stamps, Wilt collected women.'

Wilt Chamberlain

Rod Roddewig, a friend of Chamberlain's, has shed some light on the origins of the 20,000 figure. While the two were staying in Chamberlain's penthouse in Honolulu during the mid-1980s, Chamberlain decided to keep count of his encounters over a ten day period. Every time Chamberlain slept with a different girl he put a mark in his diary and, after the ten days were done, Chamberlain counted 23, a rate of 2.3 different women per day. This number was divided by two to be conservative and to account for variation. Chamberlain then calculated the number of days he had been alive, minus 15 years, and multiplied the two figures. Thus Chamberlain arrived at the figure for which he has become so renowned. Though we may naturally be sceptical about the enormity of this figure, it is clear that Chamberlain was a dedicated and prolific womanizer.

In 1999, shortly before his death, Chamberlain commented in an interview: 'All of you men out there who think that having a thousand different ladies is pretty cool, I have learned in my life that having one woman a thousand different times is much more satisfying.' Chamberlain is amongst an exclusive few who have had the opportunity to so confidently compare the two options. GE

'Some people collect stamps, Wilt collected women.'

Wilt Chamberlain's lawyer, Seymour Goldberg

BRIAN CLOUGH

Brian Clough was a talismanic and charismatic football manager whose successes on the pitch were often overshadowed by his outspoken commentary off of it. A highly divisive figure, he was revered by the people of the East Midlands where he not only re-invigorated their football but also restored pride in their region.

Brian Howard Clough was born at Middlesbrough on 21 March 1935. He enjoyed a happy childhood but was the least academically successful of his five brothers and two sisters, being the only one not to make it to grammar school. He began his career in football as a player with his hometown club, signing as an amateur in 1951 and going on to score 204 second division goals in 222 games, reaching the total faster than anyone before him. Clough had a better scoring record than the great Jimmy Greaves, but despite his proficiency in front of the goal, Clough only won two England caps, something that he would see as a disappointment throughout his career.

Clough moved to nearby Sunderland in 1961, but a bad tackle during a match on Boxing Day 1962 ruptured his knee ligaments, and despite an 18-month rehabilitation, he never regained his prior form. Clough was appointed youth coach but this didn't last long. After a period of drinking and desperation, he landed a job as manager at another North East club, Hartlepool. Here he was joined, for the first time, by his former team-mate Peter Taylor, with whom he would achieve everything as a manager. Of his new employers, Clough, in what became typical fashion, said: 'Describing Hartlepool Football Club as a tip would be giving a bonus to a tip.'

After only modest success, Clough and Taylor left in 1967 to join then 2nd Division Derby County. Relying very much on instinct and a terrific work ethic, Clough instilled character and spirit into the Derby side which in his second season won the league and with it promotion to Division 1. In 1972, Derby became league champions for the first time in their history in a campaign that Clough described in modest fashion as 'one of the miracles of the century'. In the following year, Clough took Derby to the semi-finals of the European Cup, but after yet another fall out with his chairman Sam Longson in October 1973, he resigned. He had resigned many times before but Clough had called Longson's bluff for the last time and finally he was gone.

A surprise call then came from Leeds United and Clough took over from the hugely successful Don Revie in July 1974. Clough had long vilified the players of 'Dirty Leeds' as cheats, and the lack of admiration flowed both ways. Clough lasted just 44 days before he was ousted unceremoniously from his position. Demoralised and deflated, Clough was at least financially secure. He took time off to be with his family, to spend time on the golf course, play cricket, and appear on television where he was increasingly called into action as a football pundit. But his period in the wilderness did not last long, and in January 1975 he was signed to manage Derby County's great rivals Nottingham Forest. Joined in the summer of 1976 by Peter Taylor, Clough's spark returned and he once again set about transforming an average side into winners. He led Forest to a Second Division title in 1977, winning the First Division in 1978 and, most astonishingly of all, the European Cup in 1979 and again in 1980.

Clough was an often unpleasant and difficult man, prone to bullying players, but he was without a doubt touched by genius, and knew it. 'Conceit and arrogance are part of a man's make-up,' he once said. 'Perhaps I've got too much.' Clough was considered a bit of a clown by some, he was brash and at times not particularly eloquent. He was very outspoken in his criticism of the football press whom he accused of being dogmatic and overbearing, and guilty of sucking the life out of football with their over-analysis.

In the late 1980s, his powers were clearly beginning to wane and increasingly Clough took to drinking. His behaviour became more erratic and his outbursts frequently incoherent. With Forest fans invading the pitch after a league cup quarter-final victory over Queen's Park Rangers in 1989, an enraged Clough took to the field and in plain view of the television cameras hit several fans, earning a season-long touchline ban and a £5,000 fine for bringing the game into disrepute. In 1991, he took Nottingham Forest to the FA Cup Final, the only major honour he had failed to win. Forest lost in overtime and Clough later regretted not retiring on that day. Instead, he continued for a further two failing years, retiring finally in 1993 with Forest already consigned to relegation.

Clough was made OBE in 1991 and in 1993 was granted the Freedom of the City of Nottingham. Commenting on the honour, Clough said: 'It's a beautiful city with lovely people. I'm particularly fond of the River Trent—blow me, I've been walking on it for the last 18 years.' Whatever else Brian Clough did, he certainly brightened up a good many people's lives. He once said, 'When I go God's going to have to give up his favourite armchair.' Clough died in 2004. Who knows what God is sitting on now. PG

Brian Clough

JAMES HUNT

James Hunt's Formula One career started with him joining the Hesketh racing team in 1973, founded by Thomas Alexander Fermor-Hesketh, an English baron whose passion for exuberance was only outweighed by his considerable wealth. The baron's interest in good times, however, does not compare to Hunt's, the man who would lead his racing team to fame and success in the early 1970s, and would cement his place as an icon not only in the sporting world, but also as one of the most original and captivating personalities of modern times.

Hunt and his team were initially not taken very seriously by their opponents on the track, and earned themselves (Hunt especially) reputations as the playboys of Formula One. This was not a label Hunt was particularly keen to lose. For much of his driving career, Hunt wore a patch on the right breast of his driving suit—usually extremely valuable advertising space—emblazoned with the words 'Sex, Breakfast of Champions'. Indeed, Hunt's appetite for sex was insatiable, and it occupied a great deal of the time he spent outside of the cockpit; much of his remaining time was spent drinking, smoking cannabis, or taking cocaine.

Such was Hunt's dedication to promiscuity that it is reported that he slept with over 30 British Airways air stewardesses in the nights leading up to the World Championship race of 1976 when staying at the Tokyo Hilton hotel. While other drivers were preparing for the race, Hunt would wait at reception for a group of stewardesses arriving for a 24-hour stopover, and it seems few could refuse the invitation of a party in Hunt's room. Knowing how Hunt would prepare for his races gives a possible explanation for his failsafe pre-race ritual: disappear beside the cockpit, vomit, and jump into the car. Though this is perhaps explainable by the inevitable nerves that come with Formula One racing, Hunt's lifestyle can only have weakened his constitution on the early morning of the race. In any case, Hunt would win the Japanese Grand Prix in 1976 with McLaren, and with it the championship by one point. Certainly a commendable achievement for a man who we can fairly assume was grappling against a potent hangover.

Though Hunt never won another drivers' championship, his racing career continued for many years, each one as controversial as the last. Before the 1976 championship, Hunt refused to sign a clause in his contract that required him to wear suits to official functions. Instead, Hunt would usually wear jeans and a T-shirt, would arrive visibly drunk more often than not, and rarely wore shoes or socks. In 1977, Hunt attended a function hosted by HRH the Duke of Kent in this exact attire. That same year at the Canadian Grand Prix, Hunt was forced to exit the race early after a crash. Hunt was subsequently fined $2,000 for assaulting a marshal and a further $750 for refusing to walk safely to the pit lane. Hunt won the Fiji Grand Prix the same year, but decided not to take the podium at all, which cost him a further fine of $20,000.

Hunt stopped racing in 1979 (aside from a few stilted attempts to race in order to escape bankruptcy), yet he continued to pursue a very similar lifestyle. Whilst doing so, Hunt carved a career as a commentator for the BBC, and it is through this role that he has earned much of his adoration from the wider public. During the Monaco Grand Prix in 1980, Hunt's first live broadcast in earnest, he placed his leg, which was in a plaster cast, on the lap of his fellow commentator and proceeded to drink two bottles of wine. This set the tone for a fiery spell in the box which lasted for fourteen years. Hunt's performances in the commentary box continued to be as colourful as those he had delivered on the track; he criticized French driver Jean-Pierre Jarier for perceived bad racing, calling him 'pig ignorant', a 'French wally', and claiming he had a 'mental age of 10' during live broadcasts.

Hunt continued on this career path until he died. He commentated on the 1993 Canadian Grand Prix just two days before his death, on 15 June 1993. At the age of just 45, Hunt died the way he had lived: fast, fearless, and with spontaneity. It is hard to imagine he would have had it any other way. One of the most prolific British sportsmen, drinkers, romancers, and crowd-pleasers, Hunt's mark on the world is one which will not easily fade. GE

'My first priority is to finish above rather than beneath the ground.'

James Hunt

T. E. LAWRENCE

The reputation of T. E. Lawrence, perhaps better known as Lawrence of Arabia, stems mostly from the work of American journalist Lowell Thomas, whose multimedia presentation *With Allenby in Palestine and Lawrence in Arabia* ran for six months starting in August 1919 at the Royal Opera House, London. The presentation served to ignite public interest in the extraordinary life of the man. Lawrence filled many roles: war hero, intellectual, and storyteller, to name just a few. He combined charming manners with embellished accounts of his adventures and achievements, represented a world lost in war, yet was also a modern man.

At the outbreak of the First World War, Lawrence's knowledge of the Arab world (gained through his time as a researcher in Oxford and extensive personal travelling) earned him a posting to serve in Cairo during the Arab revolt. Lawrence's distinctive appeal becomes evident in the tales which have emerged of his time serving in this war, often relayed by the man himself. In November 1917, for instance, Lawrence led a party into Syria with the aim of disrupting Turkish communications. Lawrence was captured in Deraa, and after the removal of an elaborate Circassian disguise, was identified by a Turkish officer. The subsequent imprisonment saw Lawrence flogged and raped before he eventually escaped. This tale, which emerged in 1919, has been the subject of some debate amongst Lawrence's biographers, and whilst some accept its validity, others discredit it on circumstantial grounds. Whether the tale is true or not, Lawrence lost none of his exuberance, and in April 1918 he ventured into the garrison town of Amman under a different disguise, choosing to dress up as a woman. In a war which professional soldiers had found so difficult to manage, Lawrence's intellect and character earned him immediate success even as an amateur.

After the war, and following a spell at the Versailles Conference as a diplomat, Lawrence returned to England and accepted a fellowship at All Souls College, Oxford. This opportunity enabled him to focus on one of his main passions, writing. All Souls facilitated the publication of much of Lawrence's work such as *Seven Pillars of Wisdom,* an autobiographical account of his time serving in the desert. It was not long, however, before he was drawn to service once again, this time in a starkly different capacity. Lawrence joined the RAF in August 1922, under the pseudonym John Hume Ross. In December, while he was working in the RAF School of Photography at Farnborough, the press discovered his deceit, and he was discharged and re-enlisted in another unit, the tank corps, in March 1923. This time Lawrence labelled himself T. E. Shaw.

Two years later, after persistent petitioning and with help from his connections including John Buchan and George Bernard Shaw who pressured Prime Minister Stanley Baldwin, Lawrence was allowed to rejoin the RAF. Lawrence remained enlisted until 1935, prompted in part by a genuine interest in machinery and in the technical nature of the work, but more so by the challenge of imparting influence from the bottom of the hierarchy as he had from the top. His enlistment also provided Lawrence, or Shaw, with a means of escape from the press, whose interest in his life had not waned since the war.

It was Lawrence's keen interest in machinery that led him to love the motorcycles which would eventually kill him. Lawrence was thrown from his Brough Superior, the eighth he had owned, just two months after he left military service. Coming over the brow of a hill, Lawrence's vision was obscured and he did not see the two boys on bicycles that were headed toward him. Though he tried to avoid them, the ensuing swerve threw Lawrence over the handlebars of his beloved bike, and he died six days later, on 19 May 1935, aged 35.

Lawrence was commemorated in two places, rural Dorset and St Paul's Cathedral, and in many ways there were two men to bury, each with their own appeal. The private, amateur Lawrence whose intellect had earned him his reputation in the east, and Lawrence of Arabia, the war hero and celebrity who could not escape the limelight. It is the way that Lawrence combined these two men that makes him fascinating. 'He may have been a "show-off"', Lord Vansittart put it in the *Daily Telegraph* twenty years after Lawrence died, 'but he had something to show.' GE

'All men dream, but not equally. Those who dream by night in the dusty recesses of their minds, wake in the day to find that it was vanity. But the dreamers of the day are dangerous men, for they may act on their dreams with open eyes, to make them possible.'

T. E. Lawrence

SPIKE MILLIGAN

Spike Milligan was a troubled but uniquely gifted comedian and comic writer. His brand of surreal and chaotic humour helped define alternative British comedy.

Terence Alan Milligan was born in 1918 at Ahmednagar in India. His father served in the British Army and was something of a fantasist, telling young Milligan tales of catching cobras and choking tigers. Milligan was educated first in a tent in the desert and then at a series of Indian Catholic schools. At age 13 his family returned to southeast London. He loved music and taught himself to play many instruments, most notably the trumpet. He enjoyed the stage, performing as a jazz vocalist and trumpeter in a succession of bands, once winning a Bing Crosby Crooning Competition at the Lewisham Hippodrome. Leaving school at 15, he floundered through a series of dead-end jobs.

Upon the outbreak of the Second World War, he enlisted in the Royal Artillery. He fought and was nearly killed in Italy. Suffering from shellshock, he was transferred to Africa where he met Harry Secombe with whom he instantly formed a great friendship. Despite the horrors he encountered, Milligan enjoyed the companionship and camaraderie. He wrote of his wartime efforts in a series of five hugely acclaimed memoirs, beginning with *Adolf Hitler: My Part in his Downfall.* Their tone was distinctly subversive but deeply humorous. 'A man called Chamberlain who did Prime Minister impressions spoke on the wireless; he said: "As from eleven o'clock we are at war with Germany." ... The people next door panicked, burnt their post office books and took in the washing.'

Milligan entered into a period of flânerie in Soho and London's West End during which time he became re-acquainted with Secombe, who introduced him to Michael Bentine and Peter Sellers at the pub run by ex-Major and theatre agent Jimmy Grafton. Here they began working on a comic act full of iconoclasm and the decidedly absurd. After initial rejection, and amid heavy scepticism from BBC bosses, *Crazy People (featuring radio's own Crazy Gang 'The Goons')* was finally commissioned. *The Goon Show* (as it then became known as) was an instant success and made household names of all of its stars, running for eight years and 157 episodes. Milligan wrote and starred in almost every single one. The strain of it placed enormous pressure on his fragile mental condition. Later he said, 'I'd had a terrible nervous breakdown—two, three, four, five nervous breakdowns, one after another. *The Goon Show* did it. That's why they were so good.' From the very beginning Milligan had an uneasy relationship with the BBC, he raged against it, claiming that fighting the corporation had driven him mad.

Spike Milligan

His output was prolific and almost inconceivably varied, both in genre and in quality. He scripted eight series of his own television show, he wrote for and performed to enormous critical success in the theatre and with lesser success in the cinema, he was a cartoonist for *Private Eye,* and made television commercials for, amongst others, the English Tourist Board. He published over eighty books, including verse for adults and children (in 1998 *On the Ning Nang Nong* was voted Britain's favourite comic poem) and his war memoirs were insightful, touching, but also deeply critical.

Milligan was also a great writer of letters. A collection of his more memorable missives, entitled *Man of Letters,* which was published posthumously in 2013, showed him to be part conservative curmudgeon, part ardent anarchist. He tackled the trivial; muzak, punctuality, dog mess (one letter is titled 'Milligan versus Dog Shit'), the introduction of round tea bags; and the serious, campaigning for nuclear disarmament, a ban on blood sports and successfully for the preservation of the Victorian lamp posts outside Buckingham Palace.

According to Milligan, 'nothing could be as mad as what passes for ordinary living'. He looked at the world obliquely and reveled in its oddity. His comedy trod a fine line between infuriatingly infantile and beguilingly surreal, the best was often both.

Said Hamlet to Ophelia,
I'll draw a sketch of thee,
What kind of pencil shall I use?
2B or not 2B?

Milligan received a Lifetime Achievement Award at the 1994 British Comedy Awards. The Prince of Wales sent a congratulatory message which Milligan interrupted calling the Prince a 'little grovelling bastard.' He later faxed the palace saying, 'I suppose a knighthood is out of the question?' It wasn't. He was made honorary KBE in 2001. John Cleese, acknowledging his vast comic legacy, described him as 'the great god of us all'. Milligan died in 2002. Upon his gravestone, at his own request, is written 'I told you I was ill.' PG

ROBERT MITCHUM

Nobody ever seemed to know exactly what set Robert Mitchum apart from the other actors of Hollywood's Golden Age. He was grizzled, seen-it-all, slobbish, and thuggish, but also charming, funny, urbane, and cultured. 'The embodiment of film noir' was how Roger Ebert pegged him, but Mitchum's co-star Deborah Kerr had him differently: 'An extremely sensitive, poetic, extraordinarily interesting man.' Only Mitchum seemed to think Mitchum was straightforward. 'The only difference between me and my fellow actors,' he once explained in his sleepy New England accent, 'is that I've spent more time in jail.'

Robert Charles Durman Mitchum was born in Bridgeport, Connecticut on 6 August 1917. His sea captain father died in a railway accident when Mitchum was two and his subsequent childhood took strange turns. At age 7 he wrote poetry. The following year the family moved to a farm in Delaware, where Mitchum set about hospitalising the local bullies. The family then moved to Hell's Kitchen. Mitchum and his brother John became involved in running battles with the New York gangs. Robert left home for good at age 15, heading off to California in hope of Jack London-esque adventures. He was arrested multiple times en route.

The first arrest came in Savannah, Georgia, where he was accused of robbing a shoe store. His defence was that it couldn't have been him because the store had been robbed on a Wednesday, and Mitchum had been in jail since the previous Sunday. Mitchum still ended up on a chain gang, an indeterminate sentence for vagrancy intended to straighten him out. Mitchum later recalled fleeing the sentence while wardens shot at him.

After years of odd jobs (one of which temporarily rendered him medically blind from sheer hatred for the work), Mitchum finally settled in Long Beach, California in 1937. Once there, he was encouraged by his older sister Annette to take up acting in a bid to curb his wildness, which had by now swollen to heavy drinking and the first stirrings of a lifelong pot habit. After scrubbing through a series of low budget films, Mitchum began to be pushed by Howard Hughes's RKO production company in 1944, which saw in his hard-drinking everyman persona the makings of a new kind of anti-hero for the post-Second World War audiences. An Oscar nomination came for his work as Lt Walker in *The Story of GI Joe* and further plaudits began to accrue before the run was interrupted by compulsory military service in 1945: punishment for breaking a policeman's nose in a fight. Mitchum was forced to work on the medical wards of Fort MacArthur. 'I was a pecker checker checking recruits' genitals for venereal disease,' Mitchum remembered. 'But my speciality was rectal examinations ... searching soldiers' asses for abnormalities—piles, haemorrhoids, bananas, dope—you name it.' He was honourably discharged the following year.

When he could be bothered, Mitchum was a star, particularly when cast as a villain. His 1955 role as Reverend Harry Powell in *The Night of the Hunter,* a psychotic travelling preacher come killer, is full of snake oil and malevolence. Max Cady, the vengeful killer who pursues straight-laced Gregory Peck in 1962's *Cape Fear,* appropriated Mitchum's own slouched, slobby charm and cut it through with a crocodilian menace. Mitchum's somnambulistic acting style (all lazy motions and shop-shutter eyelid drops) was unique, but what really made him memorable, beyond the calypso album he insisted upon recording in 1957, was how much he disliked Hollywood.

Mitchum assessed a Steve McQueen performance as naturally 'lending itself to monotony' and Greer Garson as taking 'a hundred and twenty-five takes to say no'. He was similarly unimpressed by John Wayne's machismo: 'He had four-inch lifts put in his shoes. He had the overheads on his boat accommodated to fit him. He had a special roof put in his station wagon. The son of a bitch, they probably buried him in his goddamn lifts.' The only person Mitchum was more acid about than his peers was himself: 'I have two acting styles: with and without a horse.' Once asked what acting meant to him, Mitchum told an anecdote about a horse farm in Arizona he bought early on in his career. 'Years ago, I saved up a million dollars from acting, a lot of money in those days, and I spent it all on a horse farm in Tucson. Now when I go down there, I look at that place and I realise my whole acting career adds up to a million dollars worth of horse shit.'

When Mitchum died in 1997 from lung cancer—a near inevitability given the magnitude of his tobacco intake—it prompted reflection from Paul Gregory, his producer on *The Night of the Hunter.* 'He was a man of great charm yet there was this sense of evil lurking beneath the surface,' said Gregory, and it was precisely this sense of contradiction that made Mitchum so appealing as an actor. As a report in the *Saturday Evening Post* had it, Mitchum the sophisticate was perpetually at risk of being bludgeoned by Mitchum the primitive.

It is a combination that Gregory remembered well. One day while filming *The Night of the Hunter,* Mitchum staggered onto set so puffy-eyed as to be near blind. It prompted Gregory to suggest he go home. Mitchum's response was pointed. 'He opened his fly and whipped out his dick, then staggered behind my Cadillac's door, which was open,' Gregory remembered. 'I looked back and saw him pissing on the front seat of the car where I'd been sitting. And it went on and on filling up the seat with piss ... And then he put his cock back in his pants with a look on his face that was as if this was the dearest thing he had ever done in his whole life.' OS

'I have two acting styles: with and without a horse.'

Robert Mitchum

BERNARD MONTGOMERY

Is it possible to be a great man without being a good one? Countless artists and writers have been praised for their talent while their lives have been severely criticized. Yet it is more rare for those in positions of power to experience such a dichotomy. Bernard 'Monty' Montgomery might be the best example of such a contrast. As a man, he was arrogant, petty, bigoted, and proud. Yet as a military leader, he was a visionary. He was responsible for the legendary victory at El Alamein that first indicated to the Allies that they might yet defeat their opponents. Montgomery was blessed with an innate understanding of strategy that could be presented simply as a head-to-head battle between two hugely talented leaders—a gift for propagandists. As he said, 'A battle is, in effect, a contest between two wills: yours and that of the enemy general.' Monty was nothing if not strong willed.

Bernard Law Montgomery was born on 17 November 1887 in London, in an impoverished and grim household where punishment was frequent. Montgomery did not dwell on this in later life, saying briskly, 'I was a dreadful little boy … I don't suppose anyone would put up with my behavior these days.' Like many of his generation, it was thought that he needed a military career for discipline, and after training at Sandhurst he saw action in the First World War, where he was wounded but was also ordered to the Distinguished Service Order for conspicuous gallantry in 1914. He ended the war a lieutenant-colonel, and led a glittering military career for the next two decades, specializing in subjugating nations such as Ireland and India, which he took pleasure in doing. When recalled to England after the Arab War of 1939, he said, 'I shall be sorry to leave Palestine, as I have enjoyed the war out here.'

Perhaps because of his frankness and general disdain for his superiors, he spent the early years of the Second World War sidelined, concentrating on domestic defence rather than on what was happening overseas. However, he got his chance in August 1942 when Churchill appointed him as Commander of the Eighth Army in the Middle East, pitting him against the 'Desert Fox', the apparently unbeatable Rommel. Montgomery was said to have remarked, 'After having had an easy war, things have now got more difficult,' and upon being offered consolation, snapped 'I'm not talking about me, I'm talking about Rommel!' He proved to be a dedicated and courageous leader, making himself popular by associating with the men on equal terms while wearing the black beret that became his trademark. Within days, he had revitalized a tired and low-spirited army with his charisma; it was typical of both the man and the general that one of his first actions was to cancel any plans for a retreat, claiming: 'If we cannot stay here alive, we will stay here dead.'

He transformed the fortunes of the Eighth Army, eventually winning a stunning victory against Rommel in December 1942, which prompted Churchill's famous statement that 'This is not the end. It is not even the beginning of the end, but it is, perhaps, the end of the beginning.' This led to Montgomery's promotion to general and a glittering succession of victories, including a crucial role in the D-Day landings. However, he antagonized many of the Allied commanders, such as Patton and Eisenhower, due to his refusal to compromise or believe he was anything other than right. It was this arrogance which led to his major strategic blunder during his involvement in the Battle of the Bulge in late 1944. While it ended in an Allied victory, it incurred far greater loss of life than it should have, probably because Montgomery had ignored the strength of the German resistance.

Nonetheless, he ended the war as a hugely popular figure, 'Monty of El Alamein', became Commander-in-Chief of the British Army of the Rhine, and was given the title of 1st Viscount Montgomery of Alamein. Yet, his boldness and lack of diplomacy, which had served him well in conflict, now became less of an asset, as he continued to antagonize those he dealt with. His tenure as Chief of the Imperial General Staff from 1946–48 was a particular disaster. He maintained the position until his retirement in 1958, but there was a general sense that he, like Churchill, had excelled in the field of battle, but was now something of a relic. It is impossible to imagine Montgomery dealing with the Cold War with any finesse; diplomacy was something Monty regarded as a chore to be dispensed with before the action could begin in earnest. He died in 1976 at the age of 88 at home in Hampshire; his last public pronouncements of any note were to support apartheid and to condemn the Sexual Offences Act of 1967, 'as charter for buggery', memorably adding, 'This sort of thing might be tolerated by the French, but we're British—thank God.'

Never a man with close ties to his family—he did not bother attending his mother's funeral on the grounds that he was too busy—he was nevertheless devastated by the death of his wife in an operation for septicaemia in 1937. Typically, he dealt with his grief by immersing himself in work. His only son, David, co-wrote a memoir of his father,

The Lonely Leader: Monty 1944–45, which offered a valuable insight into his vanity, vulnerability, and pettiness, as well as his military brilliance. It comes as little surprise to find that his great hero was Napoleon. And yet, for all his flaws, his abilities as a military leader are without parallel in the twentieth century; when Eisenhower's chief of staff Bedell Smith was asked in 1976 about the Normandy invasions, he replied, 'I don't know if we could have done it without Monty. It was his sort of battle. Whatever they say about him, he got us there.' AL

Bernard Montgomery

RUDOLF NUREYEV

Rudolf Nureyev was the most outstanding male dancer of his generation. One of the great cultural icons of the 1960s, his influence on his art was immense.

Rudolf Khametovich Nureyev was born on a train crossing Siberia on 17 March 1938. At age 7 he was smuggled into his first ballet performance by his mother who could not afford the tickets. He lived a deprived existence in a crowded one-room apartment, wearing his sisters' clothes, and collecting bottles to trade in for money. He enjoyed watching the Tarzan and Charlie Chaplin films brought to Russia by the troops at the end of the Second World War. He learned to dance at the Children's Social Club and began ballet with the Ufa Theatre. At 17, he joined the Leningrad Ballet School, manoeuvering himself into the class of legendary Alexander Pushkin. Always confident, he proclaimed 'I will be the number one dancer in the world.' He made friends with local intellectuals and artists, educating himself on impressionism, poetry, and American literature, and fell in love with a Cuban dancer who encouraged in him new ideas and a lust for life. When he turned down a contract with the Bolshoi, prima ballerina Ninel Kurgapkina persuaded the Kirov to hire him. Demanding and arrogant, Nureyev was constantly at odds with the Kirov authorities. He was famed for his short temper, was intolerant of less accomplished colleagues, he wore tights, and danced half point to better exhibit his physique. 'I don't think anyone can hold a candle to me,' he said. But his talent was unmistakable and caught the attention of Khrushchev who invited him and Kurgapkina to dance at his dacha. 20-year-old Nureyev drank champagne and rubbed shoulders with the Soviet elite.

Well-known across Russia, he achieved worldwide fame on the day he defected to the West at the tiny Le Bourget airport in Paris in 1961. Having wowed the Parisian audiences touring with the Kirov, and revelling in the lifestyle, he had again come to blows with the Kirov's top brass. Visited one evening by the KGB, he was told that Khrushchev wanted to see him dance at the Kremlin. Fearing that this signalled an end to his international career, he made immediate plans to defect.

Having danced in France and the United States in February 1962, he went on to dance at the Royal Opera House in Covent Garden with Margot Fonteyn. At 24 he was 19 years younger than Fonteyn, but despite the disparity in age and culture they had a chemistry that was unmistakable. Theirs was a partnership that would transform ballet from elitist to popular, and would enrapture audiences of all backgrounds for over a decade. Choreographer Sir Frederick Ashton described them as 'the world's most exciting dance partnership'.

He became a hugely fashionable character, relishing the extravagant peacock fashions of the 1960s and 1970s. He lived a lavish lifestyle of helicopters and private jets, keeping homes, all opulently furnished, in London, Paris, New York, Monte Carlo, Virginia, Saint Barts, and the Galli Islands. He kept up a social circle, much as he had in Leningrad, that included celebrated artists, musicians, designers, and writers. David Bailey, an arbiter of cool, included a photograph of Nureyev in his iconic 1964 *Box of Pin-Ups*. On one short trip to New York he simultaneously adorned the covers of *Time* and *Newsweek,* appeared in the *New York Times* and *Vogue,* attended The Factory's 'Fifty Most Beautiful People' party, and danced with Fonteyn on the Ed Sullivan Show, twice. He also appeared on the *Muppet Show.* In 1975 Warhol, who claimed to be terrified of him, painted his portrait. Marianne Faithful said of him: 'He had that quality of being lost in his own thing. He was staggeringly beautiful and somewhat removed. There's something about artists like him that you can't catch and never will.'

Nureyev's love life was a source of great interest. He and Fonteyn were intimate friends but not sexual partners. Nureyev was highly promiscuous. There are unsubstantiated claims surrounding several high profile sexual partners including Jackie Kennedy (whilst First Lady), her brother-in-law Bobby Kennedy, and Mick Jagger. Nureyev confided to long-term partner Robert Tracy that he had slept with just three women in his life. 'Romance is nice,' he once said, 'but my romance is my dance.'

He continued to dance a punishing schedule but also attempted, with less success, sorties into the arenas of film acting, choreography, and eventually conducting. In 1983, he was appointed Director of Ballet at the Paris Opera. With his commanding presence he refreshed their roster, revitalised their repertoire, and restored the company to international significance.

Nureyev contracted HIV perhaps as early as 1979. Despite his fading physical prowess, he continued to dance almost until his final days, and though much more frail, he could still captivate an audience. He had a profound influence on the world of ballet, asserting the prominence of the male dancer, and bringing modern and classical dance into the same sphere. He believed that he was put on earth simply to be a ballet dancer. 'As long as I dance, I remain alive,' he once said. He performed his last dance in Budapest in March 1992. He died from complications relating to AIDS on 6 January 1993. PG

VIV RICHARDS

A cricket ball consists of a solid piece of cork covered in toughened leather, which at the current record can reach up to 160 km/h during a game, explaining why batsmen wear a protective helmet with a mouth guard to boot. Not Viv Richards though—it was simply not his style. Richards abhors the modern game's protection or as he calls it 'pampering' of players, calling for batsmen to abandon their 'suits of armour' and adopt a no-fear approach to the game.

Born in Antigua in 1952, Richards was the son of Antiguan fast-bowler Malcolm Richards and brother of two other cricketers; the game truly runs in his family. Encouraged to play and train not just by his family, but also his headmaster and sports teacher at school, Richards began playing for St. John's Cricket club while simultaneously working at a local restaurant. It was the restaurant owner who would supply Richards with new cricket gear, pads, gloves, and a new bat. Richards switched clubs to Rising Sun C.C. after a few seasons and garnered the attention of Len Creed, the vice chairman of Somerset C.C.

Creed arranged for Richards to play for Landsdown C.C. in the second team, while also working as assistant groundsman to support himself financially. After dispatching his second team status with considerable pace, Richards moved swiftly into the first team, finishing his premier season with the top batting averages (not that he would pay much attention to the figures), and finally negotiated a move to Somerset on a two-year deal.

International cricket, however, is where Richards really made his mark and defined himself as a global cricket star. Representing the West Indies, Richards quickly became known as a strong opening batsman in the early part of his career. His performance with the bat helped the West Indies to win the very first Cricket World Cup in 1975. This would rank as one of Richards's proudest moments, and he would help the West Indies go on to repeat this feat in the 1979 World Cup scoring a century at Lord's. Richards was an indomitable presence at the crease, a batsman so fearlessly intense that bowlers fell one by one to his intimidation as he hit boundaries as though he were fly-swatting. Nothing attests to this more than the century he scored off 56 balls against England in 1986, completing the world's fastest ever century.

After being central to the West Indian team during the 1970s (the sometimes revered and other times reviled group of players who ferociously made the world of cricket look

Viv Richards

up from their tea cups), Richards became their captain in the mid-1980s. He would not lose a single one of his 50 test matches between 1984 and 1991, an exceptional achievement by a captain whose single-minded desire to win was his defining feature.

Richards was also a strong believer in Rastafarianism and wore a red, gold, and green band while playing, given to him by Bob Marley, to symbolise his faith. The West Indian cricket team, particularly the emergent team of the 1970s, brought fierce hope and anti-colonial inspiration to their play that some consider central to their success. Many of them, like Viv, were dedicated Rastafarians fighting against oppressive systems, and Richards himself notes that his bat was a sword. This political and spiritual profundity would endear Richards to his countrymen, who would run onto the pitch and ceremoniously hold aloft their prize-winning batsman.

Ahead of their 1976 tour to the West Indies, England's cricket captain Tony Greig made what he throught was a rousing address to his team and country. In this he used the ill fated remark 'We'll make them grovel'. Richards, talismanic amongst this most talented group of players, took this as a personal affront. He stood in stark contrast to the old-style ingrained colonial racism that was still pervasive in the world of international cricket. Throughout the series, with every smashing stroke of his bat, Richards knocked away at the racism that surrounded sport. He forced the world to think of the West Indians as more than just calypso cricketers, but as serious sportsmen brimming with skill and fiery passion. Richards, the biggest star of his day, later turned down a blank-cheque offer to play for the rebel West Indian cricket team in apartheid ruled South Africa. He talked the talk, and he also walked the walk.

Richards's retirement led to a lull in the West Indian cricket team's fortunes. Few players had quite the combination of charisma, quality, and sheer intensity that Richards had to drive the team. Few could state 'I won the glare with the bowler every time' and even fewer could be named one of the (if not the) greatest batsman in cricket history. HB

ANDY RIPLEY

In an age characterised by enthusiastic sportsmen whose careers were driven by little more than a desire for self-improvement and a deep love for the game, Andy Ripley epitomised everything that was so wonderful about the era of amateur sport. An exceptionally talented number eight throughout his career as a rugby player, Ripley continued to excel even after he retired and earned significant achievements in rowing, academia, and business, to name just a few areas on which Ripley left his imposing mark.

Ripley played for the Rosslyn Park Rugby Club throughout his entire career, dedicated to maintaining the spirit of the amateur game in a period when many others felt the allure of growing financial incentives. Winning 24 caps for England at number eight between 1972 and 1976, Ripley's life on the pitch played host to a dark time for English rugby, fluctuating wildly between the truly awful and inspired. Ripley won on eight of his 24 appearances in a white shirt, winning only the wooden spoon in the Five Nations tournament, but beating southern hemisphere giants New Zealand and South Africa.

Ripley cut an iconic shape on the field, with his trademark locks flowing behind his sizeable six-foot-five frame as he gambolled through defensive lines with a rangy, hurdler's stride. His individuality was not confined to the pitch, however, as Ripley shirked convention and ignored the demands of authority figures throughout his career. During the Lions tour of 1974, during which the Lions team journeyed to South Africa and returned victorious, Ripley refused to accommodate the desires of the organisers, who insisted that he wore the formal tour attire to the myriad public functions. After the first event, to which Ripley arrived in casual dress and with classically dishevelled hair, he was ordered to make sure he wore the tour blazer, trousers, and tie in the future. Ripley complied, wearing the three items he had been told and nothing else, arriving at the next function barefoot and bare-chested.

During the same tour, Ripley caused even more trouble when he discovered two starving kittens on a South African street. Ripley adopted the animals and spent much of the tour nurturing them back to life. The two kittens eventually regained their full health and, upon realising that they couldn't be brought back with him, Ripley sought to find them a home. The following day, the team's hotel was a picture of chaos, as the lobby was reportedly flooded with locals responding to an advert in the paper for two 'lion cubs' free to a good home.

On a day off from playing on the South African tour, the squad travelled to a nearby township. When the time came to leave, all but one were on the team bus. Ripley remained behind as night fell, reappearing later that evening wearing only a leopard's skin: Ripley had given away his entire tour kit collection to the locals, from shirts to shoes.

Ripley's playing career was relatively short, but his desire to improve and to achieve never lessened. At the age of 50, Ripley enrolled at the University of Cambridge to study for an MPhil. While at university, he began training for the Boat Race crew among men thirty years his junior. The training regime, which involved over four hours of training per day, forced his weight down from 17st 9lb to 16st 5lb, and his heart rate to 38bpm. Ripley was ultimately dismissed from the crew, though he made the 28-man squad, but his clear dedication and sheer ambition when he had nothing left to prove epitomises the man and his attitude toward life.

By this stage, Ripley had made a name for himself in many other sports, becoming a top 400-metre sprinter and hurdler, reaching the UK Amateur Athletics Champions' semi-finals in 1978. He also won the BBC's Superstars competition in 1980, and competed in a triathlon, canoeing, sailing, water-skiing, and playing tennis and basketball. As a talented linguist, Ripley returned to rugby as a commentator on French television. And throughout, Ripley managed to earn a very good living working in London, operating a chain of health clubs and marketing his own rugby equipment, before eventually becoming the deputy general manager of the United Bank of Kuwait.

Ripley is perhaps the only modern sportsman who can lay claim to a body of talent and achievement reminiscent of the great C. B. Fry. He was a true polymath and, what's more, he embraced the sporting world with the attitude of a great amateur. Few other players give off a stronger sense of love for sport than Andy Ripley—his is a mould to which modern greats should aspire. He was a truly original character, the likes of whom appear far too rarely. GE

Andy Ripley

AYRTON SENNA

For the racing driver Ayrton Senna, there was no such thing as second or third place. Instead, there was winning or losing. As he said, 'When you are fitted in a racing car and you race to win, second or third place is not enough.' What might have seemed arrogant coming from another man seemed like a perfectly rational statement by someone who was undeniably one of the greatest drivers who ever raced—and quite possibly the greatest. He was attracted to the adrenaline of the sport like a moth to a flame, claiming 'the danger sensation is exciting … the challenge is to find new dangers'. His premature death was both a tragic end to an illustrious career and a realization of every rule that he ever stuck to in his brief, glittering life.

Senna was born on 21 March 1960 in São Paulo, and began racing from the age of 4, when he developed an interest in go-karting. A runner up in the Karting World Championships of 1979 and 1980, he moved to England to begin his career in racing, eventually participating in his first Formula One race in 1984 in Brazil. He finished ninth, but his fearless, near-visionary approach to racing, where he seemed entirely at one with his machine, led to his being noticed and tipped for greater things. These duly arrived in 1985, when he scored his first victory in the Portuguese Grand Prix, and in 1986, where he won the Detroit Grand Prix. It was here that he established one of his signature gestures, namely driving a lap waving the Brazilian flag every time that he won a race. A man who genuinely loved his country, taking every opportunity to extol its people, character, and setting, he was a truly beloved son of Brazil. The only blemish to a flourishing life and career was a divorce from Liliane Vasconcelos in 1983, after a two-year marriage.

Putting his personal difficulties behind him (he quipped 'women—always in trouble with them, but can't live without them'), Senna was in the big leagues of motor racing, transferring to the Marlboro-McLaren team in 1988, and collecting accolades and trophies by the score, most notably winning the World Championship in his first year. He also encountered the man who became his greatest rival, his teammate Alain Prost. Prost, a man nicknamed 'The Professor' for his cool, analytical style of racing, could not have been more different to the fiery and instinctive Senna, and their bitterly heated clashes, most markedly in the 1989 penultimate race of the season, became the stuff of legend. Senna, in particular, blamed the FIA for what he perceived as a bias against him. Controversy continued; when interviewed by Jackie Stewart in 1990 and asked why he was so prone to colliding with other cars, Senna angrily disputed the question, claiming that Stewart should understand the pressures drivers were under.

Ayrton Senna

Despite a growing reputation for hot-headedness, his winning streak continued, seeing him attain his third World Championship position in 1991 and build his name as a man who seemed to innately understand, and feed on, the challenges and dangers of the racetrack. He commented that 'racing, competing, it's in my blood. It's part of me, it's part of my life; I have been doing it all my life and it stands out above everything else.' He was nothing if not ambitious, taking the decision to leave McLaren in 1993 for Williams-Renault, where he hoped to establish himself as the greatest racing driver of the time, especially as his arch rival Prost had recently retired.

It was the 1994 San Marino Grand Prix that proved his undoing. On Saturday, 30 April, during the qualifying races, the Austrian driver Roland Ratzenberger was killed when his car crashed into a wall. A distraught Senna, who headed to the accident site immediately when he heard of the news, was deeply shaken by the accident, and even went so far as to engineer a reconciliation of sorts with Prost by discussing re-establishing the Grand Prix Drivers' Association, in order to make the tracks safer places. He stated, presciently, 'there are no small accidents on this circuit'. The hideous irony was that the following day, on Sunday, 1 May, Senna himself crashed under similar circumstances, and died of skull fractures and brain injuries. He was mourned by millions, and Brazil recognized one of its greatest sons by declaring three days of national mourning.

A devout Catholic and a discreet but committed philanthropist, Senna was an enormous credit to a sport that was often associated with buccaneers and daredevils. He was largely uninterested in the financial rewards that the sport offered, preferring 'work, dedication and competence'. Yet it was his addiction to the adrenaline rush of racing that led to both his success and eventual fate. His life was the subject of an acclaimed BAFTA-winning documentary, Senna, which dealt with both his rivalry with Prost and his career. Produced with his family's approval, it was nevertheless criticized by Prost, who felt that he was portrayed in an unfair light and that it eschewed discussion regarding their later reconciliation.

Senna lived fast, and died all too young. And yet the quote that defines him was his statement that 'winning is the most important. Everything is the consequence of that.' In public opinion, and in his legacy, Senna remains a winner. AL

Ayrton Senna

ERNEST SHACKLETON

When times are tough, it is hard to find a more inspiring persona than Sir Ernest Shackleton. There have been many adventurers, indeed some with greater exploratory achievements, but there are few examples that match Shackleton's resolve, determination, and self-belief.

Born in County Kildare, Ireland, Shackleton and his family moved to Sydenham in suburban London in 1884, when the young Ernest was 10. His first encounter with the Polar Regions, which would provide the stage for the most demanding experiences of his life and would define his legacy to this day, were as third officer on Captain Robert Falcon Scott's *Discovery* Expedition in 1901–04. Shackleton became seriously ill during the expedition and was subsequently sent home. This appeared to have a significant impact on the young man who was determined to recover from this perceived failure, returning to Antarctica to lead the *Nimrod* Expedition in 1907. The expedition failed to achieve its main target, the South Pole, but set the record for the southernmost distance ever achieved by man, a little over 100 miles from the pole. Shackleton was awarded a knighthood from King Edward VII upon his return, but his ambition was not diminished.

At the culmination of the race to the South Pole, which ended in December 1911 when it was won by Roald Amundsen, one could be forgiven for thinking that man had overcome the greatest challenge imaginable. Shackleton thought differently, and began preparations for the Imperial Trans-Antarctic Expedition, which would start in 1914. The plan was to conquer the continent by navigating through its centre, via the pole, from one coast to the other. On 1 August, the very same day Germany declared war on Russia, Shackleton started his third battle with Antarctica. The ordeal that would follow secured Shackleton's place in history, a heroic figure with seemingly inexhaustible supplies of courage and endurance.

In January 1915, some four months after Shackleton and his team had set off, disaster struck their ship when it was irretrievably trapped in sea ice. The crew was forced to leave the ship and establish camp on the floating ice surrounding them. The ship was eventually crushed and sank 10 months later, leaving the crew with a daunting journey ahead of them if they were to have any chance of rescue. In April, Shackleton led the men in three small boats on a five day voyage across 346 miles of freezing seas to Elephant Island. Their arrival was the first time any of the men had stood on firm ground for 497 days.

Hero

Shackleton became increasingly concerned with the health of his men, choosing to donate his mittens to the team photographer, Frank Hurley, and suffering from serious frostbite as a result. Shackleton's concern only grew, and he decided to embark upon an open boat voyage to South Georgia, 800 nautical miles away, in order to organize a rescue effort. Shackleton refused to pack more than four weeks' supplies for the voyage, which was to be undertaken with a small crew of five, knowing that if they could not reach their destination by then, all hope would certainly be lost. The journey pitted the six men against some of the roughest seas in the world in a 22-foot-long wooden boat, with few supplies, and ever-dwindling resources of energy. Sixteen days later, however, the crew arrived on desolate the desolate beaches of South Georgia.

Relief was to be denied the crew for some time yet, and their journey was far from over. Shackleton and two others, Worsley and Crean, began a 32 mile journey over a previously unexplored mountain range, armed only with 50 feet of rope and a carpenter's adze between them, to reach the nearest whaling station. It was nearly 40 years before the next successful crossing of this South Georgian wilderness, in October 1955.

Shackleton arrived at the whaling station on 20 May to an audience of startled Georgian whalers, and immediately began to organize a rescue mission. The first three attempts to rescue his crew were foiled by the ubiquitous sea ice, but Shackleton was undeterred. On 30 August 1916, more than two years since the *Endurance* had left home, and four months since Shackleton had left his crew isolated on Elephant Island, all men were retrieved alive and well.

Shackleton's adventurous spirit was indefatigable, and he died whilst setting out on an expedition to circumnavigate the Antarctic continent, suffering from a heart attack on 5 January 1922. Shackleton's ability never to lose sight of his goals, never to abandon the desire to push the limits of human endeavour, and to rescue not only himself but others too when all hope seemed to have been lost, cements his place as one of the most inspirational and extraordinary men the world has ever seen. GE

TOM SIMPSON

Britain's greatest road cyclist of the twentieth century, Tom Simpson's story is one of the most tragic and misguidedly heroic in all of sport's history.

Born in the mining town of Haswell, County Durham, Tom Simpson was one of a generation of tough working-class cyclists. Moving to Harworth on the Nottinghamshire-Yorkshire border, Simpson was schooled on the empty northern roads of the 1950s, quickly developing winning habits in local time-trials.

In the early 1960s, he burst onto the continental cycling scene, the first Brit to succeed in the closed world of European professional cycling. In the 1962 Tour de France, he became the first British rider to wear the yellow jersey, finishing sixth in the general classification. In 1963 he won the Bordeaux-Paris race, crossing the line six full minutes ahead of the second placed rider. In 1965 he became the first Brit to be crowned World Road Race Champion, and that year was named BBC Sports Personality of the Year, another cycling first. In the 1965 Tour, he started the race with a cut hand which developed into a blood infection spreading to his kidneys and lungs, but despite all this he had to be forced by team doctors to stop. In 1966 he crashed, hit by a car on a descent. He carried on but was injured so badly that he couldn't break, finally forcing him to quit.

He was charismatic and flamboyant, often sporting a bowler hat, suit, and tie—he played up to the stereotype of the self-made Brit from the mines. With his great hook nose and slender face, he was an imposing character. He learned French and was loved by the peloton for the warmth of his personality, his joviality, and a beaming smile that few could resist.

In 1967 Simpson's sole ambition was to be the first Brit to stand on top of the podium of the world's most punishing sporting event. In Simpson's day, the Tour was almost 4000 kms, nearly 1000 kms further than it is today. It was then, as now, the race that defines a cyclist. With his contract due for renewal, Simpson felt additional pressure to perform. In his mind, his financial security depended on a top three finish, or at the very least to a decent run in the yellow jersey. On the 11th stage, he fell ill in the Alps and lost ground but got back on his bike. In the 12th stage, he rode well and climbed back from 16th to 7th. The 13th stage was to cross the summit of the fabled Mont Ventoux, a barren, wind-swept furnace rising 1,617 metres to a summit at 1,912 metres.

His professional team manager Gaston Plaud saw Simpson before the start of the 13th stage. 'The face I saw was of a very tired man,' Plaud recalled. He encouraged him to abandon the race, fearing he would resort to drugs. That morning it was claimed he had shown five tablets of Tonedron, the amphetamine of choice amongst cyclists of the era, to a journalist friend of his. Towards the latter part of the race, Simpson, sitting in a chasing group with six in front, attacked unsuccessfully. Fellow riders encouraged him to sit on their wheel but Simpson attacked for a second time. In blistering heat, an isolated Simpson rode the mountain alone. Simpson had had a near death experience on a bike once before and claimed it held no fear for him. Desperately dehydrated (he twice refused water), passing out of the trees up into the full white glare, he began to lose control, weaving across the road. Collapsing for the first time not far from the summit, a broken, exhausted, and incoherent Simpson fought those trying to help him, demanding to be put back on his bike. He cycled a further 500 yards before collapsing, dead, into the stones by the roadside.

 A monument was erected on the spot where he fell. In 1970, the next time the Tour rode Ventoux, Eddy Merckx, the greatest cyclist of all time, close to collapse himself, doffed his cap as he passed the monument on his way to victory at the summit.

Simpson's death, the result of a lethal combination of drugs and a human determination seldom seen in any arena, has become cycling legend. As Brendan Gallagher wrote in the *Times* forty years after his death, 'Sport throws up some harrowing images but few as upsetting and haunting as the sight of Britain's Tom Simpson zig-zagging across the road on the slopes of Mont Ventoux before collapsing to his death. Looking at the photo you have the overwhelming urge to physically step back into history and drag Simpson off his bike, by force if necessary, and save him from himself.' PG

In the 1965 tour, he started the race with a cut hand which developed into a blood infection spreading to his kidneys and lungs, but despite all this he had to be forced by team doctors to stop.

Tom Simpson

WILFRED THESIGER

Wilfred Thesiger was an explorer and documentarian whose rejection of the machinery of Western man allowed him to experience and record a world that sadly we will never see again.

Wilfred Patrick Thesiger was born in 1910 beneath the thatched roof of the British legation in Addis Ababa, Abyssinia, where his father was Consul General. He belonged to an aristocratic family; his grandfather, a general and second Baron Chelmsford, his uncle, a viscount and Viceroy of India, took him tiger shooting at age 7. He spent his formative years exposed to the great spectacle of an imperial court and to the processions of tribal warlords. Thesiger describes how as a 6-year-old he watched Ras Tafari's victorious army march bloodied through the streets of Addis Ababa, yelling war songs and brandishing their weapons. The scene made a profound and lasting impression. 'I believe that day implanted in me a life-long craving for barbaric splendour, for savagery and colour and the throb of drums, and that it gave me a lasting veneration for long-established custom and ritual, and a distaste for the drab uniformity of the modern world.'

He did not enjoy prep school, his outlandish tales of emperors and hunting tigers did not endear him to his fellow pupils. Eton however, with its spartan regime, and ancient rituals, appealed to Thesiger considerably. He went up to Oxford in 1929 to read history. He boxed, captaining the Oxford team to varsity success in his final year. As soon as the opportunity presented itself, Thesiger chose to travel. During his first summer vacation, he travelled alone by steamer and train to Istanbul, and he spent his second one working as a trawlerman in the North Sea. During his second year he was invited to attend the coronation of Emperor Haile Selassie whose children his family had sheltered during the Abyssinian civil war. Whilst there, he undertook a journey in the Danakil country to trace the Awash River. Danakil tradition held that the testicles of their defeated enemies be taken as trophies. He described one particular boy he encountered, who had collected four such souvenirs the previous day, as a 'rather self-conscious Etonian who had just won his school colours for cricket'.

His explorations in Abyssinia aided him in securing his first position within the Sudan Political Service in Darfur. At every opportunity he would press for leave to travel, becoming skilled at camel-riding and local bush-craft. He wore local clothes, rationed himself to a daily intake of a pint of water and handful of dates, and eschewed all technology bar the rifle, torch, and the compass. He revelled in his ability to befriend the dangerous tribesmen, which he thought set him above other explorers. Thesiger gained a reputation as a healer and an adept killer of lions, a skill much prized amongst the cattle-herding nomadic tribesmen. He raised two lion cubs himself, which, quite without sentiment, he later shot. Of his travels at this time Thesiger later wrote, 'I was exhilarated by the sense of space, the silence, and the crisp cleanness of the sand. I felt in harmony with the past, travelling as men had travelled for untold generations across the deserts, dependent for their survival on the endurance of their camels and their own inherited skills.'

At the outbreak of the Second World War, Thesiger fought with the Sudan Defence Force, and under the extraordinary Orde Wingate in Abyssinia where he was awarded the Distinguished Service Order. He was recruited by David Stirling into the Special Air Service with whom he fought in North Africa. On one mission, sighted by a German patrol, Thesiger went alone into the desert where he lay in a shallow depression, covering himself with dirt, in the full glare of the desert sun. An extensive search failed to run him to ground. Later diaries revealed his hunter to be *Wüstenfuchs* Erwin Rommel. Thesiger's greatest achievement, and the one for which he will be most remembered, was his epic exploration of Arabia's Empty Quarter, one of the least explored and most inhospitable places on earth. Though he was not the first to traverse it, he was the most thorough, crossing it twice over a period of five years. He poignantly captured the lives of the Bedu people in his book *Arabian Sands*. He found the experience enlightening, writing, 'In the desert I found a freedom unattainable in civilisation; a life unhampered by possessions.'

He continued to travel throughout his long life, recording in elegant spare prose and illustrating with his own photographs. Thesiger set himself against what he saw as the corrupting forces of the Western world and its technological abominations, but was never without his camera. The sparse, bewitching black-and-white photographs he took throughout his travels form an enduring record of the tribespeople who became his family, and of the lifestyles in which he immersed himself. Less than a century later, much of what he captured no longer exists. He saw this world as few have seen it. He published a total of eleven books and was awarded many honours, including the Founders Medal from the Royal Geographical Society. He was knighted in 1995, and he died in 2010 aged 93. PG

When Chinese artist Ai Weiwei is followed by plainclothes state security agents, which happens to him more than it does to most, he knows what to do. He calls the police. Cue a knockabout farce of interdepartmental confusion. 'An absurdist novel gone bad,' as Ai put it in the *New York Times*.

Ai Weiwei might as well have been born into conflict with the Chinese authorities. His father was Ai Qing, a poet whose initially friendly relationship with the Communist Party soured under the 1957 Anti-Rightist Campaign, Chairman Mao's nationwide purge of intellectuals. The Ai family was exiled to a forest in Heilongjiang, then to frozen Xinjiang, where Qing was made to clean toilets for a village of 2,000. The family survived on severed sheep hooves and piglets that had frozen to death in the cold, before being moved to a region near the border of the Gobi desert. There, the Ais lived in an underground cavern. It had previously been a birthing place for farm animals.

It was a period that shaped Weiwei's political beliefs and, when the family was finally able to return to Beijing in 1976, he began to channel all of his energies into art. A family friend sourced prohibited books on Degas, van Gogh, and Jasper Johns, and Ai became involved in the avant-garde art protest group Stars. When Stars was disbanded following the imprisonment of its central figure Wei Jingsheng, Ai left for New York. 'I felt I can no longer live in this country,' he later remarked. Ai's tension with China—his position as both citizen subject to the caprice of the state and external critic of the state's excesses—would define his career.

In America many of Ai's familiar traits began to emerge. He supported himself as a sidewalk portrait painter, housekeeper, gardener, babysitter, construction worker, and a blackjack player so successful that he's still talked about in the gambling circles of Atlantic City. They were professions that gave Weiwei time to visit galleries, where he discovered his great artistic love Marcel Duchamp, whose Dada conceptualism proved a key influence on Weiwei's own development. Ai held his first solo show in New York in 1988 and at around the same time he renewed his taste for irritating authority by documenting the riots in Tompkins Square Park. 'Being threatened is addictive,' he later said. 'When those in power are infatuated with you, you feel valued.'

Upon returning to China in 1993, Ai was ready to apply Duchamp's conceptualism to the realities of life in the People's Republic. Ai created artworks like his self-explanatory photographic series *Dropping a Han Dynasty Urn*—in which he reflected on China's alienation from its ancient culture—as well as curating events like his counter-exhibition to the 2000 Shanghai Bienniale. The exhibition was highly experimental, displaying works such as a case of (supposedly) enough poison gas to wipe out the show's entire audience, and photographs of artist Zhu Yu cooking and eating a human foetus. Titled 'Non-Cooperative Approach' in Chinese, and 'Fuck Off' in English, Ai's exhibition was calculated for maximal infuriation of the authorities—a blunt reminder of the importance of freedom in response to the strictures of the state-run biennale.

Running alongside these projects is a commitment to rigorous documentation. Ai doesn't just present finished artworks, he presents everything that went into them and everything that resulted from them. The blog he founded in 2005 is a case in point. As well as a space for occasional essays on haircuts, it became a platform for biting social commentary. He attacked the timidity of the Chinese media ('To call them whores would be to degrade sex workers. To call them beasts of burden would humiliate the animal kingdom.') and labelled China's rulers as 'chunky and brainless gluttons' who 'spend two hundred billion yuan on drinking and dining and an equal amount on the military budget every year'. When the blog was shut down by the state in 2009, Ai turned to Twitter to continue the critique.

It is an approach that has won Ai plaudits abroad, where he is viewed as a pseudo-conscience for the human rights abuses of the Chinese state—a dissenter-in-chief leading a struggle for freedom and democracy. So too is he revered by the artists who populate his Warholian open studio in Beijing, remnant of his formative years in New York. Yet elsewhere in China, opinion is mixed. Many Chinese believe he misrepresents the complexities of modern China, preferring instead to depict the state in a demonised form that suits Western tastes, rather than seeking to engage with the government in meaningful dialogue. 'Whoever wants to pass himself off as a hero, protecting people's rights, go ahead,' wrote the artist Yu Gao in 2010. 'But it is just the mask of a clown.'

What is clear, however, is that the Chinese government doesn't see Ai as a clown. In early 2011 his Shanghai studio was demolished by the authorities and a few months later he was detained by the state and held in solitary confinement for 81 days. Ai was labelled a bigamist, a fraudster, a pornographer, and a plagiarist, and post-release he was confined to his Beijing studio. In response, Ai mounted his own surveillance cameras and started to stream his own self-surveillance video online. The police ordered him to take it down.

The defining moment of Ai's life came in 2009. In 2008, China's Sichuan province was hit by a major earthquake, a disaster that official figures reported as killing 69,000 people. Yet the state had hushed up the disproportionate number of school children killed in the quake, due to what Ai termed the flimsy 'tofu dregs' construction of schools in Sichuan; a result, he believed, of officials siphoning off funds. Ai's eventual response was an installation at the Munich Haus der Kunst, a mosaic of 9,000 children's backpacks that spelled out in Chinese characters a statement from the mother of a child killed in the quake: 'She lived happily on this earth for seven years.' It was a striking piece, but more importantly the culmination of a major online investigation, a project aimed at collecting as many of the names of the children killed in the earthquake as possible. It was a project the state disliked. During the investigation, a hotel room Ai was staying at in Chengdu was raided by police. The subsequent beating he received resulted in a cerebral haemorrhage.

Yet it was a quieter moment of the research process that proved more telling. While attempting to file suit against the Ministry of Civil Affairs for failing to provide information about the earthquake victims, Ai visited the Second Intermediate People's Court of Beijing to hand over the appropriate paperwork. The filing, after hours of queuing, was rejected. The official reason was that the filing had been written in blue ink and written materials had to be provided in black. 'Kafka's Castle', was how Ai characterised the situation. It was a fitting summation. Ever since his days in the Gobi desert birthing pit, Ai Weiwei seems to be living in an absurdist novel gone bad. OS

'Being threatened is addictive. When those in power are infatuated by you, you feel valued.'

Ai Weiwei

MALCOLM X

Malcolm X was a fierce critic of the oppression of blacks by white Americans. Accused of preaching violence and racial hatred, he was the most outspoken, feared, and revered black man of his generation.

Malcolm, one of seven children, grew up with his family in Omaha but left after the Ku Klux Klan burnt their house down. The family moved to Lansing, Michigan where Malcolm was fully integrated with white children in the neighbourhood. His father, a follower of the doctrine of Marcus Garvey, was branded an 'uppity nigger', and the Klan, 70,000 strong in Michigan, burnt their house down once again. Not long after this, Malcolm's father's body, severed almost in half, was found on the outskirts of the town. Malcolm was brought up in foster care, the only black in his class, but he excelled at school, was an A-grade student, and became class president.

But Malcolm didn't go to college. He moved first to Boston, and then to Harlem where he hustled, supplying whisky, drugs, and girls. He later moved back to Boston where, at age 20, he was arrested for burglary and sentenced to 8-10 years in prison. While in prison, Malcolm studied history, religion, and philosophy; read Shakespeare, Socrates, and Gandhi. His family introduced him to Elijah Muhammad and the Nation of Islam. He joined the prison debate team and competed against teams from Harvard and MIT; his fame spread, people wanted to hear the word of the tall, athletic, electrifying young firebrand.

After six and a half years in prison, he was released and accepted into the Nation of Islam. Within two years, his passionate zeal saw him named minister of the most important temple on the east coast, Harlem's Temple No. 7. He joined the street orators of Harlem on 125th St. and 7th Avenue and quickly became the Nation's most visible and eloquent spokesperson. In the unrest which followed the 1957 beating of a Muslim in police custody in Harlem, Malcolm X held the community completely in his sway, and from that point on the extent of X's power became obvious to Elijah Muhammad, the police, and to politicians.

Malcolm X's preaching went far beyond that of any other black leader of his day. This was the era of the civil rights movement. Dr Martin Luther King fought for equal rights, preached a policy of non-violent civil disobedience, and believed in the possibility of a 'beloved society' which was colour blind. X thought King was dreaming. He believed that black men and women in America held a deeply ingrained sense of inferiority, and he strove to drive it out. 'Who taught you to hate the colour of your skin?' he said. 'Who taught you to hate the texture of your hair? Who taught you to hate yourself from the top of your head to the soles of your feet? Who taught you to hate your own kind?' He denied his own surname claiming his family name had been stolen when slavers brought his ancestors from Africa. He hated the idea that black people were motivated by a desire to fit in with the white community. 'You are better than the white man. Your skin looks like gold beside his skin.' Historian John Henrik Clarke said, 'While other leaders were begging for entry into the house of their oppressor, he was telling you to build your own house.'

White Americans did not like to be told they were oppressors. Many black Americans feared his incendiary and confrontational views, but to many he simply voiced what they were too afraid to say. The FBI kept close tabs on X. His international fame spread, he travelled widely, befriending leaders in many countries. He debated at the Oxford Union to great ovation. The BBC televised the event.

He began to grow apart from the Nation of Islam following their failure to act after a police shooting of a young black man in Los Angeles in 1962. X wanted court justice. X believed in the power of the law of the land, whereas Elijah Muhammad believed in divine protection. X further lost faith in Muhammad when it emerged that he had fathered eight children with six of his teenage secretaries. Finally, in the aftermath of Kennedy's murder, Muhammad banned all mention for fear of a backlash, but X disobeyed him claiming that this was a case of 'chickens coming home to roost,' blaming Kennedy for failing to prevent deaths of many in the black community. He was suspended from the Nation of Islam.

Malcolm X formed his own Organisation of Afro-American Unity with the single aim of bringing about freedom for these people 'by any means necessary'. Conflict with the Nation of Islam led to repeated death threats. X lived in fear. 'I am probably a dead man already,' he said. On 14 February 1965, his house, with his wife and young daughters inside, was fire-bombed. One week later, three Nation of Islam assassins shot him multiple times as he preached. He died on the stage. The *New York Times* described him as 'an extraordinary and twisted man' who 'turn[ed] many true gifts to evil purpose' and *TIME* called him 'an unashamed demagogue' whose 'creed was violence'.

X was enormously articulate, imposing, and always immaculately dressed. He held audiences in his thrall. Always happy to debate his views publicly, in the face of direct challenges and hostile audiences, he faced down every criticism with lucid counter arguments, firmly but never rudely, and with a smile. His power came from his courage and his conviction, which was absolute. PG

CHAPTER 3

Libertine

Our libertine is a man of liberty—a hellraiser, a playboy, a bon vivant. The libertine is often criticised for being morally corrupt, dissolute, even licentious. This is true in many cases, but far from being a harbinger of moral bankruptcy, he is a necessary counter-weight to a culture of moral torpidity. His freedom from moral obligations and societal strictures, his decoupling from the drudgery of work and the tedium of sobriety, reminds us that life can be entertaining.

Challenging moral principles, as opposed to behaving without them, was what motivated the first libertines. The term was originally coined in the mid-sixteenth century by John Calvin as a catch-all for those (mostly the rich and politically powerful) who disagreed with his religious views. Calvin broke human beings into two groups; the Elect, who were good and would enjoy eternal life, and the Reprobate who were eternally damned to common misery for participating in such awful acts as dancing, drinking, or anything else bordering on entertainment. The libertine of old was anyone who stood up against Calvin, the archbishop of kill-joys.

Libertine can be considered synonymous with 'freethinker', one who is against the prevailing moral or religious doctrine of his time. This anti-establishment stance is not only commendable, but a necessity if thought and society are to evolve. Both in fiction and in history, the libertine pursues themes revolving around ideas of anti-establishmentariaism, anti-clericalism, and eroticism. Perhaps most famous in the literary type is *Les Liaisons Dangereuses,* a tale of erotic libertinism, an unsparing but ultimately not entirely unflattering account of the sexual sparring between a group of French aristocrats shortly before the French revolution. The English Restoration was counter to everything Puritanical. The most noted historical libertine of all was poet John Wilmot, Earl of Rochester, a prime mover in the court of Charles II, the very embodiment of the anti-Puritanism of the day. Rochester's life was a near continual round of carousing, ribaldry, and sexual adventure.

Libertine disappeared from everyday usage to be replaced in the 1960s and 1970s by the sobriquet hellraiser. This was a broad term describing frequently drunk, often sexually promiscuous, occasionally violent, but mostly just outrageously-behaved individuals such as Oliver Reed, Jack Nicholson, and Ozzy Osbourne. Garrulous, booze-soaked, charming, and entertaining in some instances, childish and infuriating in others.

There was something extraordinary about the extent of their rabble-rousing, the great inventiveness and ingenuity of the schemes for their own entertainment and that of their companions. The hellraiser was reacting against the prevailing rigid moral standards. He acted as he saw fit, but at a cost: there is a clear sense that these are lonely lives. The hellraiser struggles to make sense of an existence ultimately isolated by his self-absorption.

The playboy, a man of ample means and time for leisure, is also a species of libertine. Spiritual descendants of the Sybarites, in the 1920s playboys were the sons of the great industrialists. Well-educated, well-travelled, they were charming and sophisticated, owned yachts and sports cars, and reputedly had enormous penises. This was not the lonely life of the hellraiser. It was a life of adventure, childish perhaps, but one of joy. In his 1938 book *Homo Ludens,* Dutch cultural historian Johan Huizinga wrote that play is the primary formative element in human culture, that it is separate from real life. 'Play', he said, 'is free, it is in fact freedom.'

There are some men whose enjoyment of the finer things in life remains largely untouched by accusations of irresponsibility and moral decline. The *bon vivant* thrives through consumption, he has mastered the drink, and derives great joy and enlightenment through a touch of inebriation. Churchill enjoyed an occasional glass of hock with breakfast. He would sip his 'papa cocktail' throughout the morning and drank effusively at mealtimes. As Churchill said, a glass of champagne 'lifts the spirits, sharpens the wits'.

There is a glorious absence of self-righteousness and hypocrisy about these men. They remind us that morality is not a fundamental principle and may take on unconventional forms. As Alan Bennett said of his friend Peter Cook, 'a life of complete self-indulgence, if led with the whole heart, may also bring wisdom.'

GIANNI AGNELLI

It is difficult to name a man with a more impeccable style than that of Gianni Agnelli. Though his place in popular culture may be cemented by his image, Agnelli offers more than this. He was once the richest man in modern Italian history as an industrialist of measureless success, and was also a war veteran. Agnelli's style serves to draw attention to the complete package of a man whose influence spans multiple spheres, and whose legacy cannot be understated.

Born on 12 March 1921, Agnelli studied at Pinerolo Cavalry Academy and read law at the University of Turin, though he never practised this vocation. Italy's involvement in the Second World War saw Agnelli join a tank regiment in 1940, and he served on the Russian front, sustaining two injuries in the process. His most serious injury, however, came while he was serving in an armoured car division in North Africa. He received a shot to the arm as a result of a drunken brawl in a bar in which Agnelli and a German officer had been arguing about a woman.

Agnelli's passion for the opposite sex did not end with the war, and he remained a famous playboy throughout his life. In 1953 he married to Donna Marella Caracciolo dei principi di Castagneto, a noblewoman and fabric designer and they had a son, Edoardo. Nonetheless, Agnelli sustained concurrent relationships with multiple mistresses throughout the marriage. Among the myriad of women with whom he liked to spend his time were the socialite Pamela Harriman, actress Anita Ekberg, and fashion designer Jackie Rogers. But despite the evident prolificacy of Agnelli's charm, the marriage lasted until his death in 2003.

Agnelli inherited control of his family's company, Fiat, and their assets in 1966, placing him among the world's industrial elite. At one time Agnelli controlled 4.4% of Italy's GDP, 3.1% of its industrial workforce, and 16.5% of its industrial investment in research, easily making him the most important individual in Italian economics, and he was considered by much of the population to be the 'True King of Italy'. He was made an Italian senator for life in 1991. Throughout his career, Agnelli became increasingly involved with the Italian football club Juventus, of which he was ultimately the owner. During his time at the helm, Agnelli would telephone the club's president, Giampiero Boniperti, at six in the morning every day regardless of where he was or what he was doing.

His considerable industrial strength aside, Agnelli's place in history, and indeed the reason he is so widely iconized in Italy and across the world, was his style. Agnelli's talent lay in the way he would always be impeccably dressed without fault while giving the impression he had done little or no effort to achieve his look. This was largely due to a flawless combination of high quality staples, often bespoke suits, and exquisite accessories. In this way, Agnelli's style has had a huge impact on the world of men's fashion. It was typical of Agnelli to wear, for instance, a perfectly tailored suit and crisp shirt with a messy, asymmetrical tie splayed across the front, a button-down shirt whose collar was left untamed, or Gucci hiking boots with boardroom suits. He famously used to wear his wristwatch over the cuff of his shirt to avoid wasting the time it took to pull his cuff back. The cornerstone of Agnelli's look, and the one which best captivates the essence of his style, was his foregoing of the buttons on the surgeon cuffs of his bespoke Caraceni suits; this exudes the effortless combination of quality materials and craftsmanship with the casual functionality which has come to epitomize Agnelli's public image. Agnelli was included in *Esquire* magazine's list of the five best dressed men in the history of the world, and his nickname 'The Rake of the Riviera' was used for the classical menswear magazine, *The Rake*. Agnelli's style encompasses much of what menswear endeavours to achieve in modern times: the effortless combination of quality materials, expert craftsmanship, and basic functionality.

Gianni Agnelli was exceptional on many different levels. His identities as a playboy, celebrity, and style icon were all achieved while he was the most influential industrialist in Italy, and its most wealthy citizen. In fact, 'wealth' is a word especially suited to Agnelli's life. It alludes to his charm, his style, his influence, and his legacy, all of which existed and continue to exist in abundance. GE

At one time Agnelli controlled 4.4% of Italy's GDP [...], easily making him the most important individual in Italian economics, and he was considered by much of the population to be the 'True King of Italy'.

GEORGE BEST

George Best is widely regarded as one of the most talented footballers to ever play the game. Indeed, Pele once said that he was 'the greatest player in the world', something which Best himself declared was the 'ultimate salute' to his life. Best's skill was peerless and earned him 170 goals in 470 appearances over the 11 years he represented Manchester United, the club who first spotted him, when he was aged only 15. His success continued on the international stage, where he scored 9 goals for his 37 caps for Northern Ireland from 1964 to 1977. It was Best's unbelievable talent, combined with his attractive appearance and captivating charisma which earned him a reputation as 'the beautiful boy' and cemented his place as one of the first celebrity footballers. With this reputation came all the opportunities and perils of the celebrity lifestyle: the money, the beautiful women, and the booze.

Best sums up his passion for this lifestyle in this immortal quote: 'I spent a lot of money on booze, birds, and fast cars. The rest I just squandered.' Best married twice (to two models) but not before pursuing a long career of womanizing. Rumours spread that Best had bedded seven Miss Worlds during his career, a claim which he disputed in his 2002 autobiography, asserting that it had only been four—he didn't turn up for the other three. 'If you'd given me the choice of going out and beating four men and smashing a goal in from thirty yards against Liverpool or going to bed with Miss World,' Best once said, 'it would have been a difficult choice. Luckily, I had both.' A sentiment to which he added on a different occasion, 'I used to go missing a lot ... Miss Canada, Miss United Kingdom, Miss World.' He did not say who the fourth was. Perhaps unsurprisingly, these rendezvous would take place over copious bottles of the finest champagne; it seemed wherever Best went the women and drinks would follow.

At one point, Best admitted to have stolen money from a stranger's handbag to finance yet another spiralling drinking session while on holiday in the United States in 1981 with no immediate access to his own funds. His love for the bottle only blossomed as his career went on, and he received a three-month spell in prison in 1984 for drunk driving, the assault of a police officer, and subsequent failure to answer bail after a drinking binge. As a result, Best would spend that Christmas Day in the Ford Open Prison. One of Best's most public exhibitions of his tumultuous relationship with alcohol came in 1990, when he appeared on a television chat show, *Wogan*. He swore throughout the interview and, upon being asked what was occupying his time now his footballing days were all but over, Best announced, 'Terry, I like screwing.'

George Best

As time went on, Best found it increasingly hard to maintain this way of life, and fell victim to crippling alcoholism. This addiction resulted in multiple trips to rehabilitation clinics and acute depression, and Best seriously considered taking his own life on a number of occasions. Having been diagnosed with severe cirrhosis of the liver in 1999, Best was admitted into a hospital in 2000 and very nearly died. The 'Beautiful Boy' was later given a liver transplant on the proviso that he would give up drinking. This was a promise Best was unable to fulfil and his drinking, combined with the medication required to stop his body rejecting the new liver, resulted in kidney failure in 2005.

A dying Best entered Cromwell Hospital in the autumn of 2005 and spent seven weeks in intensive care before his death on 25 November. Upon Best's personal request, the *News of the World* filled their front page with a picture of him, withered and weak, lying in his deathbed. The caption he chose, 'Don't die like I did', is resonant; millions of people, from young boys to grown men, would have done anything to live like Best had done, with the cars, the girls, and the glamour, but none could escape the bitter reminder that those flying highest have the furthest to fall. Best was an Icarus: he possessed genius without equal on the football pitch, charisma which won the hearts of millions, had the world at his feet, and, as is so often the case with great men, the only person who could bring George Best crashing down to earth was himself.

Despite his tragic and untimely end, the whole of George Best's life is inspirational. In his youth Best coupled natural talent with an attitude which refused to pass up any of the countless opportunities life presented to him, and cemented his place in history not only as a great footballer, but as an exceptional personality, and it would have been easy for Best to fade into insignificance when his football career became untenable, but he remained in the minds and hearts of millions. His final message was twofold: to live to the fullest, and to learn from his mistakes. GE

**'I spent a lot of money on booze, birds, and fast cars.
The rest I just squandered.'**

George Best

JAMES BROWN

'So now ladies and gentlemen it's star time, are you ready for star time?' This is how audiences were prepared for James Brown's impending performances. From the shacks of South Carolina via every venue possible, whether it be a juvenile detention centre or the White House, the narrative of James Brown's life reads like a film script based on the old rags to riches storyline.

On the 5 April 1968, the day after Martin Luther King was assassinated, the city of Boston seemed at a tipping point. Fears of race riots were prevalent across the city and it felt as though Boston would burn. Entertainer is perhaps the broadest title to give to the man who performed a televised live show on that night, keeping people revelling in his magnetism at home rather than taking to the streets to riot. This was the power of the man dubbed The Godfather of Soul.

Humble and criminal beginnings make Brown's rise to stardom all the more fascinating. Leaving school when he was 12 years old, Brown made his living shining shoes, washing cars, and famously dancing for soldiers at Fort Gordon in Georgia. It was in this time that Brown, inspired by revolutionary bandleader Louis Jordan, learnt the guitar, harmonica, and the piano in order to become an entertainer. At 16, however, Brown was sent to a juvenile detention centre for stealing a car. In jail he formed a gospel quartet inspired by his time singing in the church and was eventually paroled, meeting Bobby Byrd in the process who would become one of his closest friends.

Brown joined Byrd's R&B band, The Famous Flames, which would be the first step in Brown's illustrious career. The band was signed and successful, reaching No. 1 in the R&B charts with their single 'Try Me'. Brown began to play a more pivotal role in the band, leading and writing many of the songs. Suddenly it was James Brown and his band, and by the early 1960s Brown had started his own label, sold over a million copies of his *Live at the Apollo* album, released 'Papa's Got a Brand New Bag', his first single to reach the Top Ten in the pop charts, and won his first Grammy Award. Just over a decade after his parole, James Brown had become a household name for R&B audiences and had begun edging his way into the mainstream. He was not a black musician crossing over to the mainstream white audience, he was compelling that audience and everyone else to follow him.

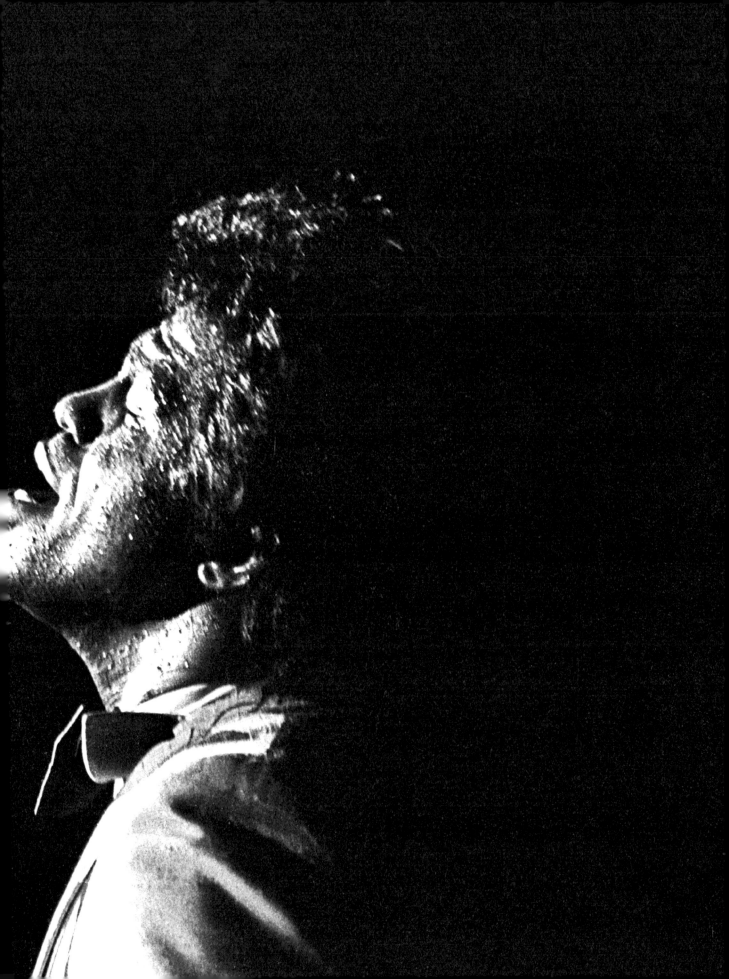

Brown began experimenting with styles, rhythms, vocal delivery, and harmonies in the mid-to-late 1960s. He crooned to audiences about breaking out in a 'Cold Sweat' in what many believe to be the first funk record. The song would become emblematic of Brown's style in later songs, including a single-chord harmony and a drum break. It is in the latter musical innovation that one can see why many believe Brown to be the Godfather of Hip-Hop too, being the most sampled musician in the genre which sprung in the late 1980s and owes so much to Brown's pioneering technique.

That is without mentioning Brown's innovative proto-rapping mode as early as 1967 on the track 'America is my Home'. The track itself shows Brown's patriotic fervour and reminds us that Brown supported the war in Vietnam, performing for troops. He notes in the song that he 'started as a shoe-shine boy and ended up shaking hands with the President'.

Brown continued to successfully record throughout the 1970s and 1980s with a stint of drug abuse in the mid-80s coinciding with various arrests for unlicensed gun possession, and most dramatically leading the police on a high-speed car chase across the Georgia-South Carolina border. His personal life could well fill this entire biography, as could his musical career, though his ostentatious stage presence should not go without mention. Draped in a cape, he would feign leaving the stage before throwing it off and performing an encore, a version of which he performed in the classic film *The Blues Brothers*. He would also star in various other films including *Rocky IV*, the *Blues Brothers* sequel and a spate of documentaries.

James Brown was a self-made man, a breathing, singing, dancing, funk-filled vision of the American dream in all its potential and in all its pitfalls. From dance to drugs, from funk to felonies, Brown's life spanned various eras, ending in 2006 from heart failure. He had been down, and implored audiences to 'Get on Up' and celebrate with him the glittering potential of music to uplift and inspire. HB

CHARLES BUKOWSKI

Few men have felt so hopelessly at odds with the world into which they were born than Charles Bukowski. His dissatisfaction with the servile nature of American bourgeois society is perhaps the greatest theme of his work. Not swept up by the wave of optimism and free expression of the sixties, Bukowski is something of an outlier. He said, 'I wasn't a misanthrope and I wasn't a misogynist but I liked being alone. It felt good to sit alone in a small space and smoke and drink. I had always been good company for myself.'

Bukowski is predominantly known as a poet, though he is undoubtedly more than that: an ideologue, a novelist, and a critic. It may come as a surprise to learn that Bukowski did not actually begin writing poetry until the age of 35. Bukowski's concurrent working life, his incredible list of odd jobs that supported his meagre earnings from writing, makes him a standard bearer for ordinary, and particularly for poor Americans. These jobs included working as a truck driver, postman, security guard, petrol pump attendant, and elevator operator. Though German born, Bukowski has become an American literary staple, penning thousands of poems and hundreds of short stories. As a child, he was beaten by his father, bullied by his classmates, and suffered from dyslexia, leading to an acute shyness and withdrawn personality that Bukowski would only begin to voice through his work. In his early teens, Bukowski would also meet his long-term mistress, alcohol.

After skipping out on military service because he was deemed mentally unfit, Bukowski began his career as a writer in New York, publishing short stories in small literary magazines. His first piece, entitled *Aftermath of a Lengthy Rejection Slip,* was published in the 1944 issue of *Story.* It was in the pages of these sometimes obscure publications that most of Bukowski's work could be found. After his initial publication, Bukowski's other early writings failed to make an impact, leading to a personal post-war depression which Bukowski describes as a 'ten-year drunk' in which he was abjectly depressed. This period would form the basis of his semi-autobiographical chronicles, exploring this state through a character named Henry Chinaski.

The turning point for Bukowski came with the discovery of an almost deadly bleeding ulcer, for which he was treated in 1955, after which Bukowski began writing poetry. He married in 1957, divorced in 1959, and resumed his drinking habit soon after. His major success came by the late 60s, the decade in which he returned to his job as a post-office clerk, had a daughter with his girlfriend, and published his first collection of poetry. His early pieces referenced a nostalgic romanticism about the past in sharp relief to the

artificial and vacuous nature of contemporary society. 1967 saw Bukowski's first major success through his contribution to a column in the Los Angeles newspaper *Open City*. His column, entitled *Notes of a Dirty Old Man* was a raging diatribe against the growing media of film and television as forms of escapism, as mechanisms to make the public sphere docile. He noted pertinently that 'The nine-to-five is one of the greatest atrocities sprung upon mankind. You give your life away to a function that doesn't interest you. This situation so repelled me that I was driven to drink, starvation, and mad females, simply as an alternative.' He would further critique patriotism, and attack the academic establishment for its conformity.

His own writings continued to display dark themes of sex, domestic abuse, low-life alcoholics, and the trap of relationships between men and women, revealing both the physical and emotional trauma of connecting with another human being. In the 1970s Bukowski began writing about male sexuality and sexual relationships, as brashly and pointedly as ever, which people labelled as misogynistic. Others have however merely noted these pieces as denouncing the moral bankruptcy of society. Bukowski continued to find success, releasing his semi-autobiographical novels and eventually dying in 1994, leaving the world with a simple adage engraved on his tombstone. Bukowski offers aspiring writers the simple dictum 'Don't Try'. HB

'**Some people never go crazy. What truly horrible lives they must lead.**'
Charles Bukowski

JOHNNY CASH

'Hello, I'm Johnny Cash.' That was the straightforward way in which Johnny Cash introduced himself at the beginning of each concert. But for a man whose career led him to become the straightforward voice of the American soul, Johnny Cash led a complicated life. Anybody who collapses into a spiral of heavy drug abuse because they were kicked in the stomach by their pet ostrich can't be *that* straightforward.

Johnny Cash was born J. R. Cash in 1932 in Kingsland, Arkansas. The J. R. didn't stand for anything—his parents couldn't think up a name—and he grew up on a farm, subject to the misery of the Great Depression and its impact on dustbowl America. Misery would become a hallmark of Cash's life. As a boy, he had a favourite dog, which one day had a litter of puppies. 'Grandpa put all the puppies in a bag with a rock in it and threw it in the river,' Cash later told his daughter. 'He made me come and watch as they drowned. Then he shot the dog.' It is an archetypal Cash story. Near-hysterical through the sheer misery and awfulness of it all.

Yet the most significant event of Cash's childhood came in 1944 when his older brother Jack was struck in the stomach by a circular saw he was using to cut fence posts. It took Jack a week to die and Cash's father blamed him for the accident, arguing that it should have been J. R. who died instead. As an escape, Cash threw himself into gospel music—a fitting start for a man whose voice would go on to become biblically baritone. Music became an outlet for his chronic world-weariness.

Cash never looked back from music, and after his short stint in the armed forces ended in 1954, he began to pursue it seriously. Cash's style was eclectic, mixing his familiar gospel with genres like pop, rockabilly, blues, and folk to create rhythms on hits like 'Folsom Prison Blues' and 'I Walk the Line', as well as taking part in jam sessions with Elvis Presley, Carl Perkins, and Jerry Lee Lewis. Cash's lyrics had a way of mythologising old-time America, singing about its corn silos, railways, prisons, and factories, all the while professing to share pathos with the beat-down and down-at-heel. It was straightforward, lyrically miserable music and it was wildly successful. In 1958 he moved to Ventura, California to sign with Colombia records. And then he went on a nine-year bender.

'I was evil. I really was,' Cash would later remember of that time, and he had a point. Cash became hooked on amphetamines and alcohol and his behaviour became eccentric.

When booked into an adjacent hotel room to the rockabilly musician Carl Perkins, Cash knocked down the wall with a metal chair so that he and Perkins could visit each other. Efforts to smuggle 668 amphetamine tablets and 475 tranquillisers into Mexico inside his guitar case were thwarted by border police and Cash frequently took so many pills that those around him mistook him for dead. Not that that stopped him. The musician Johnny Western later remembered Cash borrowing his Cadillac while whacked on pills, with a phonecall arriving hours later: 'Johnny, I lost your car. I was just going to borrow it for two or three hours and I think I left it down at the Farmer's Market.'

It all fed into an image of Cash as an outlaw. His voice was gruff, he dressed all in black, and a cyst scar on his jaw made him look like he'd just been punched. He liked to play prison concerts and his reputation for straight talking was exemplified in records like 'In the Jailhouse Now' (sample lyric: 'I told him once or twice / To quit playin' cards and shootin' dice / He's in the jailhouse now'). His offstage behaviour simply fuelled the flames of his image. In 1965 Cash was responsible for burning down 508 acres of forest in Los Padres National Forest in California, in so doing slaying 49 of the area's 53 endangered Californian condors. 'I don't care about your damn yellow buzzards,' was Cash's response, his defence being that his truck had overheated and caught fire. His nephew would later report that Cash had purposefully set fire to the truck while high on pills in a bid to keep himself warm.

Things began to turn around when Cash met his second wife June Carter (his first wife had divorced him during the bender), who helped him overcome his addictions and who converted him to fundamentalist Christianity. Carter and Cash married in 1968 and Cash subsequently got clean. He hosted the *Johnny Cash Show* on ABC, which successfully launched their careers and the early 1970s were a happy time for Cash. Yet by the 1980s Cash's star had faded and in 1983 he became hooked on painkillers after they were prescribed to him following an incident: Waldo, one of the ostriches he kept on his farm in Tennessee, had nearly disembowelled him after Cash had tried to hit him with a stick and missed. He would struggle with dependency for the rest of his life.

The latter years of Cash's career were varied. He would never again achieve the success he had enjoyed in the 1960s. Yet his fame was kept ticking with albums such as 1994's successful *American Recordings* and his reputation was stoked by the plaudits of other artists.

When Cash eventually died in 2003, it fell to no less a musician than Bob Dylan to eulo-gise his influence in *Rolling Stone:* 'He is what the land and country is all about, the heart and soul of it personified and what it means to be here; and he said it all in plain English. Listen to him, and he will always bring you to your senses.' os

Johnny Cash

WINSTON CHURCHILL

Sir Winston Leonard Spencer-Churchill secured his place in history through his role in British politics, guiding the nation to victory in the Second World War. Although he will always be remembered for this, his iconic personality, adorned with a large cigar and razor-sharp wit, has placed him amongst the most popular and well-remembered public figures of all time.

One of the most famous cigar enthusiasts, Churchill was rarely seen without a glass of whisky and a trademark stogie. Having started smoking cigars in his mid-teens, he progressed to consuming around ten a day throughout his adult life. He even had a special oxygen mask created so that, when travelling overseas, he could continue to smoke even if the airplane's cabin lost pressure. On a separate occasion, Churchill hosted a lunch for the Saudi King, Ibn Sa'ud, who did not normally allow smoking and drinking in his presence. Churchill declared in a twist of characteristically Churchillian grandiloquence, 'my rule of life prescribes as an absolutely sacred rite smoking cigars and also the drinking of alcohol before, after, and if need be during all meals and in the intervals between them,' and proceeded to smoke throughout the lunch.

Churchill produced his most famous witticisms during his career at the highest level of British politics. Pitted against the famous Labour politician, Clement Attlee, at the end of the war, Churchill launched an offensive against the man he perceived to lack the strength, charisma, and oratorical verve required from a successful politician. Attlee, Churchill quipped, was 'a modest man with much to be modest about'. In another famous comment Churchill said: 'An empty cab drew up to Downing Street, and Clement Attlee got out.' Indeed, Churchill's rhetorical sword was swung at most politicians at one time or another throughout his career. Debates in the House of Commons provided the perfect stage for Churchill's wit, and played host to some of his most memorable comments. When a member of the opposition once used more than his allotted time to make a point, Churchill disparagingly stated, 'I can well understand the honourable member's wishing to speak on. He needs the practice badly.' On a separate occasion, one particularly anguished speaker made the mistake of saying 'Mr Churchill, must you fall asleep while I am speaking?', 'No,' Churchill replied, 'it is purely voluntary.'

Outside of parliament, Churchill combined a charismatic charm, biting wit, and an enthusiasm for the other sex, consequently finding himself on the wrong side of many of his female acquaintances. 'Madam,' Churchill asked a lady one night, 'would you sleep with me for five million pounds?' 'My goodness, Mr Churchill!' she replied, 'Well, I suppose we would have to discuss terms, but of course.' Undeterred by her surprise, Churchill pressed on. 'Would you sleep with me for five pounds?' 'Mr Churchill, what kind of woman do you think I am?!' she exclaimed. He delivered the final blow: 'Madam, we've established that. Now we are haggling about the price.' Bessie Braddock once turned to Churchill after an evening of heavy drinking and exclaimed, 'Winston, you're drunk.' Unfazed by his inebriation, Churchill immediately responded, 'You are right, Bessie, but you are ugly, and in the morning I shall be sober and you, madam, will still be ugly.' Obviously a previous recipient of Churchill's uncompromising utterances, Lady Astor, the first female MP in the House of Commons, said, 'Mr Churchill, if you were my husband, I'd put poison in your tea.' Churchill rose slowly and unsteadily to his feet, but the sharpness of his mind did not match the frailty of his body: 'Madam, if I were your husband, I'd drink it.'

As Churchill grew older his wit did not wane, and he continued to shoot down anyone younger who misjudged the longevity of his mental agility. Waiting for a friend in the corridors of the House of Commons, long retired from any active role there and seemingly oblivious to the outside world, passers-by commented, 'They say the old chap's gone quite crazy.' 'They say he can't hear as well,' Churchill muttered, as the two scuttled off, scalded.

Churchill died on 24 January 1965 and left a remarkable legacy. Serving two terms as British Prime Minister, including one which placed him amongst the most widely acclaimed wartime leaders of recent history, officer in the British Army, artist, historian, and writer, and the only Prime Minister to win a Nobel Prize in Literature, he is truly a titan of the twentieth century. What binds these achievements, and what creates this unforgettable persona is his way with words. When picturing Churchill today, it is hard not to imagine the cragged face, cigar hanging from the mouth, whisky in hand, and sublime witticisms flowing effortlessly onto whoever stood in his way. GE

ALAN CLARK

To date, Alan Clark is the only British politician to have been accused of being drunk at the dispatch box. It is as good a summation of his career as any. Born in 1928 to Elizabeth Winifred Martin and celebrated art historian Kenneth Clark, Alan Clark was educated at Eton and Oxford. He seemed destined for greatness and he might have achieved it were it not for his own remarkable capacity for self-sabotage. As a young man, he wrote *The Donkeys,* a witty, vigorous, and hugely popular history of the incompetence of the British Generals of the First World War. Despite the book's ongoing influence, there have always been problems with the text. 'As history, it is worthless,' commented military historian Professor Michael Howard at the time of its release, and Clark later confirmed that he had made up a swathe of the book. Donald Cameron Watt, a professor at the London School of Economics, summed up much of the critical reaction to the text with his own acerbic assessment of Clark: 'An arrogant, self-centred man who talks bollocks.'

Throughout his life, Clark wore many hats. He was a writer, a member of the Conservative party (although only once he'd overcome being blacklisted for being too right-wing), a member of parliament (twice), Minister for Trade, Minister for Defence Procurement (disgraced) and a diarist par excellence, with his account of Margaret Thatcher's downfall becoming the definitive account of the time. Yet there was another set of epithets that always seemed to fit Clark better: roué, rogue, bon vivant, scoundrel, philanderer. Clark was charming, acid-tongued, and debonair, but with more than a whiff of brimstone about him.

Most emblematic of Clark was his liberality regarding the truth. There was his constant claim that he was vegetarian, undermined by his habit of eating melon and parma ham in interviews. His impassioned renunciation of abortion in parliament subverted by the fact he once asked his mother to arrange a termination for a ballerina he'd impregnated. Then there was the time in the 1980s when Clark was suspected as a government minister of having approved arms exports to Iraq, a claim that he denied under oath. The subsequent trial collapsed when his denial was found to be nonsense. 'Well, it's our old friend "being economical", isn't it?' Clark breezed in court. 'With the truth?' the lawyer responded. Clark's reply was perfectly weighted: 'With the actualité.'

More important to Clark than integrity or truthfulness was his own comfort or position. He once refused an interview unless the journalist could provide him with a case of Puligny Montrachet wine to the value of a lunch at Claridge's, and that was just the

tip of the iceberg. At a time when Thatcher was closing the mines and plunging the livelihood of many into crisis, Alan Clark lived in a castle in Kent. This world of aristocracy, of driving goggles, tweeds, and cravats (all of which he wore liberally) seemed to suit Clark. As a politician he never got out of the foothills of power, albeit not through any lack of talent. Clark was erudite, witty, intelligent, and quick, but in other areas he came up wanting. Colleagues knew not to trust Clark with political secrets because he inevitably leaked them to journalists over lunch. Clark could not be relied upon to discuss matters like the IRA bombing campaign, because he would say things like, 'The only solution is to kill 600 people in one night. Let the UN and Bill Clinton and everyone else make a scene.' Clark could never be put in a position of real authority, because he stank of scandal.

Alan Clark

When black communities raised concerns over the Thatcher government's compiling of data on ethnic minorities, Clark piled in with trademark sensitivity: 'They are afraid we'll be going to hand them over to the immigration services so that they can send them all back to Bongo Bongo land.' Other minorities came in for similar treatment. One of Clark's favourite words was 'spastic', while his interest in the First World War as the dominant event in twentieth-century history—a view he believed had been neglected in favour of discussion over the Second World War—prompted him to complain about people 'whingeing on about the Holocaust'. It was a comment that was typical of Clark, who was forever dogged by accusations of fascist sympathies. Clark's sister recalled that Alan had professed to admiring General Franco, while Clark himself was on record as describing Adolf Hitler as 'ahead of his time'. More telling was the diary entry that began, 'I told Frank Johnson that I was a Nazi; I really believed it to be the ideal system, and that it was a disaster for the Anglo-Saxon races and for the world that it was extinguished.' Yet Clark always seemed nonplussed by people's perception of him and the effect that his outbursts might have on his career. In fact, Clark was genuinely surprised that he had never risen to the post of Defence Secretary.

Not everyone, however, shared the belief that Alan Clark was a fascist. There were always those around him who explained away his more questionable comments as evidence of his delight in inflammatory mischief-making. 'I'm afraid that was one of his problems really,' his wife Jane later remembered. 'He was very naughty.' And naughty is a good way to describe Clark, particularly when considered in the light of his relationships with women (although Clark insisted on calling them 'girls'). There were too many to count, but Clark certainly had his favourites. Chief among them were the plump girl with 'delightful globes' he slept with on the train at Waterloo. Alternatively, there was the famous Harkness coven—a mother and her two daughters, all of whom Clark bedded in a 13-year period. The affairs were documented in Clark's diaries, all written up in his inimitable style: 'I can only really enjoy a Christmas carol concert,' he wrote, 'if I'm having an illicit affair with one of the choir.' There was little that could be done to curb Clark's womanising, although he nonetheless professed love for his wife and concern over how his affairs affected her. As a dying wish, he asked her to inscribe the phrase 'Happily married to Jane for 41 years' on his tomb. Jane Clark has yet to acquiesce to this request. Instead, she has since admitted to having another idea for the tomb: 'One of those fridge magnet type things where all the words are just jumbled up—diarist, historian, cad, philanderer, father, husband, scoundrel … everyone could choose the one they thought fit best.' os

Alan Clark

PETER COOK

Peter Cook can in all fairness be described as one of the founders of modern British comedy. His influence on the satire of the later half of twentieth century was profound, and a startling number of today's prominent British comics list him as a major influence. Cook is a man whose life was almost entirely defined by capacity for creativity; from his early days until the day he died, Cook would be unable to resist the compulsion to exercise his creative instinct, almost always with a drink and a cigarette in hand.

Peter Edward Cook was born on 17 November 1937 in Torquay, Devon. Cook summed up his experiences at Radley School, where he received his early education, as time spent trying desperately to avoid buggery, professing himself to have been 'number 3 in the charts' during his school career. Buggery aside, Cook did well in his academic endeavors whilst at school, and won a place to study French and German at Pembroke College, Cambridge. His time there would see the birth of an exceptional career in comedy, the impact of which remains without question today. As many great comedians have done, Cook joined the Cambridge Footlights company and was made president in 1960. As a student, Cook had hoped to become a diplomat like his father, but lamented that Britain had 'run out of colonies'. Cook's membership at the Cambridge University Liberal Club disguises the fact that he was politically apathetic throughout the majority of his life, especially in his later years when he expressed a serious distaste for all career politicians. Commenting on his encounters with future politicians whilst at Cambridge, Cook said, 'I spoke at the Union once, and I thought: I can do this, but I don't want to do this. The people who went into politics were those who couldn't get in the Footlights or were no good at journalism.'

Political apathy did little to stop Cook from producing some of the most poignant political satire of his time. As the driving force behind the stage show *Beyond the Fringe,* Cook harnessed the powerful zeitgeist of suspicion and distrust of British politics in the 1960s and created a seminal moment in the progression of British comedy. The show, in which he starred alongside Jonathan Miller, Alan Bennett, and Dudley Moore, was a dry, intelligent attack on the political status quo, the likes of which had not been seen before. Opening in London in May 1961, *Beyond the Fringe* was an overnight success and drew large crowds for the duration of its run. The decision of Harold Macmillan, Prime Minster, to attend one of the shows went seriously awry when Cook, who performed a damning impersonation of Macmillan during the shows, went off-script and launched into a public attack of the man in front of a packed house, to rapturous applause. The

event was indicative of a number of prominent aspects of Cook's persona. He was unafraid to speak out for what he believed, able to infuse political polemic with a peerless, razor-sharp wit, and he was in possession of an intellect which could put even the most successful politicians to shame within seconds.

Cook was a major supporter of *Private Eye* magazine and, although not a founding member, became its largest shareholder. He relished the opportunity to support a publication which engaged with politics in a way that made the establishment extremely uncomfortable, particularly enjoying the opportunity to appear in court in the various libel cases brought against the magazine by statesmen and celebrities alike. The magazine benefitted from more than Cook's money, and bears his stamp to this day. The famous front cover, for instance, which shows a photograph of a public figure with an imaginative speech bubble superimposed, was Cook's idea and continues to define the magazine's image.

Cook continued creating comedy throughout his life, which tragically ended with liver failure in 1995 when he was just 57. Major projects such as the satirical TV programme *That Was the Week That Was* sat cheek by jowl with Cook's more eccentric comedic offerings. One particularly entertaining example came when Cook adopted the persona of Norwegian fisherman, 'Sven', and began calling a late-night radio talk-show hosted by Clive Bull. Sven expressed his anguish about being abandoned by his wife, Jutte, who had run away to London, and was consistently anxious and confused. After much stilted discussion, Sven would always return to the subject about which he knew most, fish. It took Clive Bull a number of months to realize Sven's true identity.

Sven provides an example of the sheer power of the creative drive incarnate in Peter Cook. The man, who was consistently drunk and smoked 60 cigarettes a day, could not resist the urge to create for creation's sake. His performances, from enchanting imagined radio personalities to revolutionary political comedy, are indicative of a figure whose ability to think, imagine, and create are without match. Alan Bennett sums him up thus: 'In him morality is discovered far from its official haunts, the message of a character like Peter's being that a life of complete self-indulgence, if led with the whole heart, may also bring wisdom.' GE

ALEISTER CROWLEY

Aleister Crowley was a hugely divisive figure, prone to controversy and polarization of opinion. For some, Crowley was the embodiment of inhuman behaviour, debauchery, and evil, and for others he was the poster boy of a lifestyle everyone desired, but that no one could have. Regardless of perceptions, one is forced to admit that Crowley stands alone as one of the most original, fearless, and unconventional men of recent times. Crowley's life was driven by the pursuit of excess. This attitude involved a plethora of different drugs, sex with men and women, and eccentric activities including black magic and the supernatural, but whatever Crowley did, he cut no corners and never stopped short of full immersion. Crowley has thus become an icon of rebellion, with fans such as the Rolling Stones and Led Zeppelin. He stands as a perfect example of the powerful combination of genius and nonconformism.

Born Edward Alexander Crowley on 12 October 1875, he grew up amongst a strict Plymouth Brethren family in Royal Leamington Spa, Warwickshire, and attended an evangelical boarding school in Hastings, the Ebor Preparatory School in Cambridge, and later the Tonbridge School. Though clearly a talented intellectual, with strong passions for chess, poetry, and mountaineering, Crowley left Tonbridge after just a few months, allegedly after he developed gonorrhoea from a local prostitute. During his time at school, when he was just 11 years old, Crowley's father died of tongue cancer, and this proved a seminal point in his development for two reasons. First, Crowley began to recant the devout Christian beliefs of his parents, moving quickly towards a life of smoking, masturbating, and having open sex with women, including numerous prostitutes. Second, Crowley inherited a third of his father's wealth, a considerable sum, and this served to fund the adventures and misadventures of the years that would follow.

In October 1895, Crowley began a course at Trinity College, Cambridge in moral science, but quickly changed to English literature, reflecting his growing enthusiasm for poetry, especially that of Richard Francis Burton and Percy Bysshe Shelley. Crowley also briefly considered a career playing professional chess, before thinking better of it. The main purpose of Cambridge was to facilitate Crowley's extracurricular activities, and he continued to maintain an extremely active sex life, with men as well as women, although homosexuality was still outlawed in Britain. In 1897, Crowley travelled to St Petersburg, and later claimed that he was trying to learn Russian as he was considering a diplomatic career there. This claim is disputed by biographers Richard Spence and Tobias Churton,

'The joy of life consists in the exercise of one's energies, continual growth, constant change, the enjoyment of every new experience. To stop means simply to die. The eternal mistake of mankind is to set up an attainable ideal.'

Aleister Crowley

Aleister Crowley

who have suggested that Crowley had gone to Russia as a spy for the British Secret Service, alleging that he had been recruited while at university.

It was also while at Cambridge that Crowley began to explore magic, as he was exposed to groups within the university that explored spirituality and the supernatural. Shortly after leaving, in 1898, Crowley became involved with The Golden Dawn, an occult society involving literary and intellectual figures including the great poet W. B. Yeats. After moving to London, Crowley invited a senior member of the Golden Dawn, Allan Bennett, to live with him to serve as a personal magic tutor. Bennett would teach Crowley about ceremonial magic and the ritual use of drugs, and he progressed quickly through the ranks of the order, soon becoming ready to enter the inner 'Second Order'. Crowley was to fall out with the Dawn, in part because he considered their attempts at magic not serious enough, and left in 1899.

The next fifty years or so, until Crowley died, saw his interest in magic, occultism, drugs, sex, and subversion grow, and Crowley became internationally famous for his beliefs, with the British periodical magazine, *John Bull,* describing him as the 'wickedest man in the world' in the 1920s. After an incident in Italy in 1923, in which a 23-year-old Oxford student called Raoul Loveday died at Crowley's occult centre in Italy, the Abbey of Thelema, Crowley was expelled from Italy. It was reported that Loveday had died after drinking the blood of a cat in a ritual, though it has recently transpired that his demise may be attributed to water drunk from a nearby spring. Those who flocked to Crowley in Italy, and indeed wherever else he based himself, engaged in the wild orgies of sex, drugs, and supernaturalism which epitomize Crowley's excessive nature. Crowley was determined at all times to defy conformity and push the boundaries of human experience and consciousness. A genius and a heretic, Crowley was a man for whom the status quo proved no boundary, and one whose life has become an icon of youthful and impassioned rebellion. GE

Aleister Crowley

KEITH FLOYD

Widely seen as the father of television cookery, one of the most successful broadcasting topics of recent times, Keith Floyd holds an important place in modern popular culture. His programmes, in which he was known to spend as much time talking to the cameramen and crew as the audience, implanted Floyd in the mind of the nation; the image of a dishevelled, disorganized, and usually drunk man whose appetite for fine cuisine was only superseded by his love for red wine. When watching Floyd's programmes, viewers were likely to see as many moments of Floyd drinking as cooking, and as such Floyd's identity was forged as a chef and a drinker on largely equal terms.

Floyd was born in Somerset and schooled at Wellington, before beginning a stifled career in journalism and the army, earning a commission in the Third Royal Tank Regiment in 1963. Though Floyd maintained later that his move to the forces was inspired by his admiration for the heroics of Stanley Baker and Michael Caine in the film *Zulu,* which was in fact released the year after in 1964, his role was mainly as a chef for the officers' mess. Stationed in Germany, Floyd was happy to provide cuisine pleasingly different from the standard army fare.

After the army, Floyd pursued a career in restaurants. His results were mixed as, although Floyd was an incredibly talented cook, he was a spectacularly poor businessman, and could rarely keep the books in order or his customers happy. It is perhaps fortunate, then, that while cooking at one of his restaurants in Bristol, Floyd was to meet David Pritchard, the director with whom he would build his television career until 1994.

Pritchard's direction was perfectly suited to Floyd and the combination of the two personalities spawned a booze-fuelled hurricane of broadcasting which lasted for decades. Floyd's television appearances were often adventurous and never dull, and he was nearly drowned on one occasion while filming aboard a boat on the Great Barrier Reef. On a separate occasion, Floyd was forced to prioritize his love for booze over almost everything else when he elected to use the butane gas bottle from a hot air balloon, aboard which he was filming, to cool a bottle of fine champagne, as opposed to powering the aircraft with it. The balloon was destined to land on a busy motorway, and Floyd recalls being certain of his imminent demise. Thankfully, the traffic stopped and the passengers were saved, as was the champagne. The Pritchard and Floyd combination never strayed too far from controversy, finding themselves in trouble on one occasion with the Norwegian government after an enthusiastic cooking expedition to the country led to the unfortunate flambéing of two protected puffins.

Keith Floyd

Floyd also became known for his temper, and his occasional outbursts could scald nearly any target. Floyd suffered throughout his life from recurring depressive episodes and was increasingly distressed by the burden of his fame, perhaps the reason he drank so much in his later career. He said, for instance, that one of the most irritating by-products of international renown was being woken on the train by drunken city workers in need of advice on how best to cook goose. He grew to view diners at his restaurants with contempt, not least as they increasingly sought to take advantage of his abilities and his generosity, contriving to complain in search of discounts and apologies. Floyd told the story of a repeat offender at one of his establishments, to whom he elected to serve a delicately prepared beer mat, disguised as an escalope of veal. Floyd reports that the beer mat was greeted with enthusiasm, but the gentleman disagreed with the topping of his crème brûlée.

Floyd continued to grumble as his life went on, developing a particularly strong distaste for the celebrity chefs who followed in his footsteps. In 2001 he said, 'We've become a nation of voyeurs,' not flattered by the repeated imitation of his work. 'We don't cook anymore, we just watch TV programmes about cookery. Nobody takes cookery seriously now, it's just cheap entertainment. I'm totally to blame. I started it all and now I'm going to go down in history for having started a series of culinary game shows. It makes me terribly sad.' What Floyd captured, and what so many others could not, was the soul of popular entertainment. The imitators who followed could not repeat Floyd's rapport with his audience, nor his love affair with the bottle. Booze was the perfect on-screen companion for Floyd; he could fill pauses by consuming of innumerable fine wines, sought inspiration from it on his wild culinary adventures throughout the world, and used it to secure his image in popular memory. GE

'Food is life, life is food. If you don't like my approach you are welcome to go down to McDonald's.'

Keith Floyd

OLIVER REED

A self-proclaimed hellraiser, Oliver Reed is perhaps as famous for his behaviour off-screen as he is for his performances on it. An overwhelmingly talented actor, heavy drinker, and outspoken public personality, Reed is a character that is hard to overlook.

Robert Oliver Reed was born in Wimbledon on 13 February 1938, and attended a number of schools, 14 of which he was expelled from, before settling down and becoming captain of athletics and the junior cross-country champion at Ewell Castle. Some time as a bouncer at a strip club and compulsory military service in the Royal Army Medical Corps served as a precursor to an illustrious acting career which started with television work, where Reed was notably cast as Richard I in a children's serial. The bulk of Reed's work, however, was in cinema. His most famous role were in films like *Oliver!*, *Women in Love*, *The Jokers*, and *The Devils*, as well as Ridley Scott's *Gladiator*—his last film. In fact, Reed took some persuasion to start acting and ignored suggestions that he should join the Royal Academy of Dramatic Art founded by his great-grandfather, until he discovered that many of his drinking companions were making a decent living as film extras. Reed was catapulted to fame after some largely unnoticed leads in Hammer horror films, thanks to his role in the 1968 musical film *Oliver!*, in which Reed played the softly spoken menace, Bill Sikes. The film won six Oscars and Reed became an actor of international renown. By the end of the 1960s, Reed had become Britain's highest-paid actor with the world at his feet and a bottle in his hand.

Reed's next role earned him an accolade for being the first actor to appear fully nude in a mainstream film. The film adaptation of D. H. Lawrence's *Women in Love* required Reed to partake in a naked wrestling scene, a role for which he claimed to have prepared by drinking a bottle of vodka and 'staggering' onto the set. Nudity became something of a motif throughout Reed's career, with a myriad of stories of drunken, naked antics characterizing his legacy. One famous instance of the man's misadventures in a state of undress took place in the early 1970s at a hotel in the Caribbean, where he was keen to show off a recently acquired tattoo. Reed proceeded to drop his trousers to reveal a cockerel's claw emblazoned on his penis. Unbeknownst to him, the onlooking crowd perceived Reed's new acquisition as an involvement in Voodoo magic, and he was forced to make a hurried escape over a nearby balcony. In 1974, the police were called to Reed's house in Surrey after neighbours reported sightings of crowds of naked men galloping across the countryside. It later transpired that Reed had invited 36 rugby players back

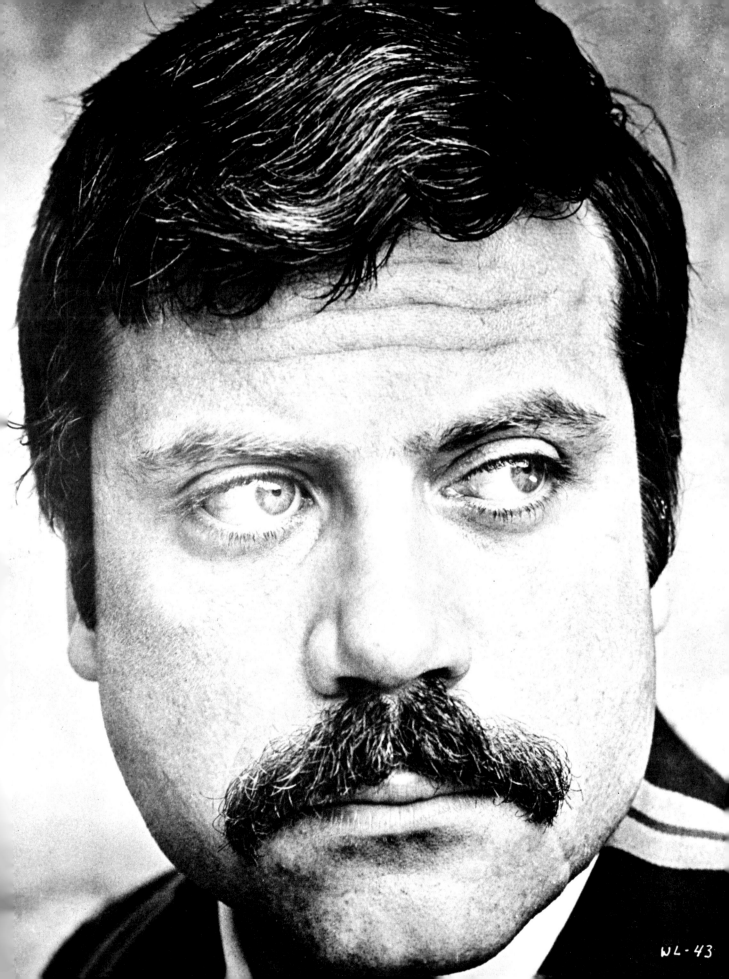

WL-43

to his house to commence a mammoth drinking session, lasting a day and a half, during which the group would consume 60 gallons of beer, 32 bottles of Scotch, 17 bottles of gin, 4 crates of wine, and a single bottle of Babycham. Reed leading the team on a naked run across the adjacent pasture at dawn brought the festivities to an end.

Reed soon became synonymous with alcohol. Rumour had it that during his stag weekend before his second marriage, to Josephine Burge, in 1985, Reed had consumed 104 pints of beer. Keen to dispel untruths about his famous drinking, Reed corrected the story in an interview. The feat, he said, had taken place during an arm-wrestling competition in Guernsey some 15 years earlier.

It is perhaps apposite that Reed's death came whilst he was drinking. During a break from filming Scott's *Gladiator* in 1999, Reed went to a pub in Malta where he suffered a sudden heart attack. Reed once summarized his career as 'shafting the girlies and downing the sherbie'. This statement does little to reflect the actor's impact on the British and international film industry, and the fondness with which he is still remembered by many today. There can be little doubt of Reed's acting prowess; his on-screen presence was captivating and he enchanted audiences across the world. That said, Reed was much more than an actor. He was, in every sense of the word, a character. Reed proclaimed that 'awe and respect are two different things', and he was right. Oliver Reed prompted awe from all, and respect from not many fewer. GE

'I have two ambitions in life: one is to drink every pub dry, the other is to sleep with every woman on earth.'

Oliver Reed

Oliver Reed

ERNEST HEMINGWAY

Ernest Miller Hemingway was born on 21 July 1899, in Cicero, Illinois. Cicero was a quiet conservative area, with not many distinguishing features. Frank Lloyd Wright, another famous resident of the community (which is now better known as Oak Park), once said of the area, 'so many churches for so many good people to go to'. Hemingway seemed determined to stray from this mould, embarking on a life of dangerous adventures and copious drinking.

It is how Hemingway spent his time when he was not writing which makes his personality so inescapably captivating. Hemingway was an adventurer. He travelled extensively and seemed scarcely able to avoid danger, drink, and distraction in equal measure. He once said, 'An intelligent man is sometimes forced to be drunk to spend time with his fools.' In fact, Hemingway took a great deal of pleasure from engaging in the right quantity of drunken foolishness, and tales of these misadventures are not hard to uncover. Stories tell of a boozy fishing trip in 1931 during which Hemingway took issue with sharks which were trying to steal his catch. In response to the unwelcome guests, he took to firing a submachine gun into the water around the boat. The sharks retreated and the catch was saved, but Hemingway had managed to shoot himself in both legs and the trip had to be cut short. It was not only sharks which incurred his wrath, however; during the Second World War, while living in Cuba, Hemingway reportedly engaged in the hunt of German U-boats, his primary weapons still alcohol and a submachine gun, but with the addition of hand grenades. Hemingway's wife at the time, Martha Gellhorn, argued that he was using these 'booze patrols' aboard his boat as an opportunity to escape from her view, fishing for marlin and becoming incapacitated with his friends instead of engaging in the war. Hemingway replied, 'Honey, drinking *is* war.'

In 1954, Hemingway's adventures in Africa involved two airplane crashes and a near-miss with a raging bushfire: As a Christmas present to his wife Mary, Hemingway chartered a sightseeing plane over the Belgian Congo. En route, the plane struck a pylon and was forced to crash land in the African bush, leaving a drunken Hemingway with multiple injuries, including one to the head. The following day, in an effort to reach medical attention in a nearby town, Hemingway and his family boarded a second flight. The odds seem to have been against the group, and the plane exploded on the runway. Hemingway added serious burns to his injuries, and a further concussion, which caused leaking of cerebral fluid. Undeterred, Ernest continued his booze-fuelled adventures with his son, Patrick, and wife, Mary, but encountered a bushfire through which he sustained second

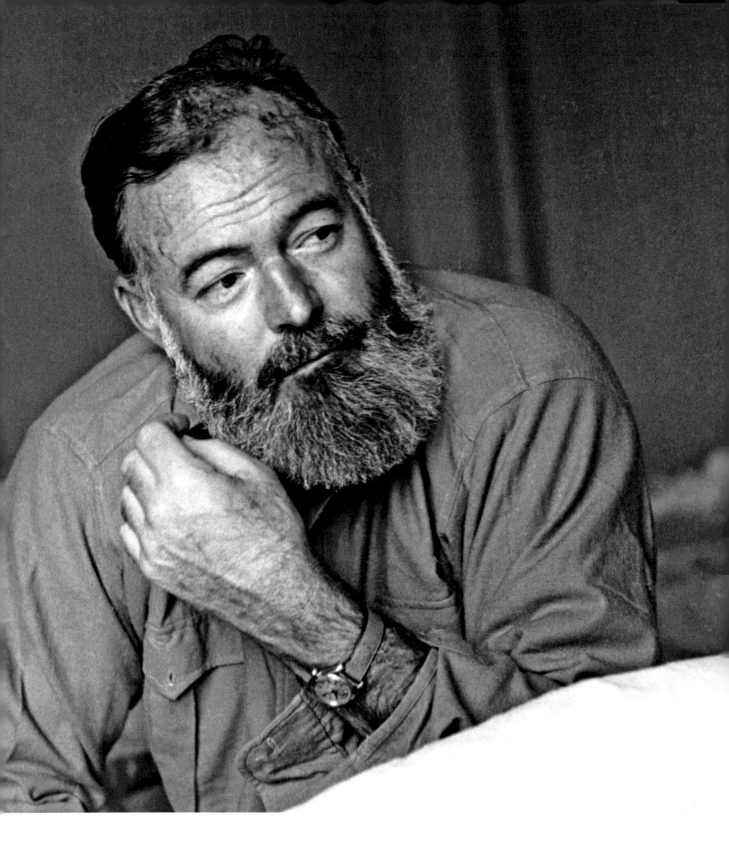

Ernest Hemingway

degree burns on his legs, torso, lips, left hand, and right forearm. Mary revealed some time later the extent of Hemingway's injuries from the ill-fated African adventure: a dislocated shoulder, ruptures to his liver and a kidney, two cracked disks, and a broken skull. Alcohol provided the bulk of pain relief for these injuries, and his ever-growing dependence on drinking likely contributed to the mental and physical decline which preceded Hemingway's suicide in 1961.

Hemingway lived the tales he wrote, his experiences inspired his narratives, and his stories enflamed his hunger for adventure. None of these adventures, whether immortalized in fiction or lived in truth, would have been the same without Hemingway's passion for alcohol. 'Sometimes I wish I'd went through those good times stone cold sober so I could remember everything,' he once reflected, 'but then again, if I had been sober, the times probably wouldn't have been worth remembering.'

'Modern life,' Hemingway mused in 1935 in the postscript to a letter to Ivan Kashkin, a Russian translator and critic, '... is often a mechanical oppressor and liquor is the only mechanical relief.' Hemingway's relationship with alcohol was one of love; he loved the doors to adventure which could be opened by a heavy session, and the relief which could only be found at the bottom of a bottle.

Hemingway managed to combine pioneering literary achievement (notably winning the Pulitzer Prize and the Nobel Prize in Literature) with an inexhaustible adventurous spirit, which earned him an equally impressive medical record and an unquenchable thirst. He was an intellectual titan, a decorated war hero, an indefatigable explorer—all of this whilst at least half-drunk. GE

'There is nothing to writing. All you do is sit at a typewriter and bleed.'
Ernest Hemingway

ALEX HIGGINS

Alex Higgins was one of sport's first anti-heroes. A flamboyant playmaker, he played with a speed that blew away the stuffy world of snooker, but possessed a self-destructive streak that overshadowed everything he achieved in his sport. Higgins was a quiet, nervous-looking, sad-eyed man, the sort who never stood out in a crowd, but in the twilight world of the working man's club and the backstreet snooker hall, he was to become a god.

Higgins grew up in Belfast and began playing snooker at age 12. After school, he would gulp down his tea, head to The Jam Pot and play standing on a box. He claimed that he developed his twitchy, nervous style as a result of the threat of violence in the Belfast Billiard Halls. Living on a diet of fizzy drinks and sweets, he hustled on Falls and Shankill Roads, usually losing to older men very willing to strip him of the little money he had.

Higgins's first love was not snooker. Sent to place bets for his father, he developed a love of horses and horse racing, and at 15 he went away to become a jockey, but lacked the discipline for stable life and was soon back home.

In 1968, Higgins won the British Team Championships for Belfast YMCA and was crowned Northern Ireland Amateur Champion in the same year. Moving to Blackburn, Lancashire, Higgins was playing for cigarettes and meat pies for his lunch until a pair of local bingo hall entrepreneurs took him under their wing. His hard drinking, chain-smoking, staccato style was thrilling to watch. In one game, Higgins scored 67 in 1 minute and 34 seconds. John Taylor, who wrote for a local paper in Blackburn, dubbed him Hurricane Higgins. His managers kitted him out in new clothes, fixed his teeth, and began to arrange exhibition matches which gained cult status. Higgins turned the previously stuffy world of professional snooker on its head and audiences loved it.

In his first year as a professional, Higgins went to the World Championship final. Playing at the British Legion in Birmingham, the audience sat on beer crates and the prize was £400. Higgins beat John Spencer by five frames with a display of dazzling virtuosity. With his sweeping hair, floppy Stetson hat, bright-coloured shirts, and velvet suits, Higgins emerged as the sport's great showman. Always contemptuous of authority, he smashed up a hotel room on a trip to Australia, and would frequently be fined for challenges to referees. He played every match like it was an exhibition, thrilling crowds with rapid, reckless play, caring more for style than results, but always swift to blame the conditions for his losses. It was to be another ten controversy-strewn years before Higgins would make another World Championship final.

'I've never played my best in front of the TV cameras.
People just don't know how good I am.'

Alex Higgins

Alex Higgins

In 1982, Higgins met Jimmy White in the semi-final. With both players at the top of their game, prodigious potting from White saw him move 15-13 in front, needing just a single frame for victory. Higgins pulled one back before White took a commanding 59-point lead in the 30th frame. Higgins then produced a 69 point clearance of such sublime jaw dropping genius that many believe it to be the single finest break in snooker. Higgins went on to win not just that match but the final against the great Ray Reardon with a dramatic clearance in the final frame, which left Reardon rooted to his chair throughout. The final scenes where Higgins, overwhelmed with joy, calls his wife and daughter down from the crowd to kiss them, set a new precedent. The image of Higgins, weeping uncontrollably and hugging his daughter and the trophy, will be remembered as one of the most poignant moments in sport.

That was to prove to be Higgins's last triumph. He would succumb to the grip of alcoholism, making strange bedfellows in Oliver Reed and Keith Moon, become addicted to gambling, and lose all control of his mouth and temper. Left out of the big money Matchroom team, he spiralled further out of control. The threat of violence was never far away with Higgins and in 1986 he headbutted a tournament referee. Fines and suspensions followed. In an attempt to pre-empt his punishment, a visibly drunk Higgins spoke to the cameras telling the authorities 'You can shove your snooker up your jacksy, I'm not playing any more'. For a long time abusive of the style of other players, he plunged to new depths when he made death threats to former friend and teammate Dennis Taylor. In 1990, his girlfriend told police that Higgins had pinned her to the floor and broken her cheekbone with a hairdryer.

At the end of his life, Higgins cut a sad and pathetic figure. Ravaged by illness and drink, and toothless, he asked for no help but ended his days living in sheltered housing in Belfast hustling for small sums of money in the very snooker halls where it all began. He never gave up his dream of regaining a place at the top of the world of snooker. At his best, Higgins was mesmeric, charismatic, and flamboyant, a deeply kind and gentle soul. At his worst, he was volatile, egotistical, petulant, and explosively violent. To himself and to his many fans he was simply the greatest snooker player that ever lived. His funeral in Belfast in 2010 was a mass outpouring of grief the likes of which is very rarely seen in the world of sport. PG

HOWARD HUGHES

When Martin Scorsese made *The Aviator* about Howard Hughes, starring a typically committed Leonardo DiCaprio as the protagonist, there were grumblings that the film dealt more with the glamorous early years of Hughes's life of squiring actresses and engaging in daring feats of aeronautic brilliance, rather than with his descent into obsessive-compulsive disorder late in life. It is easy to see that the dashing Hughes at his peak made for a more likeable character than the long-haired, urine-drinking recluse of legend, and the film did at least acknowledge his many eccentricities, ending in 1947 with Hughes helplessly repeating the words 'the way of the future' as he is sedated.

Howard Robard Hughes, Jr was born on 24 December 1905, the son of a wealthy industrialist. Both his parents died before he was 19, leaving him to inherit the family fortune. He promptly decided to head to LA with his first wife, Ella Botts Rice, and started making a name for himself in the nascent film industry, most notably with his first major success, the 1930 action film *Hell's Angels*. An early precursor to many subsequent blockbusters, it attracted a female audience with its tale of a love triangle, contained revolutionary special effects and, despite being hugely over budget at $4 million, made double the money at the box office.

It was also an opportunity for Hughes to explore both of his other great interests, aviation and women. He directed several of the combat scenes himself, disregarding the potential risks, and was linked to the film's glamorous star, Jean Harlow. Ironically, Harlow was one of the few actresses of the day with whom Hughes didn't have an affair, on the grounds that he found her tedious, but he instead pursued flirtations with many of the leading actresses of the day, most notably Katharine Hepburn (who left him for Spencer Tracy) and Ava Gardner. There was something of a mechanical aspect to his seductions, fittingly for a man who advised, 'Play off everyone against each other so that you have more avenues of action open to you.' One unsuccessful attempt was with the starlet Gene Tierney, who claimed, 'I don't think Howard could love anything that did not have a motor in it.'

His obsession with flying and technology led him to set several world records for speed, and also to build and pilot the largest aircraft ever made, the 'Spruce Goose', in 1947. However, he injured himself severely while pursuing his hobby, most notably in 1946 when he sustained third-degree burns and many broken or crushed bones. This led to an addiction to painkillers and exacerbated his erratic behaviour, which manifested itself

Howard Hughes

in a variety of strange ways; he refused to cut his hair, take baths, or change his clothes, and kept his urine in jars that he stored in sealed hotel rooms. It is likely that this initially came about because of an exaggerated response to the pain of his injuries, a condition called allodynia, but it soon developed into a habit. Hughes was no longer mentioned in the gossip columns in connection with technological advances or glamorous women, but for his eccentricities instead.

Nonetheless, even though he was physically incapacitated and reclusive, he remained involved in the workings of his empire, even down to the most minute details; this was, after all, a man who specifically designed the brassiere of Jane Russell in his notorious 1943 film *The Outlaw.* The last years of his life were spent in moneyed isolation in various penthouses in grand hotels, most notably in Las Vegas, where he bought the Desert Inn to prevent anybody else from staying there. His notoriety was such that the author Clifford Irving wrote a fraudulent autobiography about him, which was widely believed to be true; only Hughes's intervention via teleconference saw the book's status as a hoax exposed. He claimed earlier in his life, 'I'm not a paranoid deranged millionaire', but there seem to be few better ways to describe him. His status was such that Willard Whyte, a character in the 1971 Bond film *Diamonds Are Forever,* was based on him; Hughes, perhaps amused by the comparison, allowed his hotel, the Las Vegas Hilton, to be used for the filming.

Hughes died in 1976—he was on board a plane at the time. At his death, he was unrecognizable from the suave and handsome playboy of the 1930s, with long hair and beard, extremely long toenails, and with severe malnutrition. Fittingly, there was added difficulty after his death in the form of a mysterious so-called 'Mormon Will' that made virtual strangers huge beneficiaries of Hughes's billion-dollar fortune.

If Hughes represents the American Dream at its strangest in his decline, he also represents the excitement and opportunity that stem from it in his early innovations in the fields of film and aviation. He remains as enigmatic and distant today as he ever did in his lifetime, mythic and perplexing in equal measure. AL

KEITH MOON

In a *Rolling Stone* poll, Keith Moon was voted the second-best drummer of all time. *The New Book Of Rock Lists* ranks him number one. But few people remember that he ever even played the drums, for Keith Moon is primarily remembered as the worst-behaved rock star of all time.

Keith Moon was born in Northwest London in 1946. An unruly boy, his school career was not a success. Described by his art teacher in one report as 'Retarded artistically. Idiotic in other respects', his music teacher was a little more prescient, writing that Moon 'has great ability, but must guard against a tendency to show off'. In 1964, aged 17, he auditioned and was hired as the drummer for The Who. Moon's arrival heralded a change in the band both temperamentally and musically. Tensions flared but the music breathed new life. Of Daltrey and Townshend he later said, 'We really have absolutely nothing in common apart from music.'

At a gig in London, Townshend broke his guitar and with the crowd baying for more, Moon smashed up his drum kit. Moon began destroying hotel rooms on a trip to Berlin. In Copenhagen, his hotel room contained a giant waterbed; in an attempt to get it out of his room and into the lift he ruptured it spilling hundred of gallons of water and collapsing the ceilings of the rooms on the three floors below. He threw televisions from windows and exploded toilets with cherry bombs. When a hotel manager complained about the noise from the band's music, Moon treated him to dynamite in the lavatory, turning to him post-explosion and saying, 'That, dear boy, was noise. This is The Who.' On one English tour, Moon caused so much destruction that he netted just £47.75 for the entire run.

Moon's legend has become obfuscated, leaving a trail of urban myth in his wake. One story has Moon driving a Rolls-Royce into a swimming pool. *The Who by Numbers* author Steve Grantley claims it was merely reversed into his garden pond at home. Roger Daltrey claims it was a Chrysler Wimbledon, a hotel in Michigan, and more of an ornamental pond. Another story has Moon befriending a homeless man in London's Soho and checking into a Hilton with him for an extended drinking session. Weeks later, Moon had forgotten all about the man when his record company received a phone call from the hotel asking what they should do with him and who would be taking care of the bill. Oliver Reed recalls being at home in his Surrey mansion during the spring of 1974, taking a bath, when out of the window he noticed his horse going berserk in its paddock. The cause was a chopper, containing Moon, his chauffeur/sidekick Peter Butler, and a Swedish blonde attempting to land in his garden. According to Butler, 'He was trying to make people laugh and be Mr Funny, he wanted people to love him and enjoy him, but he would go so far. Like a train ride you couldn't stop.'

Reed and Moon became friends, working, drinking, and carousing together endlessly. Reed gave Moon a tortoise, which they used as a drinks trolley, and occasionally an ashtray. When Moon moved to the United States. he left a life-size fibreglass rhinoceros and a real Great Dane on Reed's drive with a note attached saying, 'Gone to America, please look after my pets.'

Bad behaviour and foolishness turned rapidly into self-destruction. On the *Quadrophenia* tour, Moon took to drinking brandy and taking tranquillisers, and to passing out on his drum kit. Frequently helped off stage, he was hospitalised after smashing up a hotel room and cutting himself so badly he nearly bled to death. Fearful for what might happen, the band decided not to fire an increasing desperate Moon. Moon seemed to want the world to destroy him, his intake of drugs and alcohol so prolific, but time and again he emerged unscathed from vicious sessions that would have crippled most humans. Abusive and sometimes violent towards his wife, and tragically inept as a father, his family life was a disaster. 'He had no idea how to be a father,' his wife Kim Kerrigan once said. 'He was too much of a child himself.'

Moon's legacy is written large across rock music. His frenetic, unorthodox drumming style was integral to the sound of The Who, and to bringing drums to prominence in rock and roll music. The list of extraordinary drummers who cite Moon as their influence is a long one, his drumming had a dynamism and passion that was entrancing. Rock author Nick Talevski says of Moon, 'He was to the drums what Jimi Hendrix was to the guitar.'

In 1978, aged just 33, Moon died of an overdose of pills prescribed, ironically, to cure his alcoholism. His death was treated by many of the tabloid newspapers as just another amusing tale of Moon the Loon. Little mention was made of his prodigious talent. To many who knew him, he was a gentleman of generosity and vivacity, and Ozzie Osbourne remarked after his death, 'God bless his beautiful heart.' But Moon was less kind and generous with those closest to him. The jokes had worn thin, promises of sobriety broken too casually and too often. His bandmates couldn't live with him, but without him their band lost much of its soul. PG

JACK NICHOLSON

The class of 1954 at Manasquan High School, New Jersey named their classmate Jack Nicholson 'class clown', and with his decision not to pursue higher education, very few of them could imagine the success that he would encounter. He worked odd jobs around New Jersey before moving to California. There, he worked as a gofer for MGM studios while also working part-time in a toy store. A strapping young man coming into and out of MGM studios everyday was bound to be noticed, and it was not long before Nicholson was sent to acting classes and given an apprenticeship at The Players' Ring theatre.

Nicholson performed in a spate of films throughout the 1960s that were relatively unsuccessful, excepting perhaps his small role in *The Little Shop of Horrors*. Unperturbed, Nicholson made his breakthrough performance in the 1969 film *Easy Rider*. Nicholson played an unhinged, paranoid alcoholic, earning an Oscar nomination for Best Supporting Actor. Only a year later, he starred in the film *Five Easy Pieces* in which he played a disaffected piano prodigy whose rebellious streak leaves him disenchanted with life. His portrayal of his character's social seclusion won him a second Academy Award nomination, this time for Best Actor in a Leading Role.

In 1974, Nicholson appeared in Roman Polanski's neo-noir *Chinatown,* the script having been written with him in mind. The film was both a commercial and critical success, earning Nicholson his third nomination for Best Actor at the Academy Awards within five years. He had recently begun his relationship with Anjelica Huston at the time, whose father Nicholson was acting opposite. In one scene, John Huston's character interrogates Nicholson's, asking pointedly, 'Are you sleeping with my daughter?' One suspects many other fathers might have wished to ask the same question.

With *Chinatown* regarded as one of the greatest films of all time and Nicholson's superlative performance a defining contribution, it became clear that Nicholson would be seen as one of the best American actors of his generation. It turned out that Nicholson's generation would span more than four decades.

Nicholson's first Academy Award winning performance came only a year after *Chinatown* with his leading role as McMurphy in an adaption of Ken Kesey's novel *One Flew Over the Cuckoo's Nest*. Nicholson plays an anti-authoritarian rebel, a likeable character whose eventual lobotomy gave the actor a chance to dabble in the madness that he would deploy in future films. His next big role was in the iconic psychological thriller *The Shining* directed by Stanley Kubrick. He then won the Academy Award for Best Supporting Actor for *Terms of Endearment* in 1983, and went on to portray the Joker in Tim Burton's 1989 *Batman*.

The 1990s and 2000s marked a maturity of performance for Nicholson. The controlled intensity that was bursting in previous performances was reined in and guided for films such as *A Few Good Men,* supplying pop culture enthusiasts everywhere with the dictum 'You can't handle the truth!' and films such as *As Good As It Gets* giving narcissistic misanthropy a suitable persona (and a second Best Actor Oscar). Nicholson even delved into directing, going behind the camera for *The Two Jakes.* While the latter was not a great success, Nicholson's acting chops could not be denied. In 2002, he looked far removed from the handsome, young, part-time toy store worker breaking into the acting world. His character in *About Schmidt* in his own words was 'the man that I might have become if I wasn't lucky enough to wind up in show business'. This portrayal of a hypothetical self earned him another Best Actor nomination. His turn to act in a supporting role again, demonstrating his tireless versatility, came in Martin Scorsese's *The Departed* in 2006. Another nomination came and went for Nicholson, as he continued his oscillation between sublime support acting and indomitable leads.

What of the man he did become after being lucky enough to wind up in show business? Short-tempered perhaps, but with enough wily charm to survive the media storm that has followed him around since becoming an American icon. There is a playful faux-villainy about him that most audiences will recognise in his personality and in his characters. Nicholson has been in and out of relationships with a few overlaps but only had one marriage. Always a great avoider of publicity, the company he kept might be instructive. His relationship with Hunter S. Thompson reveals an ease with the unusual, while the autobiography of legendary producer Robert Evans hints at his being a hard-drinking ladies' man, as the old cliché goes.

Not too much should be noted of Nicholson's personal life for in his own words, 'There is no way you can get people to believe you on screen if they know who you really are.' HB

Jack Nicholson

OZZY OSBOURNE

As the lead singer of Black Sabbath, Ozzy Osbourne was a heavy metal pioneer. Famous for earlier acts of alarming inhumanity and for a self-destructive lifestyle, Osbourne later invited the world into his living room through television, displaying a touchingly addled humility and honesty that endeared him to millions.

John Michael Osbourne was raised in a poor family in Birmingham, U.K. He left school and went to work in a car horn factory, and then an abattoir, and was imprisoned for a bungled burglary during which he dropped a television set on himself and stole children's clothes thinking them to be for adults. He claimed not to have had a holiday until he was 14, 'and that was to Sunderland to stay with an aunt. I saw the ocean and I thought, fuck that, where are the palm trees?'

In 1967, Ozzy joined his first band Mythology at age 19. He did so because he loved the Beatles. After they disbanded he joined another, originally named The Polka Tulk Blues Band. In 1969 they became Black Sabbath. Named after a continental horror movie, they deliberately played up to a dark, gothic aesthetic and employed a gloomy occult-themed lyrical style. The band rose to almost instant success, their album *Black Sabbath* remaining in the Billboard charts for a year. By 1974, they were touring the world. Their final gig, the California Jam festival, saw them play alongside Deep Purple and The Eagles to a crowd of 200,000 fans. Towards the end of recording their second album, Osbourne was admitted into Stafford County Asylum, and the band began unravelling. In 1977 he suddenly quit.

In Osbourne's words, 'When we started out we were a rock band meddling in drugs, at the end of the day we were a drug band meddling in rock.' But it was Osbourne who was doing the majority of the meddling. 'I never went out in my life for a drink. I went out to get fucked up. I never had a social line of coke. There wasn't enough on the planet for me.' After leaving the band, Ozzy holed up in a cheap hotel for what might be the greatest binge in history. For three months he didn't see daylight, surviving on booze, cocaine, and Domino's pizza. 'I lived like a rat in a box. I thought, I might as well have one good bang before it's all over.'

His manager's daughter Sharon Arden brought him back from the edge of total self-destruction. She tried to clean him up and get him started on a solo career. They hatched a plan to impress the bosses of CBS records during a meeting by releasing two white doves from under his coat. But 'by the time I got there I'd drunk about three bottles of Courvoisier and I'm arseholed'. With tensions high, Sharon attempted to straighten him

out, tipping him over the edge. Shouting 'Fuck you, and fuck them!' he took the doves out of his coat, let one go and bit the head off the other, tossing its body on the conference table. In January 2002, at a show in Des Moines, Iowa he famously bit the head off a bat. The 1980s were a decade that embraced clean cut, healthy looking pop stars with tans and coiffed hair. Against this backdrop, the ravaged lanky-haired Osbourne was to many young people the perfect antidote. Long accused of being a negative influence on teenagers, he had now elevated himself to the state of public pariah.

Things got worse in 1989. Deeply intoxicated, he lost control and tried to strangle his wife. He was charged with attempted murder. About this, he said, 'I mean, you can guarantee one of three things if you drink like I did: death, if you're lucky, insanity, or jail.' Sharon chose to stand by him, but his self-abuse didn't stop.

In 2002 Osbourne's life changed entirely. He and his entertainingly dysfunctional family became household names by letting television cameras into their Hollywood home for TV's reality series *The Osbournes*. The soft-hearted, quietly mumbling, bespectacled Osbourne came as quite a shock to many. In one scene, preparing for a concert, he is informed that there will be a bubble machine on stage. 'Bubbles,' he howls, 'Oh come on Sharon, I'm Ozzy fucking Osbourne, the Prince of fucking Darkness,' but he couldn't be further from it. His topsy-turvy family life where his children are the grown-ups, along with his touching devotion to his wife Sharon and the menagerie of demented dogs and cats all of whom he adores, created an entirely new image for Osbourne.

Eventually, he even managed to rid himself of his addiction to alcohol and drugs. He claims to have lost about 30 years of his life to it, but in 2010 managed to recall enough to pen an autobiography. 'I was bad for a very long time: I beat my wife and the rest of it … but the autobiography was cathartic—it helped me get rid of some of the guilt.'

Now in his mid sixties, Osbourne claims to be genuinely baffled by his ongoing success, 'For some reason people keep wanting to hear me and see me.' MTV named Sabbath 'the greatest metal band of all time'. They've sold over 70 million records. Osbourne is philosophical about the end of his career (or perhaps he meant his life); 'When the Big Man upstairs wants you to stop, you'll stop. And he hasn't wanted me to yet.' Osbourne's touring festival Ozzfest attracts enormous crowds and is now in its thirteenth year. PG

Ozzy Osbourne

IGGY POP

Who else, in the span of one career, will have performed on *American Idol* at the age of 63, advertised car insurance (only to see their advertisement banned on the grounds that they themselves would be uninsurable), developed a reputation for unfettered live acts that have included self mutilation, and become an acknowledged semi-authority on Gibbon's *Decline and Fall of the Roman Empire*? None other than Iggy Pop, dubbed 'the indefatigable Pop'. He remains unabashed about his reputation, claiming, 'What some people would call antics, I would just call a good show.'

James Newell Osterberg Jr was born on 21 April 1947 in Muskegon, Michigan. He later said, 'I was who I was in high school in accordance with the rules of conduct for a normal person, like obeying your mom and dad. Then I got out of high school and moved out of the house, and I just started, for lack of a better term, running free.' This newfound freedom was inspired by The Doors whom he went to see live while a student at Michigan University. Mesmerized by Jim Morrison's on-stage charisma, Iggy Pop (as he now christened himself, derived from briefly playing in a band named The Iguanas) made an early career out of high-voltage performances that often involved exposing himself to audiences and even vomiting on them. Impressed by his dedication, Elektra signed Pop's newly formed band The Stooges in 1968, but his first two albums, made under the influence of heroin, were unsuccessful, leading to a disbandment.

Pop's (and, arguably, pop's) unlikely saviour proved to be none other than David Bowie, who had enjoyed immense success at the beginning of the 1970s with a similarly provocative, although less dangerous, persona. Bowie convinced Pop to head to Berlin in 1976, where both men replaced their heroin addictions with a lust for alcohol. In turn, Bowie produced and largely co-wrote Pop's first two solo albums, *The Idiot* and *Lust For Life*. Many of his best-known songs, such as 'The Passenger' and 'Sister Midnight' were found on these albums, and *Lust For Life* became his most successful album in Britain.

Separating from Bowie, he resumed his drug addiction, and his next few albums were commercial failures. His 1980 autobiography *I Need More* was not a success either, but financial ruin was avoided when Bowie, a loyal friend, recorded their song 'China Girl' from *The Idiot* on his multi-million selling *Let's Dance* album in 1983, bringing some much-needed royalties to his bank account. The Bowie collaboration continued with a new album co-produced by him, *Blah Blah Blah,* which was commercially successful but too tasteful for Pop who commented 'I like music that's more offensive … I like it to sound like nails on a blackboard.'

For the third time, Pop's career was revived in association with David Bowie in 1996, although this time it was through the use of the song 'Lust For Life' in the instantly iconic opening of the film *Trainspotting,* which brought him to mainstream attention. He might have claimed that 'the stuff that has become more commercial doesn't have any edge', but he flirted with greater mainstream exposure than ever before, even making a cameo appearance in *Star Trek: Deep Space Nine* as a clone. Only the hard-hearted might have murmured that the 'indefatigable Pop'—beginning to show his age at 50 after a lifetime of hard living—was more other-worldly than any sci-fi alien.

Growing old disgracefully as a near-anachronistic presence—he said, 'I find it hard to focus looking forward, so I look backward'—he reformed The Stooges to much acclaim in 2007. Pop now promotes a lifestyle of clean living in Miami where he lives, claiming 'this place is fundamentally spiritual ... there's a quicksilver quality about this place', and his respectability seemed confirmed by his recent appointment to present a show on BBC Radio 6, replacing Jarvis Cocker. Yet the inner fire still burns, and a new and revived Pop can still cause discord; even his *American Idol* appearance, at the age of 63, was said to be 'enthralling and dangerous'. AL

'When they started calling it "Punk" - I moved on'

Iggy Pop

ELVIS PRESLEY

Raquel Welch (of doe-skin bikini fame) said that she first understood sex in 1956 while on a trip to the San Diego Arena in southeast USA. Welch, 15 at the time, was in the crowd when Elvis Presley took to the stage. He was wearing an open white jacket, satin shirt, loose trousers, and black loafers. And then he started gyrating, purring his way through 'Heartbreak Hotel'. 'Something about his voice on that song made me think, "This must be what sex is all about",' she wrote. 'My girlfriends and I didn't have a lot of experience in that department, but you just knew Elvis had it all.'

Elvis Presley was born on 8 January 1935 in Tupelo, Mississippi and he reached maturity at a time when America was yearning for liberation after the gloom of the war years. It was the beginnings of the sexual revolution and Presley packed what America wanted. His early days of cutting rockabilly tracks at Sun Records in Memphis were a revelation: hair slicked into a greaser pompadour, his hips swinging and pumping, Presley seemed to be the spirit of post-war liberation—a nice southern boy given over to the evils of rock and roll.

Presley went to the top of the charts with singles like 'All Shook Up' and 'Jailhouse Rock', which mixed pop, country, and R&B, while films like *Love Me Tender* and *King Creole* got him onto cinema screens. When he was drafted in 1958, his fans' reaction was telling. 'Dear President Eisenhower', wrote Linda Kelly, Sherry Bane, and Mickie Mattson, 'We think it's bad enough to send Elvis Presley in the Army, but if you cut his side burns off we will just die ... Presley. Presley. IS OUR CRY. P-R-E-S-L-E-Y.'

When he was discharged from the army in 1960, Presley picked up where he had left off. He had hits like 'Are You Lonesome Tonight' and '(You're the) Devil in Disguise', and jazz singer George Melly described Elvis's charm in typically florid terms. He was 'the master of the sexual simile, treating his guitar as both phallus and girl, punctuating his lyrics with the animal grunts and groans of the male approaching an orgasm'. Offstage, Presley had similar appeal. He had affairs with everyone, from girls-next-door and groupies, to stars like Cybill Shepherd and Anne Helm, the latter of whom he met while shooting 1962's *Follow that Dream*.

Yet by the mid-1960s and early 1970s, Presley's star had begun to fade, dimmed by a series of B-movies and rising competition from more contemporary acts like the Beatles and the Rolling Stones. There were comebacks—the *Elvis: Aloha From Hawaii* TV

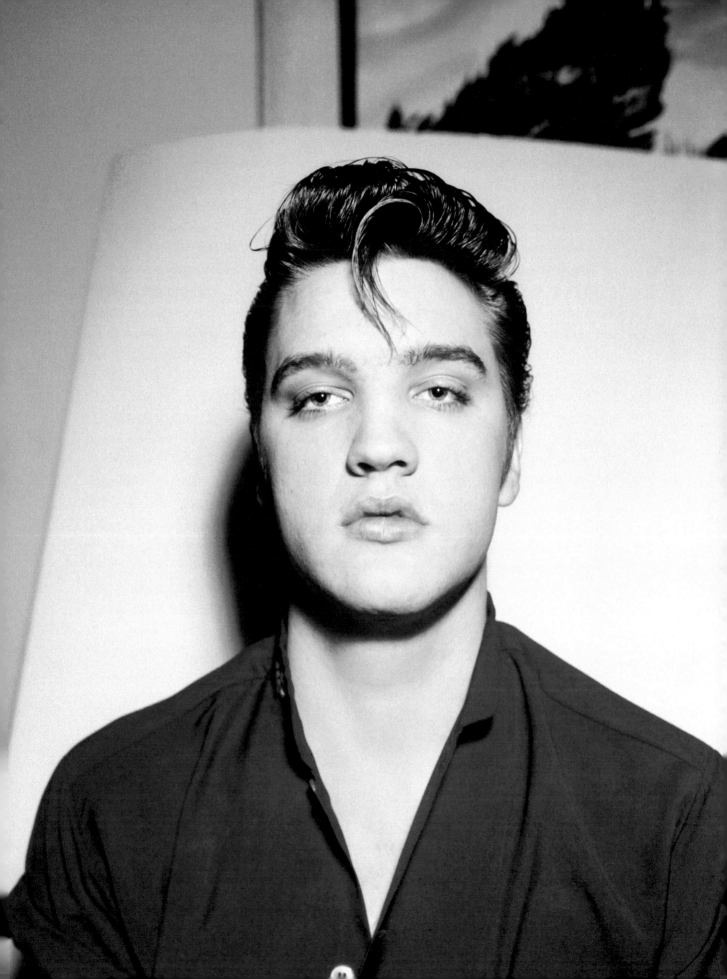

special among them—but the excitement and raw sex appeal of early Elvis was lost. The denim trousers and cotton shirts of his Memphis years gave way to the extravagantly bejewelled jumpsuits that characterise his Vegas residencies. The jumpsuits had individual names—'White conquistador', 'Mad Tiger', 'Chief'—but all struggled to contain Presley's growing girth. The lithe young Elvis who had danced in the folk and bluegrass bars of Memphis had given way to an Elvis so determined to eat his favourite sandwich from a restaurant in Denver that he was willing to fly a private plane late at night across America to get there. The Fool's Gold Loaf sandwich, consisting of a hollowed-out loaf of bread layered up with a jar of peanut butter and grape jelly, topped off with a pound of bacon, became an emblem of the latter-day Elvis. By the time he was found dead in his bathroom in 1977, pants round his ankles, Elvis's fall from the youthful symbol of burgeoning American sexuality was complete.

But in truth, Presley's sexuality had always been too nuanced to fit such easy characterisation. Several exes claimed that he disliked penetration—a hang-up from a fear of STDs he developed after discovering call girls while on military service—and that he preferred less committal pleasures instead. Pyjama parties were a favourite, with multiple girls reporting being brought back to Elvis's bedroom for make-out sessions that included pillow fights, tickling, and Presley-led classes in applying mascara and eye shadow. Meanwhile, his predilection for feet meant that his entourage, the Memphis Mafia, sometimes screened prospective partners to ensure they lived up to his preference for small, delicate toes. At least two Presley girlfriends later recalled receiving the nickname 'Bitty' in honour of their itty-bitty feet.

Quirks like these were typical. Presley preferred foreplay to fruition, with a 1956 meeting with Natalie Wood—the star of *Rebel Without a Cause*—supposedly ending when she stormed from the room to confront Presley's minders: 'What's the matter with your boss? He's all hands and no action.' Presley's fame and sex appeal meant that he could have whoever he wanted, but what he wanted was a different matter.

The oddity reached its peak in the shape of Priscilla Beaulieu, Presley's wife whom he had met at a party in Bad Nauheim while still on military service in Germany. Beaulieu was 14 when they met and although it was reportedly years before the two consummated their relationship, Presley's attraction to Priscilla was typical of his tendency towards younger women. 'He was insecure about his sexual prowess and wanted virgins so they

wouldn't have anyone to compare him to as a lover ... He wanted to mould them and mentor them and they adored him,' writer Alanna Nash later theorised.

Presley put it in less academic fashion when describing Priscilla to his friend Joe Esposito: 'She's a beautiful girl. I wouldn't lay a hand on her. But to have her sit on your face!' If Presley was the embodiment of America's post-war sexual liberation, then America's post-war sexual liberation was certainly complicated. OS

PORFIRIO RUBIROSA

Porfirio Rubirosa, dubbed 'the greatest playboy who ever lived' was perhaps the ultimate seducer, displaying a list of conquests that even Casanova would have envied. He offered the world little more than his legendary large endowment, yet that seemed to satisfy hundreds, possibly even thousands. Rubirosa's sexual exploits took precedence over everything else. He once quipped, 'Work? I don't have the time!'

Rubirosa was born on 22 January 1909 in San Francisco de Macorís in the Dominican Republic. Fittingly, it was the year of the rooster in the Chinese Zodiac. He was born into a wealthy family, with a diplomat father who was also well known for his romantic prowess. The son, learning from the paterfamilias, would sit shirtless on the curb and wolf-whistle at passing women. After some years in Paris with his family, Rubirosa returned to the Dominican Republic and became a lieutenant of Rafael Trujillo's Presidential Guard. Trujillo was already a notoriously violent and quixotic leader, and when Rubirosa began making advances towards his daughter Flor, he might have had him tortured and killed for the insult. However, he was sufficiently in thrall to Rubirosa's charm to offer him his daughter's hand in marriage instead. Their union started inauspiciously; on their wedding night, Flor was so terrified by Rubirosa's enormous penis that it was several days before they could consummate their marriage, an event that she said left her 'sore for a week'.

Good-looking and self-assured, but by no means a man of his word, Rubirosa soon made a near-heroic commitment to bedding the opposite sex. Trujillo was said to have forgiven him the ongoing insult to his daughter as Rubirosa had done him a big favour (rumoured to be a double assassination) and he was made an ambassador. Trujillo claimed that Rubirosa would make an excellent diplomat 'because women like him and because he is a liar.'

Rubirosa first headed to Berlin, where he met Hitler at the 1936 Olympic Games, and then to Paris, where his sexual prowess soon became legendary. As Flor later said, 'He was out every night, and would come home at dawn, covered in lipstick.' Perhaps unsurprisingly, her father allowed her to divorce her unfaithful husband, and he found himself out of favour with Trujillo, knowing that to return to the Dominican Republic meant suicide. He was then reduced to various acts of subterfuge to survive, most notably feigning a sniper attack on a visit to Spain to account for the mysterious disappearance of 180,000 dollars worth of jewellery.

'I will risk everything to avoid being bored.'

Porfirio Rubirosa

Porfirio Rubirosa

The advantage of dealing with an insane and whimsical dictator is that their moods can shift at a moment, and when Trujillo himself visited Paris in 1938 with his wife and son, Rubirosa was his first choice for a tour guide. After having facilitated a trip that allowed Trujillo sexual freedom, he was rewarded with the position of Commercial Attaché and set about having, by any standards, an extremely good Second World War. When back in Paris, he pursued an affair with the leading film star Danielle Darrieux, whom he eventually married in 1942. Notorious for her Nazi sympathies, Darrieux was the target of an assassination attempt, leading her and her husband to sit out the rest of the war on a farm west of Paris.

After the war ended, Rubirosa's womanizing continued in earnest. It was great news to his various conquests that he was sterile (either as the result of a childhood illness or an unfortunate blow to the testicles during a polo match) and he soon met the woman who would become his third wife, the unattractive but ludicrously wealthy heiress Doris Duke. Doris showered Rubirosa with gifts and money, but he—who had once claimed that the difference between him and other seducers was that 'all of them pay their women, and all my women pay me'—continued a tireless pursuit of other women. He travelled the world from one diplomatic post to another, being of negligible use as an ambassador. He had affairs all over the world with the leading women of the day: Eva Perón in Argentina, Zsa Zsa Gabor in New York, and Marilyn Monroe in Hollywood. Marrying again, this time to socialite Barbara Hutton, he also took up car racing with some distinction. He claimed, 'I will risk everything to avoid being bored', and finally his lust for excitement led to his downfall, as he died on 5 July 1965 crashing his Ferrari after an all-night celebration in Paris.

The man who was suitably nicknamed 'Toujours Prêt' ('Ever Ready') could have become one of the peerless figures of the twentieth century thanks to his swordsman abilities alone, but instead remains unrivalled on an entirely different playing field. It is not for nothing that the oversized pepper mills used in French restaurants are known as 'Rubirosas', providing an ongoing epitaph that its progenitor would undoubtedly have appreciated. AL

GUNTER SACHS

If it is possible to be both a playboy and a figure of substance, then Gunter 'Sexy' Sachs was that man. Epitomizing the jet-set lifestyle of the 1950s and 60s, he also had serious interests in art, photography, and astrology that marked him out as rather more than a rich dilettante. Nonetheless, his reputation as a St Tropez lounge lizard, stunning blonde on his arm as he surveyed his playground from a yacht, persisted, even as he simultaneously admitted and denied his reputation with the legendary quote, 'Playboy? Moi? I would rather call myself a gentleman.'

Sachs was born on 14 November 1932 in Bavaria. His father, Willy, was a wealthy industrialist and automobile manufacturer with suspected links to the Nazis, although these were never proved. Nevertheless, the rumours lingered, and he shot himself in 1958, leaving his 26-year-old son a rich legacy, derived from the Opel automobile millions. Sachs promptly set about enjoying himself, becoming a well-known figure in the Riviera both for his penchant for fancy dress (he once appeared at a party as Kaiser Wilhelm) and his generosity to both hard-up gamblers and beautiful women. Suave, good-looking, and self-assured, his veneer of sophistication disguised personal tragedy, both in his father's death and that of his first wife, Anne-Marie Faure, who died during surgery the same year.

Although he boasted that he had never done a day's work in his life, he was no idler. A lifelong interest in astrology began when he founded the grandly named 'Institute for the Empirical and Mathematical Examination of the Possible Truth of Astrology in Relation to Human Behaviour'. If he believed that his fortunes were written in the stars, he was proven right when he met Brigitte Bardot, then at the height of her fame, in 1966. Both were smitten; Bardot wrote that Sachs was 'magnificent' and that she was 'hypnotized' by this charming and beautiful man. They even had matching Rolls-Royces. Realizing that courting La Bardot would entail spectacular effort, he rose to the challenge magnificently by hiring a helicopter to fly over her Cote d'Azur mansion and dropping hundreds of red roses into her garden.

While his wooing of Bardot worked wonders—they were married within two months—the marriage soon foundered. Sachs might have surrounded his new bride with his powerful and influential friends, who included everyone from Salvador Dalí to Edward Kennedy, but Bardot, who had already been married twice and had had numerous affairs, soon reverted to type, most notoriously in her entanglement with the roué libertine Serge Gainsbourg. She and Sachs eventually divorced in 1969, but there was no ill-will on his part; he not only made her a gift of a diamond worth 1.2 million francs years after their divorce, but said 'A year with Bardot was worth ten with anyone else.'

Bouncing back from his failed marriage—he soon wed again, to the Swedish model Mirja Larsson—he ploughed his energies into art collecting and photography. He was a noted collector of many of the pop art pioneers such as Lichtenstein, Warhol, and Mel Ramos, often buying the pieces from the artists in person. He also had a civic conscience, being jointly responsible for the foundation of the Modern Art Museum in Munich, and organizing Warhol's first European exhibition in 1972. His interest in photography extended to then-shocking images such as the first nude photograph in French *Vogue* in 1973, but he was serious about his work, winning the prestigious Leica Award in 1976. (Self-deprecatingly, he claimed to have taken up capturing women because an early attempt to photograph a hippo had taken 'days and days'.) He continued his photography throughout the rest of his life, most notably working with a young Claudia Schiffer in 1991. He also remained a keen sportsman, and was the chairman of the St Moritz Bobsleigh Club from 1969 until his death.

As his life went on, he seemed more and more ambivalent about a world in which new, aggressive wealth had replaced old money. He said in an interview in 1998, 'There were only 12 playboys—not more—in the world. They were charming and spoke languages and behaved well with women. I think that today most of the fun has gone.' Sachs, of course, implicitly included himself in the not-so-dirty dozen. He segued elegantly into his twilight years, pursuing his interest in astrology and even publishing a book about it, *The Astrology File: Scientific Proof of the Link Between Star Signs and Human Behaviour,* in 1999. It was not taken seriously by mathematicians. His glamorous life came to a sudden end on 7 May 2011 when he killed himself at home in Gstaad; in his suicide note, he blamed 'hopeless illness A' (thought to stand for Alzheimer's), and said 'The loss of mental control over my life was an undignified condition, which I decided to counter decisively.' His peerless collection of pop art and art nouveau was sold at Sotheby's in 2012.

Dignified, charming, and above all, a gentleman, Sachs was one of the rarest examples of the playboy breed, someone whose every action epitomized old-fashioned courtesy. His life was an enjoyable one, and it's hard to hold it against him. AL

CHAPTER 4

Stylist

The stylist is a man of amplified character. His thought, speech, action, and dress have been cultivated and refined. A complete construction. Some men appear to be born with such style. Most, whether deliberately or not, add to their style over time. Quentin Crisp wrote, 'Style is not the man; it is something better. It is a dizzy, dazzling structure that he erects about himself.'

Crisp's 1975 book *How to Have A Lifestyle* is a manual to help understand this notion of style in all its complexity. Crisp spelt out in clear terms a number of fundamental principles. Firstly, that style is so much greater than mere dress, it is all of the man. Secondly, that fashion and style are not easy bedfellows. And thirdly, and most importantly, that style is never natural—it is acquired, developed, studied, and refined.

Outward appearance, possessing a veneer of fine dress without substance, is not style. It is arguably the opposite. The wits of the seventeenth century labelled such men as Fops. In an era when style was everything, they were the butt of all jokes. The Fop did not lack knowledge, indeed he was an expert on all courtly aspects; the correct sword knot, the fashionable way to arrange his cravat, the right hair-do or dance step; but this was all he knew. He was devoid of inner substance, an empty vessel; great affectation concealing a void where style should have been.

Having style is not the same as being fashionable (though it is possible to make fashion one's style). Fashion is almost the antithesis of style, since by its very nature fashion is transitory and requires uniformity, while style is about consistency and singularity. Fashion magazines are not the tool of the stylist, arguably they are a crutch for those still searching for their own idiom.

Fashion was a Georgian invention. The fashion magazine detailed the ways of the fashionable society, whose mannerisms readers were encouraged to ape. Eighteenth century fashion, like style, was not simply about clothing. It concerned itself with deportment, dance, language, diction, the correct curtsey, the right hand gesture. Nothing has changed: clothes, music, walk, and talk are clearly codified as part of the fashions you follow. Style, in the same way, is a complex construct of the various disparate elements of personality, many of these elements arising from an individual's natural character, but quite consciously and deliberately maintained. Great men make the best use of every attribute they have. As Crisp says, 'The finishing touches of style are best self-taught but the basic exercises that lead to style can be learned from others.' Like a boy scout collecting badges, we gather stylistic souvenirs by the armful; taking tea, wearing a moustache, a regional accent, drollness, eschewing jeans, riding a bicycle, the wearing of spectacles, being polite, wearing hats, bashfulness, obtuseness, rowdiness, bookishness, misery. We borrow a little here and there but the ultimate creation is original and greater than the sum of the parts.

History provides us with plenty of role models. Kings, emperors, military leaders, politicians, and notable men of all descriptions have had their lifestyles painstakingly documented. Wardrobes, pastimes, peccadilloes, tailoring bills, venereal diseases, snuff consumption, all laid bare for the would-be stylist to absorb. Amongst the best documented of all lifestyles was that of George 'Beau' Brummell (1779-1840). The destroyer of flamboyance, he was the arch stylist *du jour*. His dress was monastic in its simplicity but its precise purity required a ritual of devilish complexity. Brummell's elaborate toilette—his boots polished with champagne, his neckwear repeatedly tied until impeccability was achieved—are all part of the myth. Dandyism was more than the perfection of the result, it was also about how that result was achieved.

Historically, stylish living was almost exclusively the preserve of the upper strata of power and wealth. They had both the time and the means. But social reform has leveled the playing field, allowing for the rise of a new breed of stylist. According to Crisp, 'A modest sufficiency cramps style; extreme poverty, like great danger, enriches it.' There does seem to be a dearth of middle-class stylists. Perhaps they have more to lose by sticking their heads above the parapet. Certainly offices offer little encouragement for the demonstration of advanced style. But then some would argue that you should not let a bad job stand in the way of a good life. As Oscar Wilde said, 'I have put my talent into writing. My genius I have saved for living.'

Almost every one of our men—artist, hero, libertine—could equally be considered a stylist. Original Man is in reality man of original style.

WARIS AHLUWALIA

When heritage meets humour, Waris Ahluwalia emerges in all his diamond-encrusted glory. He is an actor and designer, regal and resplendent, unassuming and yet bursting with confidence in his creative powers. Whether gracing the big screen with frequent collaborator Wes Anderson or tracing a legacy of craftsmanship in India for his jewellery collection, Ahluwalia seems impossible to categorise. He seamlessly drifts from one passion to the next and back again whenever he so desires.

Born at the foothills of the Himalayas, he moved to New York with his family at the age of 5. Ahluwalia's story bears the hallmarks of a Hollywood tale: cutting out a Gucci advertisement for a red shoe was Ahluwalia's self-proclaimed awakening, and it is from here that his obsession with beauty began.

A liberal arts college life in upstate New York didn't quite satisfy the young Ahluwalia, though a year abroad in Manchester, England did a little more. Struck by the ubiquity of the turban in the Sikh community in the U.K., Ahluwalia began donning the religious garment on a daily basis. Neither a desire to be different nor to conform has shaped Ahluwalia's debonair distinction—he has merely grown to be urbane and unabashed.

Upon his return to New York, Ahluwalia tried a variety of different occupations, professing that if something held his interest for more than a day, then he needed to know how it worked. In his twenties, he learned how a music magazine was run, how to organise parties for the New York City art scene, and how to meet then up-and-coming film directors with a penchant for the odd.

Wes Anderson was one such film director and over a dinner in 2003, Ahluwalia was offered a role in Anderson's latest film, *The Life Aquatic with Steve Zissou*. Despite having never acted before, Ahluwalia agreed based on the faith that Anderson had shown in him, and flew to Italy to begin shooting. When asked why he had not taken acting classes, he replied, 'When I signed on for *The Life Aquatic with Steve Zissou*, Wes never asked me if I could act. He asked me if I would come to Italy and be in his movie.'

Ahluwalia's role in the movie led to further appearances in other Anderson films such as *The Darjeeling Limited* as a stern and sublimely dressed train manager, and most recently in *The Grand Budapest Hotel* as one of many big-name cameos playing hotel concierges. It would be fair to say that Ahluwalia is known as one of Anderson's go-to actors, part

Waris Ahluwalia

of a brilliant troupe in which he shares the screen with the likes of Bill Murray, Jason Schwartzman, and Owen Wilson. Yet Ahluwalia is not only colourful whimsicality—he is almost unrecognisable in Spike Lee's *Inside Man*. In the cool hue of Lee's vision, Ahluwalia becomes something that he is rarely seen as otherwise: ordinary. Ahluwalia tackles the ordinary with the same unnerving intensity than he does the extraordinary. He has since starred in a few independent films and even a few television shows.

Yet before being known to the wider world via the silver screen, Ahluwalia followed his passion for jewellery. In the nineties, to buck the trend of recession-coscious prudence, he designed two diamond rings and had a jeweller friend of his create them. Poised on his slender fingers, the rings travelled with him to Los Angeles over the winter, where in Maxfield—a renowned haunt of the Hollywood elite—they were spotted by a buyer. The fairytale concludes with Ahluwalia leaving the store with an order for more, which instantly sold out upon arrival. Thus was launched Ahluwalia's career in jewellery design, an occupation that allows him to indulge in his favourite past-time: dabbling in other careers. Be it acting, filmmaking, party throwing, or writing, Ahluwalia is relentless.

Ahluwalia's most distinctive characteristic, beyond the impeccable dress, is his general attitude towards consumption. He is a conscientious consumer, knowing almost always where his clothes are sourced from (often from friends), and travels from India to Botswana in order to appreciate genuine craftsmanship that he then incorporates into his business. His pop-up teashop in New York followed the same lines of principle, and proved Ahluwalia's truly entrepreneurial spirit. With poise and elegance on his side, Waris Ahluwalia has been called a Renaissance man by various writers. HB

'My inspiration is always love and history, and my passion to a fault is craftsmanship and responsibility. Those are the simplest things. It goes beyond jewellery. It's every part of my life.'
Waris Ahluwalia

JEAN-PAUL BELMONDO

Born on 9 April 1933 just west of Paris, Jean-Paul Belmondo did not perform well at school. Instead, he spent much of his early life playing football or, more successfully, boxing. Belmondo's amateur boxing career started on 10 May 1949 in Paris, and lasted only one year. It was, however, an incredibly successful year for Belmondo, in which he won three straight first-round knock out victories.

After this foray into amateur sport, Belmondo decided to pursue a career in acting. He was admitted to the Paris Conservatory after a number of unsuccessful attempts to study drama, although his tutors remained sceptical about his potential throughout his time there. Nevertheless, Belmondo persevered after graduating and worked for the majority of the 1950s in theatre, and later in film. He made his debut on the big screen in 1956 and appeared in several minor films over the next few years, including his first starring role, alongside Alain Delon, in *Sois belle et tais-toi* in 1957.

It was the arrival of the French New Wave movement which granted Belmondo his first opportunity to impress the wider public. His role in Jean-Luc Godard's *Breathless,* or *À Bout de Souffle* in 1960 catapulted him to national and international renown. Playing witty, handsome, and devious Michel Poiccard, Belmondo fit the role perfectly and became a national icon. A case of 'Belmondism' infiltrated the circles of Parisian socialites, and men modelled themselves on Belmondo's unconventional but captivating masculine charm, and he was frequently heralded as the French answer to James Dean.

He would again work with Godard, an icon in his own right, in 1965's *Pierrot le fou.* Belmondo was to play a tortured artist, a writer whose decision to abandon the life that makes him so unhappy results in a frenzied car journey with a babysitter, played by Godard's famous muse, Anna Karina. Belmondo embodied a number of different roles throughout the sixties, including many in which he would abandon the characters he traditionally played. *La Ciociara* in 1960, for example gave Belmondo a much kinder and more gentle role than he was used to. His decision to tackle more physical roles also gave Belmondo a chance to reclaim the athleticism of his youth, and he gained a reputation for doing his own stunts in films such as *L'Homme de Rio* and the James Bond spoof, *Casino Royale.*

Belmondo has married three times, and fathered four children. His first marriage, during which his first three children were born, was to Élodie Constantin, but later broke

down as a result of a heavily publicized affair with the actress Ursula Andress. In 1989, when he was 56, Belmondo met Nathalie Tardivel, who was 24 years old at the time, and the two married in 2002. In 2003, when Belmondo was 70, Tardivel gave birth to his fourth child, Stella.

His career continued to flourish throughout the 1970s and 1980s and Belmondo gradually started to work once again on the stage, all the while maintaining a strong on-screen presence. He was awarded a César award in 1988 for his role in *Itinéraire d'un enfant gâté*. Following a stroke in 2001, Belmondo's career was slowed, but not stopped. Deciding to play a character with similar disabilities, he starred in the 2008 film *Un homme et son chien*.

Though now rarely seen on screen, Belmondo has maintained a public image, in part through the residual affection for his illustrious career and his iconic status during the 1960s, 70s, and 80s, but also thanks to the constant newspaper coverage of his affairs with former playboy model and nightlife magnate, Barbara Gandolfi.

Belmondo's career places him amongst the most influential French actors of all time, and his partnership with Jean-Luc Godard helped ignite the New Wave movement in France and across the world, but his ability, much like that of Godard himself, to combine his excellence on screen with his effortless cool and charisma in the real world marks Belmondo as one of the most interesting and original men of our time. GE

**'When I was 17 I dreamed about being a professional boxer.
But as a boxer you get blows both physically and psychologically.
At least as an actor the blows are only psychological.'**
Jean-Paul Belmondo

DAVID BOWIE

David Bowie is simultaneously one of the most iconic men of recent times, and one of the most enigmatic. His career spans over 40 years and has seen a progression through multiple pseudo-identities, captivating styles, musical genres, and drug binges. Now one of the most influential musicians in the world, Bowie has continued to astound with the depth and range of his musical abilities, and has done so while engaging fully with the lifestyle that only musicians of a particular ilk seem capable of sustaining.

Bowie emerged onto the popular music scene in July 1969 when his song 'Space Oddity' reached the top five of the U.K. Singles Chart, and he returned after a three-year break in 1972, embodying his most famous alter ego, Ziggy Stardust, and releasing the single 'Starman' and the album *The Rise and Fall of Ziggy Stardust and the Spiders from Mars*. Bowie's influence at this stage in his career served to challenge many of the perceived core values of popular music, and shaped the direction the industry would take for the foreseeable future. His biographer David Buckley claims that Bowie, or Stardust, 'created perhaps the biggest cult in popular culture', with fawning fans and records flying off the shelves across the world. Futuristic, androgynous, and pioneering, Bowie's iconic style infiltrated the minds of his millions of fans and changed perceptions of popular music.

This incarnation of Bowie was relatively short-lived, and he continued to innovate and progress after the 'Ziggy Stardust' years. Perhaps the most controversial and crazed period of Bowie's career to date came in the late 1970s, when he portrayed himself as the 'Thin White Duke'. Immaculately dressed in a cabaret get-up, the Duke was by Bowie's own admission 'a nasty character indeed', but continued to enchant audiences world-wide who could not resist Bowie's combination of style, charisma, and creative brilliance. Bowie allegedly survived this period existing on nothing more than red peppers, milk, and cocaine, and claims to remember almost nothing about the production of his 1976 album, *Station to Station,* though it is still considered one of his best works.

The tour that followed the album's release was hugely successful but also marred with controversy. Bowie was quoted in Stockholm as saying that 'Britain could benefit from a fascist leader', stopped on the Russian/Polish border for possession of Nazi paraphernalia, and allegedly photographed giving a Nazi salute during a public appearance in London. Though Bowie publicly disavowed his connections with fascism some years later, some explanation for his erratic behaviour can surely be found in the startling amounts of cocaine Bowie consumed. Indeed, it has been reported that at one point

David Bowie 229

Bowie was in such a haze that he lived in a house full of ancient-Egyptian artefacts, burned black candles, reported seeing bodies fall past his window, having his semen stolen by witches, and receiving secret messages from the Rolling Stones.

Bowie's popularity continued to balloon throughout these years, and 1980 hosted the album *Scary Monsters (and Super Creeps),* and the No. 1 single 'Ashes to Ashes'. Bowie collaborated with Queen in 1981 for their song 'Under Pressure', which was an instant success and became his third U.K. No. 1 single. It was the 1983 album, *Let's Dance,* however, co-produced by Chic's Nile Rodgers, which launched Bowie to greater acclaim and international success. The album went platinum in both the U.K. and the United States, and the three singles to be released from it became top twenty hits in both Britain and America, where its title track reached number one. 'Modern Love' and 'China Girl' both made No. 2 in the U.K. The latter single's video featured a naked beach sex scene which was later censored, but Bowie had already cemented his place as one of the most important producers of music videos, and of course music itself.

After the 1980s, Bowie stopped producing solo music and focused his efforts on Tin Machine, a four-piece band which enjoyed initial success, and later experimented with electronica and neoclassicism before coming full circle with the release of *The Next Day,* announced on 8 January 2013, his 66th birthday. If there is one continuous feature throughout Bowie's many incarnations and creative achievements, it is the faultless style of the man. From space-age modernism to reactionary romanticism, the image Bowie has managed to project has been iconic without fail and has marked him as one of the most influential individuals in the constant redefinition of the face of popular culture. Bowie's latest album is a testament to the power of his creative impulse, and should be seen as the latest manifestation of the talent of a true modern genius; a man whose career has produced groundbreaking work and whose life has been spent enjoying the myriad of vices and indulgences that international fame has to offer, while still maintaining startling longevity and depth of achievement. GE

JARVIS COCKER

A shy, gangly, spectacle wearer from a Sheffield council estate, Jarvis Cocker went on to become the lead singer of Pulp, and in the process a reluctant spokesperson for the musical movement which defined Britain in the 1990s. With an unerringly accurate cultural barometer and waging a constant battle against hypocrisy, he has retained a relevance that few from the Britpop era can claim to have done, and is today regarded as something of a national treasure.

Born in 1963, Cocker and his sister were raised by their mother Christine, now a Tory councillor. His father walked out on them when he was 7, and emigrated to Australia. Cocker became obsessed with music from an early age. A slightly awkward kid with specs, he felt music was a way to overcome his social ineptitude. At age 15, he formed the band originally known as Arabacus Pulp, named after a tradeable commodity he had studied in economics.

In 1985, whilst trying to impress a girl, Cocker attempted to recreate a stunt he had seen performed at a party a week before. Failing to carefully think it through and lacking physical strength, Cocker dangled from a window three floors up as buses sped past below. He eventually let go. The injuries he sustained saw him hospitalised for six weeks and in a wheelchair for months, but he did enjoy something of an epiphany. He enrolled at St Martins to study film and began to realise that his best material was the everyday stuff that surrounded him. Cocker wrote about dodgy relationships, losing one's virginity, seedy sexual activity, recreational drug use, raves, and 'mockneys'. Always insistent that Pulp was a pop and not a rock group, he thought of his music as straightforward and unpretentious, but he also wanted to use it to encourage social change at a time when the unemployed had been disenfranchised in Thatcher's Britain. Pulp was articulate and self-effacing—Cocker sang about being shallow but he was anything but.

Pulp recorded four albums to increasingly positive reviews before the release in 1995 of *Different Class,* an album that launched Pulp into an entirely new trajectory. *Different Class* rose to No. 1 in the U.K. charts, sold over 1.25 million copies, and won the Mercury Prize. The single 'Common People' was described as 'the perfect encapsulation of the Britpop aesthetic'—a description that Cocker dismisses. That year, 100,000 people sang along to it at Glastonbury.

Cocker aimed to make music with a social conscience. Protest against the hypocritical and the bland featured strongly as themes in his music. During his first appearance on *Top Of The Pops*, Cocker made a sign that said 'I hate Wet Wet Wet' (a band he thought epitomised everything that was awful about the 1980s) and taped it to the inside of his jacket. At an appropriate moment he flashed it open to reveal his message to the world. This was however a mild preamble to a protest that for a while threatened to overshadow everything else Cocker had done. At the 1996 Brit Awards Michael Jackson performed Earth Song. Thousands of screaming fans watched as a messianic Jackson sang with a chorus of bedraggled rag-clad children before a thirty foot video screen showing scenes of starvation and deforestation. Cocker registered his distaste by ambling, rather perplexedly, onto the stage and miming the wafting of a fart. He evades capture and briefly reappears silhouetted before a malnourished African baby. It was perhaps the oddest protest ever witnessed. Some found Cocker's actions deeply offensive. But to many more it made him heroic.

Jarvis Cocker

The Britpop era ended with a bang. The scene became unwholesome and the record-buying public grew tired of shots of bleary-eyed musicians stumbling out of the Atlantic Bar. 'You realise you've become a knob-head,' said Cocker, 'The world that has supposedly opened its doors to you just seems really shite, so my way of dealing with that situation was just to get as hammered as possible.' He claims that it was the worst period of his life: 'Well, I mean, you don't often hear people say, since he's been taking them drugs he's become such a nice person.' Cocker removed himself from Pulp and the scene entirely, moving to Paris and starting a family, and a solo career to much critical success.

In 2010, BBC Radio 6 Music launched the Sunday radio show *Jarvis Cocker's Sunday Service.* The idea of Sunday Radio was strongly appealing. Cocker is quoted as saying, 'Sundays have been getting too lively, I want to bring back a sense of time slowing down. I'm not wanting to depress people, but to give them time for reflection.' The show, a mix of music from across Cocker's exceptionally broad spectrum of taste with conversation and listener requests, won the SONY Rising Star Award in its first year and remains one of the station's most popular shows.

Cocker further endeared himself to England's quiet core by making an album of sounds recorded at historically important sites across Britain for the National Trust. In a project strongly reminiscent of Mario's aural love letter to his island in the film *Il Postino,* Cocker recorded waves washing ashore at Brownsea Island in Dorset, stairs creaking on the grand staircase at Chartwell (Winston Churchill's former home), gardeners gardening, clocks ticking, the sound of a big front door being unlocked by a key: further proof of Cocker's rare ability to find joy and meaning in the everyday.

Cocker's cultural relevance remains as strong as ever and crosses many boundaries. He played Myron Wagtail, lead singer of the band The Weird Sisters in *Harry Potter & The Goblet of Fire,* and Wes Anderson cast him in *Fantastic Mr Fox.* He has also appeared on the BBC flagship political programme *Question Time.* In 2011 it was announced that Cocker would take on an editorial role at legendary publishers Faber & Faber.

For a man once described as 'the Alan Bennett of pop', these activities, from Sunday broadcasting to the recording of gravel, seem to perfectly summarise a life lived wonderfully out of sync with the modern world, and fit in perfectly with a career that embraces the commonplace and celebrates the gentle ebb and flow of daily human existence as a high art form. PG

JOHN COOPER CLARKE

Once described as the bard of Salford, and more recently as a 'matchstick man from L. S. Lowry country', John Cooper Clarke was the original punk poet. Lost in drug addiction for many years, he cleaned up his act and returned as one of the most original, humorous, and forthright voices of our time.

Cooper Clarke was born in Salford, Lancashire in 1949. His father was a funny man, often to be found entertaining crowds of Manchester criminal types at after-hour lock-ins. Clarke cites his lack of encouragement as one of the reasons he became such an accomplished poet—faint praise, he claims, is the scourge of the performer. Cooper Clarke was raised a Catholic and still adheres to the faith. 'People who believe in God are happier than those who don't. I've never met a happy atheist.'

His first job was as a bookie's runner, doing illegal off-track betting round local pubs, earning enough money to fund a lavish lifestyle of Saturday matinees at the Rialto Picture House, and boxes of Black Magic chocolates. He was 'living like a king. I was pissing pure gold'. He began writing poetry at school, and had a knack for it. Cooper Clarke was inspired by a teacher called Mr. Malone who used to throw his glass eye in the pool for the kids to retrieve, and who would advise young Cooper Clarke to copy the style of the great poets but write about the things that he knew, advice he believes would benefit any aspiring poet.

He began performing his poetry in the clubs of Manchester, reciting to tough crowds of shirt-and-tie-clad working men. These crowds had no particular enthusiasm for poetry, a grounding which prepared Cooper Clarke for the punk rock crowds he would later face. He wrote about the everyday, kitchen-sink verses, almost Dickensian in his linguistic artistry. A master of the arcane and the absurd, but always incisive and precise. He wrote about vacuum cleaners and Ford Cortinas, he captured all of the absurdity of the Spanish package holiday: 'Mother's Pride, tortilla and chips, pneumatic drills when you try to kip.' Like an angry Douglas Dunn, he painted a picture of a life of down-trodden hopelessness, a life where working class folk picked each other's pockets to get by: 'The fucking scene is fucking sad, the fucking news is fucking bad, the fucking weed is fucking turf, the fucking speed is fucking surf.'

He shared the bill at punk clubs with The Sex Pistols, The Buzzcocks, The Fall, and Joy Division, always donning the same trademark slim dark suit. He adopted a leather jacket

because, he claimed, the audiences spit was more readily removed from it. In the 1980s he was a huge cult success, playing live across the country, recording albums, films, and publishing compilations of poetry. His album *Snap Crackle & Bop* reached No. 26 in the U.K. charts. At one point he even played *Sunday Night at the London Palladium,* alongside the likes of Frank Sinatra and Sammy Davis Junior.

But for most of the 1980s, he became lost. He didn't write or record, earning no money and living hand to mouth. He openly discusses his addiction to heroin and the life that accompanied it. Cooper Clarke beat his addiction in the late 1990s. He is back performing live with a motivation that comes partly from the knowledge that it can all be lost again. His work resonates with a new generation. Cooper Clarke's poem *Chicken Town* closed an episode of *The Sopranos* and he appeared as himself in the Plan B film *Ill Manors,* performing the track of the same name. Cited as a major influence by Arctic Monkeys frontman Alex Turner, his poetry appeared on the artwork for their single 'Fluorescent Adolescent' and a reworking of 'I Wanna Be Yours' appears on the Album *AM.* Cooper Clark's encouragement influenced Turner and his band to stick with their name.

In 2013, he received an Honorary Doctorate from the University of Salford. 'Well, I've obviously been a great source of inspiration to the academic population of Salford,' he said. His poetry now appears on the National Curriculum, which makes him very proud. 'I couldn't be happier that my work is being rammed down the throats of reluctant school children.' With a dispirited younger generation seeking meaning in a Britain low on prospects and high on social division, the poetry of Cooper Clarke seems as relevant today as it ever was in the 1980s. His intelligence, comedic northern familiarity, and his skilled self-deprecation make him a figure that few can fail to warm to. PG

'I was living like a king. I was pissing pure gold.'

John Cooper Clarke

John Cooper Clarke

QUENTIN CRISP

Quentin Crisp, the actor, writer, and dandy, had a talent for arousing controversy. Crisp's deliberately affected dress sense and sharp wit were on display throughout his lengthy life, but so too were an innate understanding that both London and New York—the cities with which he was most intimately associated—were elaborate stages on which a knowing performer could thrive. As he said: 'Never keep up with the Joneses; drag them down to your level.'

Crisp was born the altogether less exotic-sounding Denis Charles Pratt in Sutton, Surrey on Christmas Day 1908. His birth did not necessarily denote glad tidings; his distant father Spencer, a solicitor, was disappointed early on by his son's effeminacy, leading Crisp to comment, 'My mother protected me from the world, and my father threatened me with it.' Refusing to conform to the norms of society, he had a miserable time at Kingswood House School in Epsom, and fled to London as soon as he was able to. He briefly studied journalism at King's College London and art at the Regent Street Polytechnic—both of which proved surprisingly valuable in his later career.

Once he had established himself as a Soho flâneur in the early 1930s, Crisp took to the depravity and danger of the age like a rather well-feathered duck to murky water. He had no obvious means of support, confining himself to a small bedsit and saying, 'The poverty from which I have suffered could be diagnosed as "Soho poverty". It comes from having the airs and graces of a genius and no talent.' Denied the opportunity to serve queen and country in the Second World War on the grounds that he was suffering from sexual perversion, he instead enjoyed a rather good war picking up lonely GIs who were rather captivated by this strange androgynous figure. It was then that he moved into his flat in Beaufort Street in Chelsea, which he never cleaned, saying, 'After the first four years the dirt doesn't get any worse.'

Crisp needed some means of support and decided to divide his time between writing books and posing as an artist's model; the latter, he said, was 'like being a civil servant, except you were naked'. It was this that led to the title of his 1968 autobiography, *The Naked Civil Servant*, which brought him fame. It was nonetheless not until 1975 when his memoir was adapted for television with John Hurt as Crisp, that he went from being a cult figure to a mainstream one. There were few men in London who took such pleasure in becoming, at the age of 66, a deeply unlikely celebrity.

'In an expanding universe, time is on the side of the outcast. Those who once inhabited the suburbs of human contempt find that without changing their address they eventually live in the metropolis.'

Quentin Crisp

Quentin Crisp

Having conquered Soho in spectacular fashion, Crisp decided to head to New York with a view to achieving similar success—which inevitably occurred. He had fallen out of love with England, claiming, 'The British do not expect happiness. I had the impression, all the time that I lived there, that they do not want to be happy; they want to be right.' His decision might have been coloured by his disagreements with the increasingly vocal gay liberation movement; Crisp, a self-described 'stately homo', had no interest in lending his name to protests, regarding the attempts to normalize homosexual activities ridiculous. As he said in his memoir, 'All liaisons between homosexuals are conducted as though they were between a chorus girl and a bishop. In some cases both parties think they are bishops.'

While an Englishman in New York, Crisp became a knowing exemplar of a particular kind of effete Englishness, conducting countless one-man shows as a mixture of old-fashioned aristocrat and bawdy vaudevillian. He was a much sought-after dinner guest (never once paying for it—the pleasure of his company was enough) and became one of the most invited men in the city. He claimed that he was perfectly able to live on a diet of champagne and peanuts, despite a fairly considerable income, and his small flat in the East Village was, once again, left uncleaned.

He dabbled in acting, most notably as Elizabeth I in Sally Potter's film of Virginia Woolf's novel *Orlando*, but Crisp was his own greatest creation, and so his appearances tended more to iconic cameos than genuine attempts to play other characters. He became more reactionary as he aged, attacking both AIDS ('a fad') and Princess Diana ('She could have been Queen of England—and she was swanning around Paris with Arabs') but he remained quotable and a much sought-after raconteur until the end of his life. He died in November 1999, fittingly straddling the twentieth century like a camp Colossus.

His influence as one of the first openly gay men that the average person had heard of was hard to exaggerate. While he adopted an effeminate and controversial persona that others were irritated by, he was also tough and knowing. He said, 'Life was a funny thing that happened to me on the way to the grave.' AL

NOEL FIELDING

Much can be learned about comedian Noel Fielding from the fact that he has a favourite cape. It is black with a standing collar, crimson lining, and two red ties to fasten it at the neck. It appears in multiple video clips of Fielding and is mentioned in several of his interviews. Favourite suggests plurality. A telling fact indeed.

There has always been something of the fancy dress costume box about Fielding. Since his emergence in the mid-2000s as one of the founders of surrealist comedy troupe The Mighty Boosh, much of Fielding's appeal has been rooted in the idea that he's a daydreaming Peter Pan, a benign man-child set loose in a boring world for grown-ups. When Fielding tried his hand at painting in 2011, it was in typical child-like fashion. He donned a canary yellow boiler suit and tramped around the shop window of Waterstone's in Manchester, painting crude blue cats across the glass.

This impression of Fielding as a proto-Lost Boy is exacerbated by the way in which both he and his Boosh counterpart—the Bryan Ferry-worshipping zookeeper Vince Noir—like to dress. A Fielding outfit is a dervish of colliding styles, combining ponchos, sequinned bodysuits, fur coats, skin-tight jeans and skirts, cowboy hats, and bandanas with care-free abandon to create a kaleidoscopic whole. It's a style that is reminiscent of glam rock, but Fielding always seems too deliriously joyful to affect a genuine smoulder like Bowie or Eno. All big features and cheerful grin, Fielding looks like a *Just William* schoolboy who's broken into Mark Bolan's dressing room and is thrilled to have found the feather boas. 'It's impossible to be unhappy while wearing a poncho,' Fiedling once quipped in an interview and it might as well be his mantra.

Born in 1973, Fielding grew up in London before moving to study graphic design at Buckinghamshire Chilterns University College. It was in nearby High Wycombe that Fielding founded The Mighty Boosh in 1998, after watching the more established stand-up comedian Julian Barratt perform at the Hellfire Comedy Club. Subsequently working together, Barratt and Fielding later confessed that the main goal of their collaboration was to create a Goodies for the twenty-first century, a change in direction from the first tentative steps in solo comedy that Fielding had already taken prior to meeting Barratt, in which he liked to appear on stage dressed as Jesus Christ and descend from a cross to dance to Mick Jagger songs.

'Some people have a fear of being on stage.
I have a fear of coming off it.'

Noel Fielding

The Mighty Boosh proved a phenomenon, spanning multiple live shows, a radio programme and three television series to date. The show is always more concerned with the surrealist characters and situations that surround its leads than with any notion of plot or character development. There is Mr Susan, the guardian of a mirror world whose body is made from chamois cloths and disco ball testicles; Milky Joe, a coconut turned imaginary island friend turned lecturer on Sartre and geology; and Jacques LeCube, an avant-garde French cube. One plot point (which proves fairly representative of the series as a whole) involved Noir and Moon battling the Crack Fox, a fox whose predominant characteristic was a taste for crack cocaine.

It is difficult not to read connections into the eclecticism of Fielding's comedy and that of his dress sense. Just as Fielding's clothing is sculpted from fragmentary sources—glam rock, by way of teenage goth and Edgar Allen Poe's mortician—so too is his work a collage of whatever happens to have piqued his interest at any one time. *The Mighty Boosh* and its Fielding-penned follow-up series *Luxury Comedy* were non-traditional in every sense, more akin to flights of fancy than to any narrative-driven sitcom or punchline-led sketch show. Fielding's comedy adopts the tropes of word association and he delights in chaining together nouns and adjectives to create grammatical but nonsensical situations. Fielding dresses like a Lewis Carroll character and he writes like the Jabberwocky.

It's an attitude to life that Fielding shed a certain light on in a 2010 interview with the *Times*. 'Kids have no problem with weirdness,' he said. 'You say to kids, "There's a fox over there made of goose fat!" And they go, "Right, yeah, cool. What does he do?" And you say "He eats encyclopaedias!" And they say, "Great!" They never, at any point, go: "What!? That's just silly!" So I've got a lot of respect, and a lot of time, for kids.' You sense that Fielding feels a kinship with children, the only people who seem able to keep up with and understand the sheer glee with which he greets everything that surrounds him. Most people grow out of capes when they're young. Comedy should be thankful that Fielding didn't. OS

Noel Fielding

JIMI HENDRIX

Psychedelia, the sixties, and the sounds of the electric guitar are the watchwords for remembering Jimi Hendrix, an artist who in seven short years rose to become possibly the most prominent guitar player the world has ever known. Hendrix: the ostentatious, the flamboyantly multi-coloured, the outrageous, the over-amplified guitar player, the guitarist so bent on innovative practice that he could claim music as his religion. In retrospect, Hendrix seems like an ethereal vision. He was a drug-induced dream of a musician came from humble beginnings and defied the status quo, becoming the world's most famous performer and tragically dying choking on his own vomit. Perhaps one of the best examples of a modern tragedy, there is a Shakespearean quality to Hendrix's life—but it would be remiss to focus on his death. As Hendrix once famously crooned, 'Come on Baby, let the good times roll!'

The sixties in America had an all-pervasive character. It was a decade in which music, politics, literature, art, and drugs were not limited to their respective spheres. There is no Hendrix without Vietnam, without Dylan, and without LSD. Military service did not suit a young James Hendrix who had spent most of his young life avoiding his parents' domestic disagreements, and at 14, Hendrix found his first instrument: a single-stringed ukulele that he learnt to play by ear with Elvis Presley's 'Hound Dog'. He would soon receive his first acoustic guitar, an instrument that a young Hendrix spent countless hours practising on each day, only to be disappointed by the instrument's relative quiet once he joined his first band The Velvetones.

Hendrix prefferred to restring his guitar in order to play left-handed, yet his father's belief that left-handed people bear the mark of the devil meant that Hendrix also learnt to play right-handed on a guitar that he had restrung for his left. This small piece of trivia is immensely revealing as it speaks of Hendrix's dedication, determination, and also to his shunning of traditional methods. He would play by his own rules.

After an honourable discharge from the United States military service, Hendrix played back-up for famous acts such as Little Richard, The Isley Brothers, and Sam Cooke before forming his own band and relocating to Greenwich Village. In 1966 Hendrix moved to London, changed from 'Jimmy' to 'Jimi' and formed the Experience. 1967 was a triumphant year for the Jimi Hendrix Experience with three top ten singles 'Purple Haze', 'Hey Joe', and 'The Wind Cries Mary'. That same year, the album *Are You Experienced*

was released to raucous reviews, and two centrally important live shows made Hendrix both an internationally famous musician and a musically revered performer.

June 1967 at the Savile Theatre in London, Hendrix marched out on stage playing the Beatles. Paul McCartney said, 'The curtains flew back and he came walking forward playing "Sgt. Pepper". It's a pretty major compliment in anyone's book. I put that down as one of the great honours of my career.' McCartney would, that same year, recommend the Jimi Hendrix Experience to the organisers of the Monterey Pop Festival, and their success there would give Hendrix his breakthrough in the United States after much commercial success in England. At the festival, Hendrix would create one of the most iconic and memorable images in the history of rock 'n' roll and perhaps in music altogether: with the aid of lighter fluid, he set his guitar on fire, knelt by its burning body, and wafted the smoke upwards in a voodoo gesture of his mystic connection with the music. A poignant moment, unforgettable and epochal.

This, however, would not be the height of Hendrix's career. The Experience would go on to release two more albums, *Axis: Bold as Love* and *Electric Ladyland,* both of which saw Hendrix using new and pioneering musical techniques, showing a rising confidence in his song writing, and reinstating his position as the greatest living guitarist. After the break-up of the Experience by 1969, Hendrix was the world's highest-paid rock musician and would headline Woodstock, an historic musical moment.

Hendrix closed the three-day festival by playing at 8am on Monday morning after three sleepless nights. Hendrix took to the stage to perform an enigmatic and visionary version of 'The Star Spangled Banner' with profuse amounts of feedback and distortion. After finishing his encore with hit single 'Hey Joe', an over-exhausted Hendrix collapsed on his way off stage.

By 1970, Hendrix was disillusioned with the music industry, heavily reliant on drug-use and extremely insecure about his personal relationships. Isolated and often sleepless, Hendrix overdosed on sleeping pills and aspirated on his own vomit in September 1970. His premature death at only 27 has since added to his allure and posthumous fame. Hendrix will forever be known as one of the most eminent musicians in history, hopefully for his achievements while alive rather than his tragic death. HB

ELTON JOHN

Sir Elton Hercules John, born Reginald Kenneth Dwight on 25 March 1947, is perhaps the most entertainingly flamboyant musician of our time. A man of fairly modest origins, John has crafted a career spanning five decades, earning himself critical acclaim, enormous wealth, and vast and enduring popularity. He is hard to characterise, his life now spanning music making, political and cultural activism, dog rescuing, and philanthropy on an enormous scale.

John was brought up in Pinner in North West London. His gift for music was evident at an early age, and encouraged by his grandmother he began playing the piano at just 3 years old. By the age of 11 he had won a scholarship to study at the Royal Academy of Music. His father, with whom he had a tumultuous relationship, was against a career in music. A semi professional trumpeter and avid record collector, he wanted a more traditional career for his son. But his mother supported his ambitions and encouraged him to begin playing at a nearby pub. Aged 15 he performed covers and a few tunes he'd written himself to a rowdy drunken Saturday night crowd.

In 1967 he answered an advert in the New Musical Express. Also answering the same ad was lyricist Bernie Taubin. Initially penning songs for other artists, they began what would prove to be amongst the most successful songwriting partnerships in history. In 1970 he got his big break at the Troubadour in LA and from that point his rise was unstoppable. John didn't just write great songs and have a great voice, his live performances wowed audiences. His dynamism on stage was electric and his costumes were fantastic. Clothes of dazzling exuberance. Sparkle, feathers, hats, capes, platform shoes. Animal costumes, historical costumes, jumpsuits. And the glasses without which no Elton John outfit would be complete. There was always humour in everything he wore and did, and this is part of his enduring appeal. On tour he liked to check into hotels under a preposterous pseudonym, like Sir Colin Chihuahua, Sir Humphry Handbag or Sir Horace Pussy. But on the flipside of the humour was his terrific temper. The 1997 documentary Tantrums & Tiaras captured glimpses of his legendary rage and preposterously acid tongue. But he could be contrite too, and few people could resist his charm and broad toothy grin.

John's achievements in the music industry are far too numerous to mention but it is enough to say that he has sold over a quarter of a billion records. He has been awarded six Grammies, five Brits, an Academy Award, a Golden Globe Award, and a Tony.

Few have achieved more. But even after all of the adulation and commercial success, John was still plagued by self-doubt and the inferiority he had suffered from as a boy. He lapsed into full-blown alcoholism and serious drug abuse. He suffered from bulimia and attempted suicide, taking a huge amount of sleeping tablets. After 15 years of abuse he took himself into rehab and by 1990 he was clean, an achievement he claimed was the greatest of his life.

John earned a serious amount of money from music but equally serious is his talent for spending it. He once spent £250,000 in Versace in one day. A lifelong fan of Watford Football Club, he loved the club so much that he bought it (under his chairmanship it went from the fourth division to the first). His collection of contemporary art includes the likes of Hirst, Emin, the Chapman brothers, Gillian Wearing, Grayson Perry, Gilbert & George, and Anthony Gormley, all spectacularly housed in a copper clad gallery-cum-library built by architect Jack Schneider from his former garage at their Windsor home.

He is also perhaps one of the best connected men in the world. He counts amongst his friends an extraordinary array of stars from the worlds of art, music, film, politics, and fashion. He is the ultimate party thrower and a spectacularly generous host. His White Tie & Tiara Ball held annually from 1998 until 2103 was amongst the most photographed parties of the year, and in its time it has raised over £50m for the Elton John Aids Foundation which lay behind it.

Now half of the world's most famous gay couple, John married long-term partner David Furnish on the first day that gay marriage became legal in the UK. They began a family together and now have two sons.

John still records new material and performs live gigs, both intimate and on the grand Las Vegas scale. To watch him play, sweating, gurning, fist pumping, is to watch a man who clearly still adores every second of his time on stage. He seems finally also to be enjoying every second off it too. PG

MARCELLO MASTROIANNI

The suave, mysterious, and handsome Marcello Mastroianni is one of the great heart-throbs of modern cinema, enamouring audiences across the world, both on and off screen.

Born in Fontana Liri, Italy on 28 September 1924, Mastroianni was moved with his family to Turin and then to Rome, where he stayed until the late 1930s and the Second World War. During his time in Rome, Mastroianni had a number of casual jobs, but upon the outbreak of war, while working as a draftsman, Mastroianni was forced into work at a German labour camp in northern Italy. In a turn of events perhaps better fit for a film than real life, Mastroianni forged his escape from the camp and fled to Venice, where he lived in poverty until the end of the war in 1945. In the following years, he worked in an administrative capacity for a British film distribution company in Rome, and practised acting with an amateur group of university students in the evenings.

Mastroianni's first lead role in film was in the Italian production of Victor Hugo's *Les Miserables*, which appeared in 1947. It was his relationship with Federico Fellini, however, which generated most of his initial success. Cast as an attractive, mysterious, and womanizing journalist in the revolutionary film *La dolce vita*, Mastroianni's face was emblazoned on the minds of audiences worldwide. The relationship with Fellini continued to blossom, with Mastroianni benefiting from Fellini's inspirational work, and Fellini profiting from Mastroianni's rakish good looks. He went on to star in the 1963 film *8½* in which he appeared with Anouk Aimée, *City of Women* in 1979, and *Ginger and Fred* in 1986. He built a famous on-screen relationship with Sophia Loren, starring alongside her in 10 major films. Together, the two grew to be seen as the embodiment of the true Italian man and woman—married, in love, or just infatuated. Vivacious, romantic, and beautiful, the couple won the affections of audiences worldwide.

Through all these roles, Mastroianni cultivated a reputation as a prolific seducer, from whom even the most hardy women were unsafe. Audiences around the world came to recognize the dark Italian as the 'Latin lover' he so often portrayed on screen. Exuding class with such ease, Mastroianni toured the globe promoting movies, smoking endless amounts of cigarettes and breaking countless hearts. Once on a flight in Germany, Mastroianni began talking to, and seducing, an air stewardess. So strong was his passion for the opposite sex, and for spontaneous random encounters, that Mastroianni led them both on an eight-day adventure by air, enjoying her company on the plane and between flights.

Asked about his love for women, and their apparent love for him, in a 1965 *Playboy* interview, Mastroianni said about American women: 'I've never seen so many unhappy, melancholy women. They have liberty—but they are desperate. Poor darlings, they're so hungry for romance that two little words in their ears are enough to crumble them before your eyes.' He continues, 'American women are beautiful, but a little cold and too perfect ... What perfection—and what a bore! Believe me, it makes you want to have a girl with a moustache, cross-eyes and runs in her stockings.' It is this attitude, a lust for excitement and energy, which best encapsulates Mastroianni's views towards sex and love.

In fact, the reputation which began to precede him in his later years did not please Mastroianni. He did not want to be perceived as a womanizer and a chauvinist. Mastroianni maintained that rather than pursuing casual encounters of no meaning, he had fallen in love with each and every women who had grabbed his attention over the years. 'I am not in fact a seducer,' he declares, 'I have been more seduced—and abandoned.' In this sense, Mastroianni can be seen not as womanizer but as a true romantic. He became engrossed in the real pleasure of love, spontaneity, and excitement, refusing to be bored and uninspired. His overpowering charm and classic Italian good looks, made famous by his work in cinema, enabled Mastroianni to pursue a life of love normally restricted to fiction. GE

'I only exist when I am working on a film.'
Marcello Mastroianni

Jonathan Meades

JONATHAN MEADES

Occasional novelist, idiosyncratic documentarian, essayist, journalist, suburban travel-ler, Jonathan Meades is a man of infinite variety but singular style. He is the most origi-nal and charismatic broadcaster in Britain.

Meades was brought up in South Wiltshire in the 1950s, his parents giving few reasons for rebellion, their only serious concerns being 'bad grammar, bad handwriting, and bad manners'. Meades describes his childhood in florid detail in *An Encyclopaedia Of Myself (2014)*. This was an England we imagine in shades of grey and puce, a most unpromising of eras, but Meades pans nuggets of joy from the ordinary streets of urban and suburban Britain. Through his unique lens, ordinary subjects become magnified and grotesque. He shows us the wonder that lies just beneath our noses, a world peopled by eco-fascist fruitcakes, cold warrior boffin-gods, lesbian primary school teachers, and homosexual civil servants. Meades is a Laurie Lee for 1950s Salisbury.

Meades originally wished to become an actor, claiming he could think of nothing else to do. In 1966, he successfully auditioned for RADA. When he left, the principal, Hugh Cruttwell, told him he thought it likely he'd make a fine character actor, but not until he hit middle age. Meades, foreseeing a period of enforced rest, decided to try his hand at writing instead.

His 1984 collection of short stories, *Filthy English*, features murder, incest, and bestial pornography. *Peter Knows What Dick Likes* followed in similar vein. *Pompey* (it is set in Portsmouth) is less clean. A family saga, it is the story of a flaky pyrotechnician and his progeny; a gimpy geek, a junkie porn star, the damaged result of a botched abor-tion, and a leather-wearing gay gerontophile. Not the stuff of Galsworthy. Indescribably dirty, Meades counsels readers: 'After using this book please wash your hands.' Meades has an extraordinary capability with language leading to rightful comparisons with Shakespeare, Jonson, Joyce, and Bellow.

For 15 years he was a food critic at the *Times*. As a young man he recalls eating a small amount of whale in a pie, the taste, texture, and smell of which he can still vividly recall. Since then he's eaten brains, tripe, various sections of the pig's alimentary canal, spinal cord, testicles, and beaver. But he claims that his most exciting gastronomic experience was his first taste of Golden Wonder cheese and onion crisps.

Not long after he published his first book, he began making television programmes. *Abroad in Britain, Further Abroad (as far as Belgium), Even Further Abroad (about Caravans), Abroad Again in Britain* and finally *Abroad Again*. Places from his childhood, places discovered on his forced 20-minute bus journeys, these are potted social histories of seldom glamourised corners of Britain, and his despair at the befuddled thinking of those who build our towns and cities. Meades credits his father for developing in him 'a love of place, and a love of what makes places. Landscapes, street-scapes, rivers, heaths, chance conjunctions, field systems, the nameless bits between them all, especially those bits.' Meades describes his younger self as 'a midget autodidact'. He was not interested in nature and 'the God malarkey', but by mankind's interventions.

Off Kilter, made in 2007, is televised Meades at his best, a hypnotic and quixotic sweep across Scotland, a country he claims to have become fascinated with through the names of towns on the football pool's coupon. The style is beguiling, deliberately misaligned, clunky, shuddering, awkward. Meades from afar, suited, in a bog, or wind-buffeted on the machair. Meades in a midge hood. The cinematography is decidedly surreal, all the more so because of the dead-pan of Meades's delivery, and the suit. This is theatre, not television documentary. *Off Kilter* becomes an ode to the Island of Rust, the Isle of Harris/Lewis, a curious yet compelling love letter to transit vans rotting in peat bogs, to distressed iron cladding on ramshackle steadings. This rusting shackscape is beautiful 'in the way that lupus is beautiful, or mould on fruit'. Art born of artlessness or carelessness.

His most recent broadcast, *Bunkers, Brutalism and Bloodymindedness: Concrete Poetry* is Meades's remedy for the encroaching toxic wave of 'Ikea Modernism'. 'A main aspiration of architects over the past 40 years has been not to give offence. There is a terrible timidity, whereas Brutalism was very aggressive. It was anti focus groups and consensus.' 'The whole idea of populism,' he says 'is inherently flawed.'

Now in late middle age, Meades is hitting his stride. Like all great stylists he has refined his persona, amplified it, made himself his art. His great role, the one Crutwell predicted he would learn to play, is himself. He is a uniquely gifted performer on television, a medium which so often veers towards the lowest common denominator. Meades never attempts to please the many, he aims to delight the few. PG

Jonathan Meades

FREDDIE MERCURY

Much of Freddie Mercury's life was based around the assumption of identity. Onstage he was the mercurial frontman of Queen, a man with a predilection for black leotards with diamante crotches, hot pants, crowns, and skin-tight vests with even tighter jeans. Crowing and preening, he whipped crowds into a frenzy, strutting regally across a stage with his mic stand serving variously as royal sceptre, electric guitar, and phallus. Offstage, things were different. 'It does get tough when people spot me in the street, and want him up there,' Mercury once acknowledged in an interview. 'The *big* Freddie.'

Born Farrokh Bulsara in 1946 in Stone Town, Zanzibar, Mercury was the son of Bomi and Jer Bulsara from Gujarat. As a child Mercury grew up between Zanzibar and India, where he became known to his friends as Bucky because of his prominent front teeth. He spent his youth playing cricket and piano before the family fled to Middlesex, U.K., to escape the violence of the 1964 Zanzibar Revolution. As a boy, Mercury was quiet and unassuming; a far cry from the brush-moustached, vest-cladded Freddie of later years.

In England, Mercury's more familiar traits began to appear. He had already adopted the name Freddie while in India, but Britain allowed him to pursue his interest in music. Mercury was a natural baritone, but his near four-octave vocal range let him easily slide between low notes and high ones. It was a talent he put to good use in failed bands. Moving around Britain, he performed in Ibex and Sour Milk Sea—both glorious failures—before finding his feet in 1970 with Brian May and Roger Taylor in Queen. Freddie had picked the name himself—'it's very regal obviously, and it sounds splendid'—and around the same time he had also settled on a new surname for himself. Freddie Mercury came into being and Farrokh Balsara was purposefully buried in obscurity. 'No, Mercury isn't my real name, dear,' he admitted to journalist Caroline Conn in 1974. 'I changed it from Pluto.'

Queen was a sensation. They combined stadium anthems with glam rock, mixing in heavy metal for good measure. Throughout the 1970s and 1980s the band's live shows were replete with smoke bombs, flash pots, and May's heavy guitar, the group careering between the high-camp 'Killer Queen', march-like 'Another One Bites the Dust', and rockabilly 'Crazy Little Thing Called Love', not to mention the absurdist operetta of 'Bohemian Rhapsody'. At the centre of all this was Mercury, a frontman as happy leading raucous call-and-response stadium sessions as he was pinwheeling off into Liza Minelli-esque cabaret.

Offstage, however, Mercury's life was complicated. His long-term relationship with girlfriend Mary Austin had broken down in 1976 after Mercury came out as gay. The two stayed close, but Mercury began to become involved in the gay scenes of London, New York, and Munich, hosting in the latter a 39th birthday party so debauched and *nudity-heavy* that his ex-manager John Reid remembered it as 'the last days of Berlin, the last hurrah'. Elton John was in agreement: 'Freddie Mercury could out-party me, which is saying something.'

Mercury didn't hide his sexuality ('I'm as gay as a daffodil, my dear!' the *NME* reported him as saying in 1974), but he didn't publicise it heavily. Mercury may have been a hedonist, but offstage he was no showman. He hated interviews and was self-contained, shy, and frequently sentimental. While on tour, he would often telephone Austin to ask her to hold up the multitude of cats he owned to the receiver. He wanted to say 'hello' to each of them individually.

Mercury's domesticity, especially once he hit his forties, was telling. A photo album of Freddie with his final partner Jim Hutton shows the pair lounging around, Hutton topless, Mercury in an aloha shirt, each hugging increasingly boggle-eyed house cats to their chests. Privacy was a watchword for Mercury, particularly after he was diagnosed with HIV in the late 1980s. As he became increasingly reclusive and gaunt, it was clear to most what was wrong, but Mercury took great steps to hide the truth. He insisted upon being treated at home and medical supplies were smuggled into the house, hidden inside record sleeves and boxes. It wasn't until 23 November 1991 that Mercury finally confirmed that he was suffering from AIDS in a public statement. The following day he died.

It was a sad end, but one that Mercury handled with dignity. 'You can do what you want with my music,' he told his then-manager Jim Beach, 'but don't make me boring.' It was a remark indicative of Mercury's general fear of attention ever drifting from *big* Freddie and onto the real Freddie who lurked behind. But Mercury was a man adept at juggling identities and what was remarkable was how quickly he could slip into the role people demanded of him; how easily he could become the mischievous, gregarious Freddie Mercury so captivating on stage.

In 1987, Mercury was promoting his solo single 'The Great Pretender', forcing him to agree to a number of interviews, including one with journalist David Wigg for a TV movie.

'Do you get intimidated by the size of a crowd?' Wigg asked, sitting next to Mercury on a white leather sofa. 'No, the bigger the better ... in everything,' Mercury replied, before breaking into laughter and slapping Wigg on the knee. The interview was halted, its director asking that Mercury refrain from slapping Wigg as the sound would spoil the recording. They began a second take. That time, Mercury slapped Wigg's knee so hard that the seat collapsed. os

MORRISSEY

A singer best described as 'the Oscar Wilde of the welfare state', to borrow a description of his idol Joe Orton, Morrissey has enjoyed a career that bears a resemblance to a fairground rollercoaster. Emerging from nowhere in the 1980s with The Smiths, he had subsequent success as a solo artist, and attracted a huge amount of controversy along the way.

Steven Patrick Morrissey was born in Davyhulme, Lancashire on 22 May 1959. 'Naturally my birth almost kills my mother, for my head is too big,' he wrote. His mother, an assistant librarian, encouraged him to develop an eclectic breadth of interests. He read the celebrated poetry of John Betjeman alongside kitchen sink novels, and listened to music ranging from David Bowie to T Rex. The family moved to Stretford in Manchester, and the young Morrissey became an avid watcher of *Coronation Street;* its emphasis on a working-class Mancunian life echoed his own.

An undistinguished student at St Mary Secondary Modern (he quipped 'it may be secondary, but it is not modern'), Morrissey left with three O-level passes, and after briefly signing onto the dole, fronted a short-lived punk band, The Nosebleeds, and wrote a book about the New York Dolls. He then met the man who would become his songwriting partner, Johnny Marr, in 1982. The two of them formed The Smiths with bassist Andy Rourke and drummer Mike Joyce, and enjoyed a remarkable amount of success, thanks to the championing of the influential DJ John Peel. They wrote songs about issues that most bands of the age might have considered recherché, dealing with everything from literary plagiarism ('Cemetery Gates') to ecclesiastical perversion ('Vicar In A Tutu'). They had a cult following for their eccentric live performances, in which Morrissey sported a hearing aid and was prone to distributing gladioli.

After a few tumultuous years, the band split up, in part because of Marr's increasing unhappiness with what he perceived as Morrissey's controlling nature. Shrugging off what would have been catastrophic for other musicians, Morrissey instead launched a solo career with his 1988 album *Viva Hate*, which contained songs wishing for the death of then-Prime Minister Margaret Thatcher ('Margaret On The Guillotine') and the seminal 'Everyday Is Like Sunday', which is best described as John Betjeman's poem *Slough* updated in the shadow of the Cold War. Morrissey's attitude towards conflict was unsurprisingly dismissive, describing war as 'the most negative aspect of male heterosexuality'.

After some years of success and acclaim that rivalled his time with The Smiths, a succession of unfortunate events lowered Morrissey from the exalted position he enjoyed in popular culture. An ill-conceived performance at Finsbury Park in 1992 in which he wrapped himself in a Union Jack led to accusations of 'flirting with fascism'. It didn't help that his recent song 'Bengali In Platforms' contained the provocative lyrics 'life is hard enough when you belong here'. Morrissey, for the past decade a hero of the left, was now considered a more dubious character, a status further confirmed by a public and ugly court case in which Joyce successfully sued him and Marr for performance royalties.

After taking a significant amount of time out of the industry, he returned in triumph in 2004 with his album *You Are The Quarry,* which introduced his music to a new generation of admirers, and which saw him play an acclaimed series of concerts throughout the world. He capitalized on its success with a 2006 release, *Ringleader Of The Tormentors*, which was produced by David Bowie's associate Tony Visconti. Subsequent releases, including 2009's *Years of Refusal* and 2014's *World Peace Is None of Your Business*, have seen him smoothly plough a furrow as a suave elder statesman of rock, only interrupted by his frequent cancellation of concerts due to sporadic ill health.

Notoriously celibate throughout much of his adult life (he said 'I always thought my genitals were the result of some crude practical joke'), Morrissey appeared to confirm, at least in part, long-standing rumours that he was either homosexual or bisexual in his 2013 autobiography, referring to a two-year relationship with Jake Walters in the 1990s, and claiming 'for the first time in my life, the eternal "I" becomes "we"'. Nonetheless, he later retracted what appeared to be an unusually candid confession by claiming, 'Unfortunately, I am not homosexual ... I am attracted to humans, but of course, not many.' One of the world's most famous vegetarians, he has said, 'I see no difference between eating meat and paedophilia,' and has attempted to ban the sale of meat at his concerts, occasionally walking offstage when bothered by the odour of burgers.

Enigmatic, hilarious, frustrating, and surprising, Morrissey continues to be amongst the most Wildean of rock stars, as ready with a perfectly-timed putdown or witticism as his great hero. One of his best was, when described as a 'puffed-up prat' by the broadcaster Richard Madeley in 2006 for his objection to a vivisection laboratory, to shrug and say, 'I think it's a bit rich coming from a man who actually married his own mother.' AL

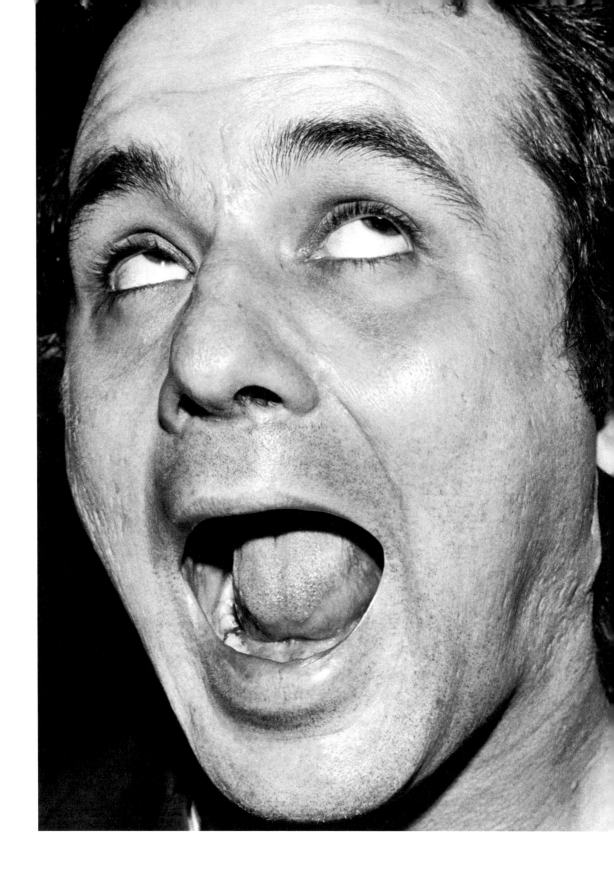

Bill Murray

BILL MURRAY

Bill Murray has developed a reputation for eccentricity. An extremely popular public figure for his on-screen appearances alone, Murray's main contribution to his popularity remains his performances in the real world. Born William James Murray on 21 September 1950, Murray had little intention of becoming an actor in the earlier years of his life. In fact, he attended Regis University in Denver, Colorado to study a pre-medical course. Murray was forced to abandon these studies, however, when he was convicted for attempting to smuggle 4.5 kilograms of marijuana through O'Hare airport in Chicago. Many have suggested with hindsight that Murray's secret baggage may never have been discovered had he only been able to rest the urge to tell other passengers that he had bombs in his luggage.

Murray's career change nonetheless proved extremely successful with well-received television performances on three seasons of *Saturday Night Live* before cutting his teeth on cinema in the late 1970s. Notable first performances included *Meatballs* in 1979, followed by *Where the Buffalo Roam* in which Murray played his friend, writer Hunter S. Thompson. The 1980s were host to a string of box-office successes for Murray, with *Caddyshack*, *Stripes*, and *Tootsie* all appearing in close succession. Perhaps Murray's most memorable performance came in the 1984 film *Ghostbusters*, which became the highest-grossing film of the year. In fact, Murray was not entirely committed to his role in the film, originally agreeing to star in order to secure funding for *The Razor's Edge*, an adaptation of a novel co-written by Murray, which would become a significant financial failure.

Murray would later receive a Golden Globe Award, a BAFTA Award, and an Independent Spirit Award, as well as Best Actor awards from several other critical organizations, for his role in *Lost in Translation*. Murray has reportedly missed out on roles in a number of other critically acclaimed films due to his refusal to employ an agent. Instead, film companies are forced to call a toll-free telephone number set up by Murray and pitch their film to an answering machine in order to secure his work.

Murray's decision to play the voice of a talking cat in *Garfield: The Movie* was a surprising change of direction for many followers of his career, not least because he had turned down a similar role in another animated film, *Toy Story*. Murray later claimed that his role in the production could be ascribed to a case of mistaken identity.

Garfield was co-written by Joel Cohen, the author of screenplays including *Cheaper by the Dozen* and *Daddy Day Camp*. Upon reading Mr Cohen's name on the script, Murray mistook him for one of the Cohen brothers, Joel and Ethan, authors, directors, and producers of numerous critically acclaimed films including *The Big Lebowski* and *O Brother, Where Art Thou?* and was quick to show his support for the project. This tale does little to explain Murray's appearance in the film's sequel, *Garfield: A Tail of Two Kitties*, in 2006.

Murray's individual style and eccentricity is most obvious when he is not in front of a camera, however, and stories of his antics abound. On the set of *Groundhog Day*, Murray was asked to employ a mediator between himself and the studio. An irritated Murray did so willingly, recruiting a deaf mute who could only communicate through Native American sign language.

Murray's passion for random encounters with strangers, often at parties, composes much of his reputation. During a trip to St Andrews for a celebrity golf tournament in 2006, Murray invited himself to the party of a Norwegian student Lykke Stavnef, whom he had met in a bar. Murray arrived at the party with Stavnef, much to the amazement of her friends, told some jokes, did the washing up, and left. It is also said that Murray often appears in fast food restaurants in New York, helps himself to fries from the plate of strangers and departs saying only the words 'no one will ever believe you'. The most bizarre encounter of this kind came in Bali, where Murray got lost in the jungle on a motorcycle. He was found hours later performing an improvised one man show to an entire village of tribespeople, the language difficulty proving no barrier to the entertainment.

Some years after his experience in Bali, Murray arrived at a bar in Austin, Texas with RZA and GZA of the Wu Tang Clan. The three hopped over the bar and proceeded to take orders for drinks. Murray decided, regardless of what was ordered, to provide all customers with tequila shots.

It is Murray's taste for impromptu entertainment of this kind which has earned him such a cult following. It is difficult to find an unfavourable tale of Murray's public appearances; his personality is bizarre, infectious, and brilliant. He is a man with an inimitable charisma and individual style. GE

BOY GEORGE

When a beautiful, androgynous young man appeared on *Top of the Pops* in October 1982 daubed in make-up and singing his band Culture Club's most recent single 'Do You Really Want To Hurt Me?', his presence divided a nation. Newspaper headlines screamed 'Is it a boy or a girl?' and defiantly heterosexual pundits were heard to call for the repeal of the decriminalization of homosexuality, so strange and gaudy was this figure. As the tabloids fulminated, Boy George raised an elegantly manicured eyebrow, sipped on a cup of tea (which he famously favoured over having sex) and watched his single go to No. 1 in the charts.

Boy George was born George O'Dowd in Bexley, Kent on 14 June 1961, one of six children. After his family moved to Eltham, he left the local school to join the then-nascent New Romantic movement at the beginning of the 1980s, inhabiting squats in central London by day and dancing in nightclub promoter Steve Strange's infamous Blitz club by night. He also dallied with the lesbian club Madame Louise's, where he danced in the company of the Clash and the Sex Pistols.

He had come out to his parents at the age of 16, possibly without a great deal of surprise on their part, and his dramatic manner and appearance drew him to the Sex Pistols' Svengali Malcolm McLaren, who set about turning him into a pop star. After an ill-fated flirtation with the act Bow Wow Wow, George formed Culture Club (so called because of the eclectic ethnicity of its members) and began an affair with the drummer, Jon Moss. Frightening off their original record label EMI, they were instead picked up by Virgin, and their 1982 debut album *Kissing To Be Clever* was a success in both Britain and the United States.

George and Culture Club were now on the verge of superstardom (the band was the first since the Beatles to have had three top 10 hits in the United States from their debut album), but George's insecurities lurked in the shadows, even though their sophomore album *Colour by Numbers* was an even bigger hit. It looked as if George might be able to do what David Bowie had done the previous decade, combining an outrageous public persona and charismatic stage presence with great commercial success.

However, self-destruction and fame went hand in hand for George, beginning with the end of his relationship with Moss in 1986, and followed by reports of drug addiction:

'I'd got very successful, everyone knew who I was, but I felt very empty.' Scandal then beckoned when the keyboardist Michael Rudetsky was found dead of a heroin overdose in George's home, and Rudetsky's family sued for wrongful death. While ultimately unsuccessful, the lawsuit and George's drug habit led to the end of Culture Club. He pursued a solo career with some initial success, despite having developed an addiction to the prescription drugs he was given to overcome his heroin dependency, but was unable to replicate his earlier hits with his debut album *Sold*.

The early 1990s saw George move away from pop music and start DJ-ing at acid house events, attracting the fame and fortune of his residencies at London superclubs that he had craved for so long. His public profile was sufficiently high by 1995 for him to publish his autobiography *Take It Like A Man*, in which he discussed his love affairs with Moss and the punk singer Kirk Brandon, who unsuccessfully sued for libel. He found fulfilment in a new public role as an advocate for tolerance and equality.

His career over the next decade remained stable, with a highlight in 2002 when he appeared in the autobiographical New Romantic musical *Taboo*, but his drug addiction returned, leading to several legal entanglements and arrests. Most seriously, in 2008 George was convicted for the false imprisonment of a male escort and sentenced to 15 months in jail. Against the odds, George rebuilt his life upon release. In 2013 he released his first solo album in 18 years, *This Is What I Do*, and announced a reunion of Culture Club in May 2014, initially for a series of concerts, and for an upcoming album in 2015.

He remains philosophical about his turbulent life, claiming, 'My life hasn't always been a disaster, but when it has, it's been spectacular.' Refreshingly uncensored and engagingly candid, George has managed to weather storms with grace and wit. AL

'I would rather have a cup of tea than sex.'

Boy George

David Ogilvy

DAVID OGILVY

The Scottish king of 1950s advertising not only created some of the most iconic and successful advertisements of all time, but also devised theories on advertising and brand building that are as simple and as wise in today's world of digital media as they were more than half a century ago. Ogilvy's was a world of three piece tweed suits, pipe smoking, and 'gentlemen with brains'. He became the stuff of Madison Avenue legends.

David MacKenzie Ogilvy was born in West Horsley, England in 1911. He was educated at Fettes College, Edinburgh and Christ Church, Oxford (where he failed to graduate.) He worked briefly as a chef before beginning a career selling Aga cookers in Scotland door to door. It was on the doorstep that he learned the art of selling, and the efficacy of simple language and getting to the point. In 1935, he wrote a manual for his fellow salesmen entitled *The Theory & Practice of Selling the Aga Cooker*. *Fortune* magazine later called it 'probably the best sales manual ever written'. It contains the usual Ogilvy mix of good sense and humourous miscellany typical of his missives: 'Dress quietly and shave well. Do not wear a bowler hat;' 'Learn to recognise vegetarians on sight;' 'Aborigines bake their hedgehogs in the ashes of a dying fire.'

In 1935, he joined Mather & Crowther where a braggart Ogilvy, at the time a junior executive, delivered an address on his theory of advertising to the entire staff. Many years later he found the address and sent it to his then Board. The accompanying note said: 'It proves two things: A) at 25 I was brilliantly clever, and B) I have learned nothing new in the subsequent 27 years. As theories they are every bit as correct today: "every advertisement must tell the whole sales story;" "the copy must be human and simple;" "every word must count;" "superlatives have no place in serious advertising;" "apparent monotony of treatment must be tolerated, only the manufacturer reads all his own advertisements."' In an era when bogus science was used to baffle consumers into buying products, Ogilvy believed in the power of simple narrative.

In 1938, he was sent to America to study the market and its methods. In 1939 he joined George Gallup's Audience Research Institute in Princeton. It was here that Ogilvy developed his belief in the value of meticulous research and in adhering to what is known, rather than presumed, to be true. After a short period during which he worked for the British Government in Washington and as a farmer with the Amish in rural Pennsylvania, he returned to New York and in 1948 he founded the New York-based ad agency Hewitt, Ogilvy, Benson & Mather.

Some of the most successful advertisements of the 1950s were Ogilvy's ideas. The owner of Hathaway Shirts approached Ogilvy but knew that he couldn't afford his fees. Ogilvy took the job on the condition that he would have total control, and that he would never be sacked. On the way to the shoot for the first of the new advertisements Ogilvy spotted an eye patch in a shop window. The eye patch made its way onto the moustachioed model in the photograph and The Man In The Hathaway Shirt was born. Hathaway went from being a small provincial shirt-maker to the largest in America. Ogilvy, adhering to his theory that monotony is never a problem in good advertising, let man, shirt, and eye patch run virtually unchanged for two decades. In a bid to grow their business in the United States, Schweppes came to Ogilvy and suggested he run ads featuring a similarly recognisable figurehead, their own advertising manager the splendidly bewhiskered 'Commander' Edward Whitehead. Ogilvy was unconvinced but The Man From Schweppes became an instant hit. 'Whitehead's bearded mug,' remarked a baffled Ogilvy 'has captured the imagination of the American Public.'

Ogilvy was a copywriting genius, though he frequently claimed it was a struggle. His solution for writer's block was simple: 'If all else fails, I drink half a bottle of rum and play a Handel oratorio on the gramophone.' In 1959, he wrote arguably the most memorable headline of any car ad ever made when he wrote, 'At 60 miles an hour the loudest noise in this new Rolls-Royce comes from the electric clock.' The line is still referred to at Rolls-Royce today.

But his ideas went far beyond advertising. His thoughts on business culture are more readable and have greater clarity than the majority of mainstream management theory. 'Encourage exuberance; get rid of sad dogs who spread gloom; if you hire people who are smaller than you are, we shall become a company of dwarfs. If you hire people who are bigger than you are, we shall become a company of giants.' Ogilvy was never short of an opinion. He was also never one to sell his own achievements short, once saying of himself, 'I doubt whether any copywriter has ever produced so many winners in such a short period.' PG

NORMAN PARKINSON

Photography is a medium of expression that promises the real, captures the empirical image, the Truth. Where then does this leave the photographer? Some would say as arranger of the Truth, selling the real in the composition of a single shot. The power of photography therefore lies in its supposed objectivity. Enter Norman Parkinson. Not content with the callous studios, the artificial lighting, the premeditated poses and postures, Parkinson sought something in photography to reinvigorate its purpose as a medium: a powerful sense of the candid. An open and true vision of reality unshackled from expectations but shackled instead to Parkinson's own imaginative vision. He took the promise of the real, gave it to the audience, and gave them also just a little bit more. As he once said, 'I like to make people look as good as they'd like to look and with luck, a shade better.'

Born in London, Parkinson, commonly referred to as Parks, took photography as his single and ultimate goal. He began as a court photographer and opened his own portrait studio at the age of 21 in Piccadilly. He would work for *Harper's Bazaar* and *Bystander* magazines for five years before becoming a reconnaissance photographer for the Royal Air Force during the Second World War. It was during and after the war, when Parkinson worked for *Vogue* magazine, that he became the iconic photographer known today.

During the war, posted on a small Worcestershire farm, Parkinson took everything in and reproduced it in his own visual language. He mainly focused on women at work, photographing them at cattle auctions, while picking fruit, or walking the dog. After the war, Parkinson unabashedly sought to 'unlock the knees' of the women he was photographing. He would photograph them running and jumping, contrasting greatly with the tedious expectations of studio photography of the time. These women were vivacious, and it was that energy that Parkinson sought to capture.

A photograph of his own wife, Wenda Parkinson, resplendent as always in cashmere and seated next to a toughened, flat-cap wearing cowman grasping a pint at Hobnail Inn was just the type of photograph Parkinson wished to take. It was also just the type of photograph that would cause concern at the offices of *Vogue*. Who of the *Vogue* readers would be seen at a public bar, let alone fraternising with such company? Well, not many apart from Wenda Parkinson, and yet it is the juxtaposition that makes the photograph, that leads the viewer to question, not the beauty or elegance of the female subject, but the reality of the image itself. It suddenly takes on an otherworldly quality, she as the subject becomes transcendental, not limited to a certain space or context.

This is the crux of Parkinson's photography that after the war became about travel, exotic locations, and pushing the limits of composition. He travelled from India to Australia, Jamaica, and Haiti. One of Parkinson's most famous photographs is of model Jerry Hall standing on a rock in the sea in a blue swimsuit and cap, holding a matching blue telephone. It was the 1970s and 1980s that inspired the bright use of colour in Parkinson's photography. In contrast with his earlier muted efforts, by the mid-1970s, Parkinson had matched models with Australia's burnt orange landscape, had brought pink floral females to Barbados, and even given London its colour with his shot of a red bus, red traffic light, and an unfazed beauty sporting a red headscarf.

Parkinson would become the Royal photographer after the death of Cecil Beaton in 1975. His notable Royal portraits include a candid image of Princess Anne, revealing a previously private beauty. Through his lens, the princess became a wistful young woman rather than another royal demonised by the British press. A 1980 portrait of the Queen Mother through a window pane, shimmering in regalia but otherwise looking like any grandmother might, shows Parkinson's skill for capturing images that are always a little more than they claim to be.

Parkinson himself cultivates a striking appearance. His self-portraits fluctuate between a moustachioed, exquisitely-suited individual and an eccentric, sometimes exotic character with his camera often prominent in shots. Parkinson's moustache has the air of a colonial official about it, and indeed, when suited, he cuts the image of the quintessential English gentleman. But his photographs are in no way conservative and in no way traditional. Parkinson died in 1990 in Singapore while shooting on location for *Town & Country* magazine. A giant of the British art scene, Parkinson preferred to be known as a craftsman rather than an artist, and indeed he did craft images of incredible quality and imagination. HB

Norman Parkinson

George Passmore and Gilbert Prousch

GEORGE PASSMORE AND GILBERT PROUSCH

The twentieth century has seen artists come and go, but there is something that distinguishes George Passmore and Gilbert Prousch from all the others. While they have spent their careers producing works of art, often provocative and always original, they have also transformed themselves into a living piece of art, developing over time, becoming more bizarre and fascinating by the day.

Gilbert Prousch was born in northern Italy at San Martin de Tor in South Tyrol. After beginning his art studies in Selva di Val Gardena he went to Austria as well as Munich, before he moved to England. George Passmore had a less varied upbringing, born to a single mother and growing up in a poor household in Plymouth, England. Passmore was educated at the Dartington College of Arts and then the Oxford School of Art. It was in London, however, that the paths of the two men would cross, at St Martin's School of Art on 25 September 1967. Members of the same sculpture class, Gilbert and George have described the meeting as 'love at first sight'. They were also drawn to each other for pragmatic reasons: George was the only one who could understand Gilbert's ropey English. Together ever since, it was the inception of their fruitful and influential artistic careers.

The duo have spent most of their working lives on Fournier Street, Spitalfields, East London, and are often seen walking through the area together, more often than not wearing exuberant matching suits. Passmore has famously stated, 'Nothing happens in the world that doesn't happen in the East End.' Gilbert and George's suits, which have become famous in recent years, have their origins in one of the very first pieces of art they produced together. *The Singing Sculpture,* created in 1970 while they were still students, consisted of both men standing on a table, singing along and dancing to 'Underneath the Arches' by Flanagan and Allen. Sometimes this would last all day. The two covered their heads and hands (the only body parts visible under their suits) with metallic powder, and though the powder has disappeared with time, the suits remain.

The Singing Sculpture, which was hosted at the Nigel Greenwood Gallery, set the tone for much of Gilbert and George's career. They have refused to differentiate their 'real' lives from their art, insisting instead that all things the two do should be considered a piece of art. The living sculptures have thus blurred the lines between art and life, and have ensured fascination with all of their behaviour. Another of their most famous works from their early career was a double portrait of the two smiling, wearing their trademark suits, entitled *Gilbert the shit and George the cunt*. The piece was designed, they say, as a sort of pre-emptive stoke against the wrath of the media. 'They could call us what they liked,' George said, 'but not before we did.'

A great deal of Gilbert and George's work has been essentially subversive of the status quo. Their main ethos has been 'Art for All', an effort to extend their creativity to a wider audience and beyond traditional conceptual boundaries. This is largely the reason they have chosen to refer to all their works as sculptures, regardless of the medium. In the early 1970s, the two produced drawings which they termed 'Charcoal on Paper Sculptures'—designed specifically to add substance to their identities as living sculptures. In May 2007, in an effort to reach an even wider audience, Gilbert and George released a new work, *Planed,* as a free 48-hour download so that everyone can own an original Gilbert and George piece.

Unafraid of upsetting an audience to prompt a reaction, the two released a particularly controversial picture as part of the 2009 'Jack Freak Pictures' exhibition. The pair appears wearing Union Jack bondage masks several times throughout the show, including next to the crucified Christ who is also wrapped with the flag. Pleased with the reaction the piece provoked, Passmore commented, 'For the first time in 2,000 years, Jesus has a union-flag halo and a union-flag loincloth.' The two claim they do not hold any anti-religious views, and that the piece merely seeks a reaction, although none specifically.

Though much of their work is composed of still images, most often photographs, the duo produced one particularly memorable film in 1972, titled *Gordon's Makes Us Drunk*. In the film, Gilbert and George sit together drinking from a bottle of gin, while romantic classical music plays in the background. As time goes on, the pair's movements become clumsy and they get, as the title foreshadows, increasingly drunk. The video captures the essence of Gilbert and George's work: The piece blurs the line between reality and art, and the audience is unsure what to make of the pseudo-hypnotic scene playing out before them—Gilbert and George, alone, pursuing self-indulgence and provocation.

The two have needed little more than each other to create this artistic brand which seems to resonate with many of the people it reaches, provoking some kind of reaction or other. Whether they seek to entertain their audiences or simply themselves is a point which is very much up for debate. GE

LITTLE RICHARD

To be known as the Godfather of Rock 'n' Roll is the ultimate poisoned chalice. In the case of the brilliant, quixotic, and perhaps ultimately unknowable Little Richard, he was father, mother, and midwife to most of the popular music of the second half of the twentieth century onwards. He was also a deeply contradictory man: a sometime evangelical preacher who also spread the gospel of sex through his music. His frequently licentious songs also stood in stark contrast to his own complex and mysterious sexual orientation. As he said, 'I was always my own person.'

Richard Wayne Penniman was born in Macon, Georgia on 5 December 1932. Both his parents were involved in the local Baptist church, but his father also made a living out of owning a nightclub in which he sold his self-produced moonshine liquor. Richard's two major influences while growing up were religion and music. He sang in the church choir and was given the nickname 'War Hawk' for his octave-spanning voice. Called Li'l Richard because he was such a small and skinny child, he also had a birth deformity that left him with one leg shorter than the other, resulting in a dragging, loping gait. Perhaps typically, he turned this to his advantage.

Never a distinguished student, he enjoyed some early success performing standards in the local clubs, but his life hit a catastrophic bump in February 1952 when his father, whom he had been performing with, was killed in a fight outside a dancehall. Richard was inconsolable, but eventually he was persuaded into recording one of the songs that he had become associated with on the circuit, a heartfelt paean to sex called 'Tutti Frutti'. Released in a more lyrically acceptable fashion in November 1955, it became an instant hit in both Britain and the United States, establishing its unusual, flamboyant creator as one of the pioneers of the new, aggressive style of popular music that was explicitly designed to make young men and women of all colours dance together.

The irony was that, in its original form, 'Tutti Frutti' was a song that celebrated gay sex; in an age when it was illegal on both sides of the Atlantic to be homosexual, to release a popular song that was a love letter to the forbidden act was brave indeed. Rumours about Little Richard's sexuality began to circulate; he fanned the flames by making statements such as 'If Elvis is the King of Rock 'n' Roll, then I'm the Queen.' Despite this, he enjoyed continuing success with songs written in the same vein, including 'Long Tall Sally', 'Lucille', and 'The Girl Can't Help It'. His charismatic public performances, in which he used his piano as if it were an unruly percussion instrument that urgently needed taming, attracted delirious fans who had to be restrained from taking to the stage to embrace Richard. A glittering career beckoned.

However, in 1957 he announced that he was retiring from rock music in order to pursue a career in the church, apparently as a result of a fiery vision he had had while on board a plane. He appeared sincere in his ambition, attending theological college and even getting married in 1959 to a secretary named Ernestine Campbell. He did not abandon music entirely, continuing to record and perform gospel music, but it seemed as if the excesses and outrageousness of the previous years had been put to bed.

He was nonetheless soon to be rediscovered by an entirely new audience, thanks to the popularity of two bands explicitly in his debt, the Beatles and the Rolling Stones, both of whom were peddling anglicized versions of the energetic, pounding music that he had made his signature sound (Richard even taught Paul McCartney to imitate his trademark soaring howl). Throughout the decade, he associated with the leading lights of contemporary music, upstaging everyone from Jimi Hendrix to John Lennon with his electrifying stage performances, wild charisma, and sexual charge. The world loved him; by the end of the decade, he had sold over 32 million records.

As musical styles and tastes changed, so Richard's popularity waned once more. His occasional dabbling in religious music was now largely ignored, despite his having been ordained a minister in 1970. However, the 70s passed in a blur of alcohol and drugs, and it wasn't until 1979 that Richard again abandoned rock and roll in favour of evangelism, without much public attention. However, by the mid-1980s, he realized that he could combine both personae with great success. Camping up his character to an extent that made him seem more comic than threatening—he claimed, 'If I had my life to live over, I would want to be a man'—he appeared in self-parodying cameos in films such as *Down and Out in Beverly Hills* and *Last Action Hero*. Refusing ever to be explicit about his sexuality, instead describing himself as 'omnisexual', he became knowingly unknowable.

He continues to perform at the age of 81, and 'Tutti Frutti' has been included in the National Recording Registry by the Library of Congress, who claimed that 'its unique vocalising over an irresistible beat announced a new era in music'. Certainly, a man who proclaims 'I am the architect of rock 'n' roll' could never think of retiring, and it is likely that he will continue to perform until his very last breath. AL

Little Richard

Helmut Schmidt

HELMUT SCHMIDT

There is much that seems ironic or even contradictory in the life of Helmut Schmidt. He was the son of a half-Jewish banker and was a lieutenant in Hitler's army during the Second World War, he was a leader of the Socialist German Student League after the war, but a rejecter of student protests and political idealism ('People who have visions should go see a doctor' he is known to have said), and a Social Democrat Chancellor who was ousted for refusing to cut social welfare during the worldwide recession in the 1980s. Something about Schmidt has always clashed with his context and perhaps this is why he is known as one of the most effective and influential politicians in Germany's modern history. Not to mention one of the most charismatic.

Smoking may kill, but it has been incapable of taking the life of 95-year-old Schmidt who's incessant puffing has become a hallmark of his old-school charisma. This irreverence has endeared him to the German nation in recent times and rarely can he be seen without the trail of wispy whiteness ascending above and away from him. He supposedly still smokes two to three packs a day 'everywhere except in a Church', in his own words. He is the idol of the hardened smoker, and the quiet envy of all those who have quit. He stockpiled 38,000 menthol cigarettes when it seemed the EU might ban them, has successfully fought off complaints, and refuses to adhere to the domestic smoking ban in Germany. His relationship with the potent mixture of nicotine, tar, tobacco, and paper provides the perfect starting point for anyone with even a vague interest in Schmidt. It speaks of his defiance, his undeterring self-belief, and his refusal to pander to a new politics of image that does not sit cosily with this Cold War luminary.

Aside from the grand literal and metaphorical smoke, the story of Helmut Schmidt is one of a firebrand politician, known for his sharp tongue and proactive attitude. As a young soldier in the Second World War, he was awarded the Iron Cross, but not before a 14-year-old Schmidt visited Manchester on a pupil exchange at the end of the Weimar Republic. He was interviewed about his time, and complained that too much over-zealous affection was bestowed upon him by the Mancunian mother he was staying with. These were the small beginnings of a man who would grow to become one of the most memorable German Chancellors in history. In 1942, during a break from his military service, Schmidt married his childhood girlfriend Hannelore, affectionately known as Loki, and only her passing would separate them after seven decades of marriage.

Their marriage persisted through the murky depths of the Cold War, through Schmidt's successive tenures as Minister of Defence (1969–72), Minister of Finance (1972–74), and finally Chancellor (1974–82), and afterwards as a co-publisher of *Die Zeit*. As Interior Minister of Hamburg in his early political career, Schmidt summoned the federal army and police to Hamburg to deal with the 1962 floods. It was an unprecedented move that contravened the German constitution's prohibition of using the army for interior affairs. Schmidt however was unrelenting, stating characteristically, 'I wasn't put in charge of these units—I took charge of them!'

Throughout the 1970s as Chancellor, Schmidt helped West Germany weather the economic crisis caused by the rising oil prices by keeping both unemployment and inflation at relatively low levels. He would further attempt to maintain strong support for the social welfare system. Yet he was not merely known for his domestic policy, his sharp tongue earned him a reputation abroad as well. Some, like François Mitterrand the then newly-elected President of France, and even his predecessor Giscard with whom Schmidt laid the foundation for greater European solidarity, received Schmidt positively. His same sharp tongue would however turn other world leaders against him. Menachem Begin, the Israeli President, once described him as 'unprincipled, avaricious, heartless, and lacking in human feeling'.

Schmidt's exit from political office was somewhat unceremonious. After his coalition split and he was forced to head a minority government, Schmidt lost a vote of no confidence in the German parliament, making him the only politician to be ousted from office in this way. He has however climbed the ranks of popularity to 'elder statesman' and is known affectionately as Schmidt the Lip due to his disarming honesty. A brilliant politician, pianist, and smoker, Helmut Schmidt's long life must be attributed to at least one of these—which one, however, is anybody's guess. HB

**'I wasn't put in charge of those units—
I took charge of them!'**

Helmut Schmidt

CHARLES WINDSOR

Of all the royal family members in the United Kingdom, it is Charles Windsor, the Prince of Wales, who often seems the most anachronistic. Knowing that his father Prince Philip once said during a recession, 'Everybody was saying we must have more leisure. Now they are complaining they are unemployed,' this is no mean feat.

While rarely as archaic as his father, Prince Charles has always seemed more like a man-out-of-time. He loathes modern buildings ('You have to give this much to the Luftwaffe. When it knocked down our buildings, it didn't replace them with anything more offensive than rubble'). He is attached to the livery companies of shipwrights, drapers, carpenters, goldsmiths, and gardeners. He has a voice so aristocratic that hard consonants go there to die, and his favourite sport is polo. The Prince, one can sense, would have been happier in another century.

But timing has been a crucial element in all aspects of Prince Charles's life. Born in 1948, Charles became heir to the throne at age 3 following the death of his grandfather George VI and the coronation of his mother Elizabeth II. It is a position that he has now held for 62 years, making him the longest-serving heir to the throne in history. His mother won't stand down and many in the British public would prefer his son William to assume the throne when she eventually does. Prince Charles often gives off the air of a man preserved in aspic; forever the heir, never the King.

Added to this is Charles's own staunch refusal to change; a facet of his character that is perhaps most evident in the way he dresses. Prince Charles is immaculate and what is telling is the sheer appropriateness of everything he wears; he gives no quarter to trends and makes no concession to fads. In the daytime he favours tailored suits and crocodile shoes, while for evening functions he dons either white tie, black tie, or military dress, his decision dependent upon dress code. On his regular trips to tropical climes in his youth, he wore crisp beige safari suits. While visiting the countryside, he tends towards English checks, tweed, and houndstooth. Prince Charles may be a self-described stopped clock, but that's precisely the point. When hosting a reception for menswear designers at Clarence House in London in 2013, he summed up his style appropriately: 'I'm finding it very hard to live with myself, Ladies and Gentlemen. Because someone suggested that I might be an icon of fashion. After 64 bleeding years! I don't know why.'

A resurgence in appreciation for the Prince is perhaps a surprise. His image was badly damaged by his first marriage to Lady Diana Spencer. They married in 1981, but both parties quickly came to regret the partnership, and both had lovers. Yet it was Diana who attracted the majority of public sympathy for the failure of the marriage. While she seemed vulnerable and caring, Charles was perceived as cold and distant, with Diana's death in 1997 only strengthening public admiration for her. It was a difficult period for Charles. His eventual second marriage in 2005 to Camilla Parker Bowles, the woman with whom he had been romantically involved for 25 years, only came after a long period of public rehabilitation.

Part of this rehabilitation has come in the form of an increasing sense of harmlessness about the Prince. When Diana was alive he was demonised by the press and public as her tormenter, an unloving jackal who was front and centre in the Royal Family's perceived campaign against the 'people's princess'. Yet with ill-feeling over Diana having subsided over time, Charles's more wholesome pursuits have been allowed to come to the fore. He champions the lot of sheep farmers and the British countryside with his Campaign for Wool, his Duchy Originals company has shown that organic farming can be brought to profit, while his Prince's Trust youth charity reports to have aided 80,000 young people in its nearly 40-year existence. It is a development that has radically altered the Prince's public image. In place of frigidity, there is warmth. In place of adultery, there is charity. Prince Charles is no longer inexorably tied to an ill-fated marriage; instead he is associated with a graceful élan and progressive youth programmes.

Perhaps more importantly, some of Charles's more controversial statements have begun to chime. While many of his more strident remarks about the 'carbuncles' of modern architecture remain archaic, his resistance to starchitecture and contextless megastructures now resonates with an architectural industry increasingly keen to work with existing communities and buildings. Similarly, his hard line on the need for climate change legislation ('The risk of delay is so enormous that we can't wait until we are absolutely sure the patient is dying') now seems prescient. When in early 2014 the Prince compared Vladimir Putin's annexation of Crimea to the actions of Adolf Hitler, it was difficult not to recall that Charles was among the first world leaders to publicly criticise the Romanian dictator Nicolae Ceaușescu, one of the worst human rights violators in Europe.

Such forthrightness however owes a debt to a surprising source. Of all the statesmen with whom the Prince has met, the three exchanges he is reported to have enjoyed the most were with Harold Macmillan, François Mitterrand, and Richard Nixon, the latter of whom recommended that Charles restrict himself to being nothing more than 'a presence' in politics, but not to avoid controversy altogether. If anyone knew controversy, it was Nixon, and Charles learned the lesson well. Yet rather than bring down a major government in a slew of dirty tricks and corruption, Charles has courted controversy through simple outspokenness, doggedly pursuing agendas that have genuine importance. Prince Charles may often seem a man-out-of-time, but he is increasingly making himself felt in the present. os

Index

DEDICATION

Agatha Christie addressed a dedication to her readers in just two of her novels. The first, in *The Secret Adversary,* might readily be applied to this book also. 'To all those who lead monotonous lives, in the hope that they may experience at second hand the delights and dangers of adventure.' And since it would be foolish to attempt to improve upon this, I shall instead make my own supplementary dedication to those who have helped in this book's conception, either recently and directly or long ago and possibly without knowing it. I am most grateful to those who have suggested names for inclusion, to those who have suggested names it might be more prudent to omit, and to those whose glorious personal anecdotes sealed the inclusion of at least five men. I am grateful also for the enormous help I have received in procuring some wonderful and rarely seen photographs. And finally to those who have simply provided moral support. Thank you Waris Ahluwalia, Anna Beattie, Hamza Beg, James Benson, Will Broome, Emily Bryce-Perkins, Felix Chabluk Smith, Stephanie Chaplin, Alexa Chung, David Coggins, Oli Cooke, Debbie Dannell, George Eyre, Jim Grant, Sue Grant, Victoria Grant, Alex Haddow, Katie Hillier, Ben Hudson, Kenneth King, Robert Klanten, Alex Larman, Jonathan Meades, John Mitchinson, David Preston, Jon Savage, Kim Sion, Emily Smith, Oli Stratford, Nick Sullivan, and Claudia Winkleman. PG

ORIGINAL MAN

THE TAUTZ COMPENDIUM
OF LESS ORDINARY GENTLEMEN

Conceived by Patrick Grant
Edited by Patrick Grant and Robert Klanten
Layout by Gestalten

Foreword by Nick Sullivan
Introduction and chapter introductions by Patrick Grant
Profiles by Hamza Beg (HB), George Eyre (GE), Patrick
Grant (PG), Alexander Larman (AL), and Oli Stratford (OS)

Copy-editing by Noelia Hobeika
Proofreading by Bettina Klein

Cover design by Floyd E. Schulze and Moya Ehlers
Cover photography by Archive Photos / Getty Images
Creative direction by Floyd E. Schulze
Graphic design by Moya Ehlers

Typefaces: Lyon Text by Kai Bernau and
Gill Sans by Eric Gill

Printed by Nino Druck GmbH, Neustadt / Weinstraße
Made in Germany

Published by Gestalten, Berlin 2014
ISBN 978-3-89955-552-3

Bibliographic information published by the Deutsche National-bibliothek. The Deutsche Nationalbibliothek lists this publication in the Deutsche Nationalbibliografie; detailed bibliographic data are available online at http://dnb.d-nb.de.

None of the content in this book was published in exchange for payment by commercial parties or designers; Gestalten selected all included work based solely on its artistic merit.

This book was printed on paper certified according to the standard of FSC®.

FSC
MIX
Paper from responsible sources
FSC® C006655
www.fsc.org

Gestalten is a climate-neutral company. We collaborate with the non-profit carbon offset provider myclimate (www.myclimate.org) to neutralize the company's carbon footprint produced through our worldwide business activities by investing in projects that reduce CO_2 emissions (www.gestalten.com/myclimate).

myclimate
Protect our planet

ORIGINAL MAN

THE TAUTZ COMPENDIUM
OF LESS ORDINARY GENTLEMEN

An original man is governed by none other than himself and the choices he makes. The men in this book hold a reputation for being peculiar, odd, or special—they are all true originals as displayed by their contributions to the arts, sports, and politics. Loosely labelled artists, heroes, libertines, and stylists, these men have shaped the world we live in, and inspire us to lead less ordinary lives ourselves.

Original Man is the brainchild of Patrick Grant, the visionary behind British tailoring house Norton & Sons and the relaunch of E. Tautz for which he has received international accolades. Grant has compiled a collection of portraits of men who go beyond a veneer of stylish attire to wring every last drop out of life with their actions, thoughts, and words.

Featuring Jack Nicholson, Elvis Presley, Gunter Sachs, Robert Mitchum, Yves Saint Laurent, Quentin Crisp, Helmut Schmidt, Jean-Luc Godard, David Bowie, Takeshi Kitano, Federico Fellini, Malcolm X, Oliver Reed, and many others.

gestalten
ISBN 978-3-89955-552-3

9 783899 555523